GARAGE SALE

Manual & Price Guide

Dana G. Morykan
Harry L. Rinker

Expert advice on how to conduct a garage sale,
shop a garage sale, and price items at a garage sale.

Photographs by Harry L. Rinker, Jr.

Antique Trader Publications
Dubuque, IA

ISBN: 0-930625-37-4
Library of Congress Catalog Card No. 95-76092

A sampling of books published by Antique Trader Publications:

American & European Art Pottery Price Guide
American & European Decorative & Art Glass Price Guide
American & European Furniture Price Guide
American Military Collectibles Price Guide
American Pressed Glass & Bottles Price Guide
The Antique Trader's Antiques & Collectibles Price Guide
Ceramics Price Guide
Comics Values Annual
Maloney's Antiques & Collectibles Resource Directory
Rockin' Records Buyers-Sellers Reference Book & Price Guide

Magazines published by Antique Trader Publications:

Antique Trader's Collector Magazine & Price Guide
The Antique Trader Weekly
Baby Boomer Collectibles
Big Reel
Discoveries
Military Trader
Postcard Collector
Toy Trader

For information about ordering additional copies of this book
or for a sales catalog listing all available titles, contact:

Antique Trader Publications
P.O. Box 1050
Dubuque, IA 52004
Phone: 1-800-334-7165

CONTENTS

INTRODUCTION

Welcome to the wonderful world of garage sales — a place to turn your recyclables into cash if you are a seller and a place to increase the purchasing power of your dollar if you are a buyer. EVERYONE IS A WINNER AT A GOOD GARAGE SALE. The seller ends the day with an empty garage. Buyers head home with one or more useful treasures.

Everyone wins at a garage sale

Let's clear the air right away in respect to garage sale nomenclature. For the purposes of this book, garage sale, yard sale, rummage sale, tag sale, white elephant sale, or whatever term is commonly used in your region are one and the same. Location is not the issue. Garage sales can occur in garages, driveways, yards, community buildings — in any number of locations.

A garage sale involves the sale of goods, usually less than ten years old, that still have a usable life. Simply put, a garage sale is a vehicle in the modern recycling process, a chance to pass along to others usable items that are no longer of value to you — and earn some spending money in the process.

Think recycle

I grew up in a large nucleated family. Hand–me–downs were a way of life. I wore many a shirt that started out life new on the back of cousin Charles. Reusing material that was "too good to throw out" was just common sense. There was no stigma attached to being a second or third owner.

Further, I lived with a family of savers. Perfectly useful objects that had been replaced by newer models were housed in basement cabinets, tops of garages, and sheds under the guise of "You'll never know when someone might need it." My cousins and I benefited from this Pennsylvania German mindset, especially when we established our first independent domiciles. Our mothers called relatives, discovered what was available, and gave us a list from which to select. My bedroom suite from home, a set of dishes from Aunt Doris, a table and chairs from Grandpop's, and glassware from Aunt Ruth helped furnish my first apartment. Our garage sales were family affairs, conducted by telephone.

Families: large & nucleated or small & scattered

Times change. The era of nucleated families confined to a small geographic region is long gone. My extended family that once lived within a fifty mile radius of my home town in the 1950s is now scattered from Massachusetts to California, Ohio to Texas. The family storehouses that served my generation so well no longer exist.

A mobile society is one reason for the enormous popularity of garage sales. There are many others. I have lost count of the number of times that I heard a person running a garage sale say "we simply have no room for this in the truck" or "it does not fit the decor of my new home." It is easier to get rid of something than to take it with you.

Garage sales are a product of our mobile society

You probably have enough to hold a garage sale

Today's young adults are technologically oriented. They like to own the latest gadgets, even though there is plenty of life left in the ones that they have. They no longer wait until something breaks or wears out before replacing it. In the mid–1990s, trendiness is in vogue.

As a result, attics, closets, the space under the beds, storage bins, and the basements have become homes to dozens of objects that still have years of use in them, but are not being used.

The post–World War II Yuppie, Dink, Me, and X generations are recycle conscious and value oriented. If something is not of use, why not pass it along to someone who can use it. This is better than storing or junking it. Better yet, why not sell it and recover some of its initial purchase price. Everyone welcomes the chance to make a few extra bucks.

Extra cash is always welcome

Garage sales are often about money. There is nothing wrong with this. Sellers are not greedy because they wish to recover some of the cash invested in the goods they are selling. Buyers are not misers and skinflints because they are constantly searching for bargains. Garage sale sellers and buyers are maximizers — individuals who make every dollar count. They are practical, thrifty people. Dana and I consider ourselves proud to be numbered among them.

ACKNOWLEDGMENTS

First, thanks for buying this book. It is designed to make all your garage sale experiences memorable. We hope it does. Your criticisms and suggestions are welcomed. There will be subsequent editions of this book; and, we want to make each better than its predecessor. Send your comments to: Garage Sale Manual, 5093 Vera Cruz Road, Emmaus, PA 18049.

Second, no book created at Rinker Enterprises, Inc., is solely the work of the individuals whose names appear on the cover. Books are a team effort. Ellen Schroy, Terese Oswald, Harry L. Rinker, Jr. , Nancy Butt, Joselyn Mousley, and Richard Schmeltzle all contributed and have our sincere thanks and appreciation.

Third, thanks to Deborah Monroe, Vice President of Landmark Specialty Publications, who saw the opportunities and possibilities in this project that several other publishers failed to recognize. We also appreciate the roles played by representatives of Antique Trader Books: Jaro Sebek in designing the cover, Ted Jones in supervising the production, and Bee Andrews in heading the sales efforts.

Vera Cruz, PA — Dana G. Morykan
August 1995 — Harry L. Rinker

HOW TO RUN A GARAGE SALE

CHAPTER ONE

The Birthing Process

There are dozens of reasons to have a garage sale. You are moving out of the area or into a smaller dwelling. There are a number of things you cannot or do not want to take with you. Your children have outgrown their things and you would like to pass them along to someone who can use them. The kids have moved out, do not want the stuff they left behind, and you are tired of looking at it. You have run out of storage space. You have to sell the old to make way for the new.

Out with the old, room for the new

The hardest garage sale decision to make is whether or not to have one. Once that decision is made, the course is clear and well defined. Those who have gone before have blazed the trail. All you need to do is follow it. Time to make that decision.

I AM GOING TO HAVE A GARAGE SALE. Great! It's settled. Forward, ho!

SET GOALS

The first step in having a successful garage sale is to set goals. Keep the number small. We recommend three:

Get rid of the stuff

Your first goal is to sell everything. If you stop and think about this, it makes perfectly good sense. There is no feeling of accomplishment if you have to repack unsold merchandise and return it to storage. You already decided it should go. Be a magician. Make it disappear.

Make the decision to get rid of your things a final one

Make money

Set a monetary goal. While familiar with the old adage of "don't spend it before you have it," your garage sale will be a far bigger success if you make a wish list of new things you will buy or family activities that will take place because of your garage sale proceeds. Now you have a motivation, a real incentive. Initially, your wish list will help you in the what–to and what–not–to sell decision making process — the longer your wish list, the

Create a monetary incentive

more you will select to sell. Your wish list also will keep your enthusiasm high and provide you with the selling edge you need. Finally, fulfilling your wish list serves as a well deserved reminder of your success.

Have fun

Make fun a primary goal

This is the most important goal of all. Garage sales are work, hard work. There will be moments in the process when you may question whether or not you have lost your sanity. You will keep your cool if fun is foremost in your mind. When you feel your sale becoming too serious, step back, take a few breaths, and relax. The celebration at the end of the day should be one to toast your sale's success, not devoted to "thank God it's over."

BECOME A SPY

We provide the basics. You add the frills

There is absolutely no reason for you to reinvent the garage sale wheel. This ***Garage Sale Manual and Price Guide*** contains the basics you need. How you put this theory into practice is another matter. It pays to do a little garage sale spying.

Before working on your own sale, read this book and then hop in your car and do a little garage sale shopping. Do it over several weekends. Check out the garage sale scene.

One or two key ideas will greatly enhance your sale

Watch for a number of things: types and placement of signs, layout of tables, crowd flow, how merchandise is grouped, display techniques, what buyers are buying, and most importantly, what they are paying. What works and sells at one garage sale generally does so at others, too. Make notes about the features you like and those you do not. Don't be shy. Take a camera with you. Pictures record things far more accurately than one's memory.

If an opportunity presents itself, talk with the individual(s) running the garage sale. Because a garage sale is a once–and–done affair, sellers generally are extremely cooperative and willing to share their experiences. Obviously, they will be far more receptive in the sale's last few hours than when it first opens. Ask them what worked well and what they would change now that they have had their sale. Compare what they said with your own observations and what we tell you.

You cannot have too many good ideas (pick & choose what is right for you)

There are few rights and wrongs in respect to garage sales. The "how–to" choices are enormous. If you have done your homework, you will have more ideas than you can use. The critical questions are: what am I comfortable doing and what will work best for me?

In the final analysis, it is your garage sale. Make certain that you are in charge. You decide what you will and will not do. Never lose sight of this fact.

LOCATING THE THINGS YOU ARE GOING TO SELL

Your field work completed, it is time to go through your house and outbuildings and decide what you are going to include in your garage sale. A typical garage sale consists of several hundred items. Are you certain you have enough things to conduct a full–blown garage sale? Hopefully, your search for material will result in a yes answer. If not, you might consider combining your sale with that of a neighbor or friend.

Check to see you have enough

Make a list of the objects that you saw sell at the garage sales that you visited. Use it as a guide when going through your own material. Never reject anything because it is not on the list. The list is only a guide, not an absolute. Use it as an aid, not a crutch. View it as a "keep your eyes open for" or "have you thought about this" list.

Nothing frustrates a person preparing for a garage sale more than going back over the same ground two, three, or even four times. Adopt a once–and–done philosophy. The key is a plan that has you on the offensive and moving forward. Keep detours to a minimum.

Avoid backtracking, minimize repitition

With this in mind, assemble the following materials *before* hunting for the items that you will be selling in your garage sale: (a) an assortment of cardboard boxes and paper bags, (b) packing material (newspaper for glass and china; brown butcher paper for the rest), and (c) marking tools, tags, and other pricing supplies. Use the boxes and bags for organizational purposes — toys in one, clothing in another, etc.

Resolve to tag and price each object immediately after you have selected it for sale. If they need to be washed, do this first. Do not wait to price objects until sale day. You will be less rushed and more level headed if you price them as you find them. Experience has shown that sellers price more realistically at this stage. Alas, it also shows that most people wait until later.

Price as you go, if possible

[If you are impatient, jump ahead and read the sections on pricing and marking starting on Page 21. The assumption is that the vast majority of you will read this book in its entirety before doing anything. Reality suggests some of you will jump in feet first and read as you go.]

The hunt

Let the hunt begin. Since fun is one of your main goals, make the hunting process a search for hidden treasures. Since these treasures could be buried anywhere, you need to develop a game plan that provides one hundred percent coverage of the hunting grounds.

Look everywhere

Be methodical. Start at the top and work your way down. Don't overlook closets, cabinets, crawl spaces, and other remote storage areas.

Once the house is finished, move on to the garage, barn, storage shed, and other outbuildings. Repeat the process of searching from top to bottom.

Make the hunt a family affair

Involve the whole family in the hunt. The what–to and what–not–to sell decision is often subjective, not objective. Making a decision to sell something is far more difficult than deciding not to sell it. Sentimentality frequently clouds the issue. Second opinions help put things into proper perspective. Get tough and get rid of your stuff.

WHAT I SHOULD AND SHOULD NOT SELL

No use - it goes

This is an easy question to answer. First, consider selling everything that you have not used or worn within the last two years or cannot imagine using in the upcoming six months. Objects that are family heirlooms, have strong personal attachment, or are part of a collection are exceptions.

Second, sell your recyclables. Do not sell your junk. Think carefully about collectibles and antiques. Send your junk to the landfill. Better collectibles and antiques are best sold at a flea market, to an antiques dealer, or at auction.

Recyclable

Pass it down

A recyclable is an object, e.g., an appliance that works or a piece of clothing your child outgrew after wearing only a few times, whose value is primarily utilitarian, not collectible or antique. Ideally, the object should be less than ten years old, but this does not necessarily have to be the case. Objects that are fifteen, twenty, or twenty–five years old, especially furniture and tools, often have plenty of life left in them.

What makes an object recyclable? First, it is in usable condition. It is all there. It works, is wearable, or still has plenty of playtime left. Essentially, there is nothing wrong with the object other than normal wear and tear. You get the idea.

Second, it is something that no longer has value to you. You have replaced, outgrown, or simply tired of it. However, just because you view it in this fashion does not mean that someone else will. One person's trash *is* another person's treasure.

Junk

Do not sell junk

As you select items to sell in your garage sale, ask yourself this question: If I had a use for this object, would I buy it? When your answer is no, you have a landfill candidate. If you would not buy it, what makes you think someone else will?

Do not waste a great deal of time deciding whether to sell or junk an object. If the object is broken, junk it. If the object is incomplete, junk it. If the object is damaged or rusted beyond repair, junk it. Why? Because when buyers attend your garage sale, you want their initial impression to be favorable — what a group of great things — not what a bunch of junk.

Junk is junk

Aren't there buyers who haunt garage sales for items that they can fix up and resell at a substantial profit? Of course there are. Air conditioners, bicycles, lawn mowers, and snow blowers are just a few of the objects they seek. However, instead of selling such items at your garage sale, sell them in advance. Check the telephone directory yellow pages for retail and repair merchants who advertise reconditioned as well as new appliances, bicycles, or lawn equipment.

Finding the fixer–uppers

Make certain that everything you sell is ready to use as it stands. Make your garage sale motto "take it home and use it," not "take it home and see if you can fix it." Eliminate any buying risk. In doing so, you remove one of the major concerns of garage sale shoppers: what happens if I get it home and find it doesn't work?

Sell it ready–to–use

Antiques and collectibles

DO NOT SELL LARGE NUMBERS OF COLLECTIBLES AND ANTIQUES AT A GARAGE SALE. Garage sale buyers expect to pay five to ten cents on the dollar for something, especially if it has been recycled several times. As the primary seller, you should sell a collectible for twenty to thirty cents and an antique for thirty to forty cents on its retail dollar. Selling a collectible or an antique for a nickel to a dime on the dollar is equivalent to giving it away.

The older something is, the more you need to question if it should be sold at a garage sale venue

If you have only a few antiques or collectibles, you may wish to give them a try. Properly researched and priced, they will serve as a good draw for your garage sale. Follow the guidelines provided. If you have a large number of antiques and collectibles, put them aside until you have the time to research them properly. You are running a garage sale, not an antiques business. Deal with them after your garage sale is over. For the moment, you have more important things on your mind.

A few antiques and collectibles lure customers

How can I identify antiques and collectibles? Assuming you are a thirty–five year old adult (if you are older or younger adjust accordingly), follow these rules: (1) if your kids grew up with it or played with it, sell it; (2) if you played or grew up with it, think twice, it is probably a collectible; (3) if your parents, grandparents, or anyone from their generations owned it, it is either a collectible or antique and should be researched before being included in your garage sale. If this is too confusing, stick with the concept of selling primarily items that you acquired new within the last ten years.

Is it an antique?

If you are research oriented, there are dozens of antiques and collectibles price guides you can consult. The following is a good basic working library:

Price guides are guides, not absolutes

Dragowick, Marilyn E. *Metalwares Price Guide.* Antique Trader Books.
Husfloen, Kyle. *The Antique Trader Antiques & Collectibles Price Guide.* Antique Trader Books.
Husfloen, Kyle & Susan Cox. *Pottery & Porcelain-Ceramics Price Guide.* Antique Trader Books.
O'Brien, Richard. *Collecting Toys: A Collector's Identification and Value Guide.* Books Americana.
Rinker, Harry L. *Warman's Americana & Collectibles.* Wallace-Homestead.
Rinker, Harry L., Jr. *Price Guide to Flea Market Treasures.* Wallace-Homestead.

When using any of these price guides, there are two important points to remember. First, make certain that you have the latest edition. Values change as collecting categories get hot or cool off. Second, the values represented in these guides are retail values, i.e., what you would have to pay to buy an object from a dealer with overhead expenses, not what you would get if you want to sell it. Use the twenty to thirty cent rule for collectibles and the thirty to forty cent rule for antiques to calculate your selling price.

Have realistic price expectations

SETTING THE TIME AND DATE

You have selected the things you want to sell, washed and priced them, and set them aside in storage boxes or bags by type. You found more than enough objects to have your own garage sale. What is the next step?

Check local rules and regulations

The answer is a call to your local city or township hall to find out what rules and permit fees apply to having a garage sale in your municipality. Many communities have garage sale regulations covering a wide range of topics, for example, frequency (often no more than once or twice a year at the same site), signs (may not be posted more than "x" hours before the sale and must be removed within "x" hours following the conclusion of the sale), duration (some communities limit garage sales to one or two days and/or ban sales on Sunday), parking (no parking signs are prohibited), and fees (permits begin at a few dollars and go up from there).

Do not ignore local regulations and permit requirements

Ignorance is no excuse. A policeman in a local municipality delights in going around on Saturday morning and shutting down garage sales without permits. Since borough hall is closed on Saturday, the offenders are out of business, their advertising and organization wasted. Do not let this happen to you.

Season

Isn't any time a good time to run a garage sale? Absolutely not. Each region of the country has a garage sale season. In the North, Midwest, and West, the ideal time is mid–April until late May and then again from mid–August until late September. The first period corresponds to the annual spring cleaning ritual and general spending mood fueled by the arrival of both warm weather and income tax refunds. The second coincides with replacing summer with fall and winter things, the start up of school, and individuals looking for a little extra money to spend during the upcoming holiday season.

Think carefully about when to hold your sale

While it is possible to hold garage sales on a year round basis in the South and Southwest, there are periods when the number of sales diminishes — mid–November through mid–January and during sport play–off seasons. Hot temperatures also can quickly cool down sales.

Is there a scientific way to calculate the absolute best time to sell in your region? Yes. Should you care? Probably not. However, for those fanatics reading this book, here are two methods for making this determination.

The scientific method

First, go to the public library and look through two year's worth of garage sale classified advertisements. Chart the advertisements on a week by week basis. The peaks show the "best" time to have a sale.

Second, check with several moving companies in your region and determine when moving activity, especially in respect to families moving into the area, is greatest. New arrivals, often having sold off many of their things instead of shipping them, are one of the major sources of garage sale buyers.

Overkill is a problem

Permit us a piece of advice in regards to these two suggestions. If you do either one of them, do not tell anyone. We know what they will think; and they may be right.

Date

One or two days?

Most garage sales last two days. Saturday and Sunday are the two most popular days with Friday and Saturday a close second. Monday through Thursday and evenings are out. The critical question is: do you need two days? The answer is no. Most of the second day is spent sitting idle waiting for 4:00 to roll around. The few shoppers that do come expect to see give-away pricing. There song is birdlike — cheap, cheap, cheap. Who needs this?

One day is all it takes

ONE DAY IS MORE THAN ENOUGH TO GET THE JOB DONE. Saturday is the ideal garage sale day. The vast majority of people are off from work. You are not fighting the church for attention. While you may go to bed exhausted, you will not have nightmares about getting up the next morning and doing it all over again. If you do your advance planning properly, one day is all you will need.

Go in ideal weather

What happens if it rains? The answer is either cancel and regroup or hold it the following weekend. Be sure to list a rain date in your ads if you plan on the latter. Even though the temptation is great, resist holding it the next day. If Saturday is the ideal garage sale day, then have your sale on Saturday. Do not jeopardize its potential by selling on a day that is second best. Make certain you are in charge, not Mother Nature.

Time

Post Time 7:00 A.M.

Most garage sale sellers advertise their sale hours as 8:00 A.M. until 4:00 P.M. A few communities have regulations that prohibit selling before 9:00 A.M. These municipal councils are out of touch with reality. Despite an advertised 8:00 A.M. kick–off, a garage sale day typically begins at 7:00 A.M. This is when the early birds will start knocking on doors.

Why create aggravation for you and your buyers? Accept the inevitable. Begin your garage sale at 7:00 A.M. and advertise this fact. This way you will level the playing field. The best sales results are achieved by giving everyone the same opportunity to buy.

All it takes is half a day

Yes, starting at 7:00 A.M. means that you will have to get up by 5:00 A.M., especially if you plan to set up on the day of the sale. Sorry. This is one of the prices you pay to have a garage sale. Be stoic. Keeping telling yourself over and over again: "It will all be over by 5:00 P.M."

Neighbors

Enlist the support of neighbors

Before firmly setting a date, check with your neighbors. A neighbor will not be thrilled if your big garage sale occurs on the same day he plans to entertain business clients in his back yard. Securing the cooperation of your neighbors is critical to making your garage sale a success.

Your garage sale, any garage sale, is disruptive. Garage sale shoppers often do not care where they park, e.g., on someone's lawn or blocking a driveway. They also have trouble sticking to established paths or sidewalks. Shoppers will trample anything that stands in their way of getting to a bargain quickly.

Alerting neighbors that you are planning to have a garage sale and when is common courtesy. Some will take the low road and beat a hasty retreat. Others will take the high road and offer to help or, better yet, have a garage sale of their own on the same day.

Neighborhood or multi–family garage sales

The more the merrier

Nothing draws a bigger crowd than a neighborhood or multi–family garage sale. It is a winning concept. Sellers share expenses. The number of people needed to run the sale is lessened. Shoppers are able to maximize their buying time.

A neighborhood garage sale takes place at several locations within a one to three block area. This is ideal because it spreads out the parking and reduces the number of people at one location. The shopping atmosphere is much more exciting. Relaxed? Let's hope not. Sales are best when buying is frenzied.

One or a series of multiple sites? Both work well

A multi–family sale generally takes place at one site. Each family either has a specific section in which to sell its merchandise or a marking code is used so that the cashier can credit each sale to its rightful family. The plus side is the tremendous increase in people power to help run the sale. The negatives evolve around the continual "whose merchandise is this" plea and the need for more detailed bookkeeping.

Tag alongs

Even though your announcement that you will be running a garage sale may not trigger a neighborhood or multi–family response, chances are you will receive numerous requests from neighbors, friends, and relatives along the lines of: "Would you mind if I brought over a few of my things for you to sell?" If you can find the courage and strength to say no, by all means do so. Most individuals cannot.

Consignment is not a great idea

Consignments are a nightmare. The consignee expects you to sell his things without charging him a cent for your time and trouble. Further, he expects you to get what he asked. Do not believe for one moment that "I'll take whatever you can get" has meaning. Everyone has a fixed price in mind.

Theft can be a problem at garage sales. While the theft of one of your objects may upset you, how will you deal with the theft of an item that you have accepted on consignment? Will you feel so guilty that you wind up paying the consignor for an item for which you never received money?

Good ideas are not always followed

Although there are dozens of good reasons why you should not take other people's goods on consignment, chances are better than even that you will. Assuming you do and the consignor is not a close friend or family

Document consignments

member, protect yourself by having the consignor provide you with a document that: (1) clearly describes what he is placing on consignment, (2) the price asked, and (3) a statement releasing you from all responsibility if the object is damaged or stolen while in your possession.

Surprises happen

In addition to consignor tag alongs, chances are that someone else in your area will schedule a garage sale on the same day as yours and not offer to share in the expense of advertising or sign production. There is only one approach to this problem. Ignore it. There is nothing you can do. Laugh about it and concentrate on making your own garage sale a success.

Call your insurance agent

The process of establishing a day and time for your garage sale began with a telephone call or visit to the local authorities to check on the local ordinances relating to garage sales. End the process by contacting your insurance agent.

Do not become insurance poor

Inform him that you are planning to have a garage sale and make certain that you have adequate insurance coverage. Cover all the bases — personal liability, property damage, and theft, loss, and breakage. If a shopper attending your garage sale destroys your neighbor's favorite shrub, rest assured your neighbor will come after you, not the shopper.

In most cases, your homeowner's insurance should provide you with adequate coverage. Why take chances? Check and double–check. If your protection is inadequate, consider buying a one day policy. The peace of mind is worth it. The expense may not be.

LET THE WORLD KNOW YOU ARE HAVING A SALE

If your garage sale is to be a success, you need to utilize three forms of advertising: the media, word of mouth, and an adequate number of signs posted the day of the sale. Each is highly effective. All are equally important. Ignore one of the three and you compromise the success of your sale.

Get the word out

The challenge is to keep your advertising costs minimal. One of the purposes of your garage sale is to make money. Profit comes only after expenses are deducted. If you are not careful, advertising can become a major expense.

Media

Confine your advertising to classified advertisements. They are inexpensive and easy to write. Display garage sale advertisements are costly and the results, more often than not, unsatisfactory. Stick with the proven winner — the classified advertisement.

Thursday is traditionally the day most daily newspapers run their classified garage sale advertisements. Twenty–five to fifty garage sale advertisements are not uncommon during early spring and late summer, the peak of the garage sale season.

Advertise when it makes sense

Your classified advertisement needs to contain two groups of information. The first includes the basics — the date, time, and exact address. If you live on a side street or in the country, also mention the section of the city or the nearest town to where you live. There is no need for directions. If you have placed your signs correctly, the shoppers will be able to find your sale once they arrive in your general vicinity.

DO NOT LIST YOUR NAME OR TELEPHONE NUMBER. If you do, your telephone will ring constantly once your advertisement hits the papers. People will call asking for specific directions, for permission to check out your sale in advance, and with an endless array of questions of "do you have this" or "do you have that." You will hear dozens of reasons why you should let "X" shop your sale early.

Include your telephone number at your own peril

In the forty–eight hours before your garage sale, you will have plenty to do. An endless stream of telephone calls only adds to your burden. Shut the door to this possibility. Do not include your name and telephone number in your classified advertisement.

The second group of information in your classified advertisement contains the buzz words and phrases designed to attract people specifically to your sale. Here are some samples: "bargains galore, dozens of brand new — never used items, enormous variety, everything must go, moving and cannot take it with us, multi–family sale, multi–generation sale, nothing held back, one bargain after another," and "tremendous assortment." The idea is to gild the lily a little. Do not be modest. It is expected.

Sell the sizzle, not the steak

Garage sale advertisements are billed at so much per word or so much per column inch. Beware of saying too much — the longer the advertisement, the less likely it will be read. Begin your advertisement with the basic information and conclude with the gilding. Here are two sample advertisements. Use them only as models. Add your own personal touches.

GARAGE SALE TO END ALL GARAGE SALES, Saturday, 7:00 A.M. to 4:00 P.M., 7002 Carl's Hill Road, just off Route 100 south of Shimersville. Maple bedroom suite, bicycles, riding mower, lots more. First time seller. Kids have left. We're moving to a smaller home. Priced to sell.

Just the facts ma'am, just the facts

GARAGE SALE, 5 Families, Saturday, 7:00 A.M. to 4:00 P.M., 5093 Vera Cruz Road, Vera Cruz, just south of Emmaus. Hundreds of items from clothing and toys to furniture and household goods. Just the sale for young couples starting life together.

Once you have written your advertisement, select the papers in which your advertisement will run. Advertise in all daily papers within a twenty–

Shoppers come from miles around

Advertise when others advertise

Know your customers

Talk up your sale

Put your flyers in windows and on bulletin boards

five mile radius of your location. If you are lucky, there will be more than one. Place an advertisement in the major daily of the city that serves as your county seat, even though it may fall outside the twenty–five mile radius.

In addition to the daily papers, advertise in the pennysavers (a.k.a., shoppers' journals) that serve your area. If you live in a rural area, also advertise in the local farm and dairy paper. Pennysavers and farm and dairy papers have large, loyal readerships.

Run your classified advertisement once in each paper. Select the issue that appears immediately before your sale date. In the case of daily papers be sure your ad runs on the same day as the majority of other garage sale advertisements. Garage sale shoppers rarely plan more than a few days in advance.

Word of mouth

A large number of your garage sale customers will consist of friends, business acquaintances, neighbors, and family. Drawn initially by curiosity, they often are among the biggest spenders. The concept is simple — the more you spread the word, the more successful your garage sale will be.

Start talking up your sale about two to three weeks in advance. Use phrases such as: "I'm selling loads of great stuff," "There is a lot of life left in the stuff I'm selling," and "I'll bet there are dozens of things you can use." The name of the game is vague but enticing. Do not take the mystery out of your sale by providing a detailed list of what you will be selling.

Spreading the news of your sale by word of mouth is aided by handing our flyers. Design the flyer to double as a sign. Keep the text simple. Only four pieces of information are needed — garage sale, date, time, and location. You may wish to list of a few choice pieces. If you do not want to take time to design your own flyer use the sample provided at the end of this book.

Every community has a number of public announcement bulletin boards, some public and some private. A few possibilities include the grocery store, community and/or senior citizen center, post office, park, and YMCA/YWCA. Do not forget church bulletin boards, the local laundromat, and bowling alley. Check with local barbers and hair dressers to see if they will put one of your signs in their window. Finally, ask your friends and relatives that belong to civic organizations to mention your sale at upcoming meetings.

All you have to do is get the ball rolling. The community grapevine will do the rest.

Signs

There are three types of signs that you will need for your garage sale — a tease, directional signs the day of the sale, and signs for use at the sale itself. You will make most of the signs yourself — by hand, with your computer, or by photocopying the samples in the back of this book. While you can buy ready made signs at a local hardware store or have signs professionally made , why go to this expense? Signs are destroyed or discarded at the end of the sale. Further, a garage sale has far more allure when its signs have a handmade, rather than professional, quality.

Save money — photocopy or make signs yourself

Keep signs simple, especially those someone will be reading through their car, truck, or van's window. If your sign has more than ten words on it, think again. Also, do not over embellish. Readability is the key. Busy backgrounds make reading a sign difficult. Check your urge to utilize all the design tools in your computer and sketch book and stick to basics.

Make signs easy to read

If your local ordinance permits it, put a sign in your yard the Monday before your garage sale stating: "GARAGE SALE HERE / SATURDAY / 7:00 A.M. to 4:00 P.M. / BARGAINS GALORE" This is all you need.

When you go to the municipal office to get your garage sale permit, buy a local road map. Use a thick marker to identify the major access roads in your area. These are the arteries from which you will have to direct people to your garage sale. Select one route from each artery. Plot this route with a thinner marker.

Make it easy for people to find you

Get in your car and drive these routes. Are they the ones you normally use? If not, why not? Shouldn't what works best for you work best for someone trying to find your house?

As you drive the routes, check each intersection where a turn is necessary for a pole or device to which you can affix your directional signs. Every turn needs to be marked. It is better to have too many signs than too few. Avoid using street, STOP, and other similar signs if at all possible. Tampering with these, and that includes hanging other signs on them, is usually a violation of the law. It is generally not enforced; but, understand the risk.

You can never have to many signs

If there is not a convenient place to hang your sign, you'll have to put it on a stake that you can drive into the ground. If this is necessary, ask permission from the property owner in advance. All is lost if an angry property owner removes your sign the morning of the sale.

The only directional signs requiring a specific address are those posted at the junctions of the side streets with the main arteries in your neighborhood. From that point forward, arrows will suffice, especially if less than half a dozen turns are involved. Once again, keep your signs simple.

Perhaps the most effective on site sign the day of the sale is a kiosk, generally a large cardboard box (a television or microwave box is ideal) set

Make a "You're Here" kiosk

on top of a trash can with a poster on all four sides touting the garage sale and spelling out the categories of objects being offered.

Do not forget operational signs

Cashier, parking instructions, and dot code identification are some of the on site signs that will help your sale run more smoothly. Keep your on site signs, such as "Everything on this table 50¢," to a minimum. Garage sale shoppers are skilled spotters. They want to see the merchandise, not dozens of signs. Further, an object might be picked up and handled over a dozen times in the course of a sale. Chances of it being returned to its original spot are minimal. Use a sign only if it helps simplify your sale. Eliminate any signs that may cause confusion.

Make a smoking or no smoking decision

Should you prohibit or allow smoking? No matter what you decide, it is a no win situation. If your sale is confined to inside a garage, a no smoking policy makes sense. If you do post a no smoking sign, either inside or out, provide a place, e.g., a can with sand, where smokers can dispose of their cigarettes. On the whole, smokers are very considerate individuals and will abide by whatever decision you make.

PREPARING YOUR OBJECTS FOR SALE

Three steps are involved in preparing your objects for sale: (1) enhancing the salability of the objects, (2) pricing them, and (3) affixing the price tags and owner's code, if necessary. Ideally, you did this when you selected the objects for your garage sale. Reality suggests otherwise. Not all good advice is followed. Most likely, you have dozens of boxes and bags loaded with things waiting to be priced. Now is the time.

Enhancing salability

Not all objects sell themselves — You need to help

The most important thing that you can do to enhance salability is to wash or clean the objects that you plan to sell. An object's sales potential is greatly reduced when it is dirty. Not only will it bring a lower price, possibly only half that of a clean example, but its chances of selling at all are greatly diminished. People want things clean and ready to use.

Some additional suggestions are:

1. Check an item for completeness. Put multi–part objects into a box or tie the parts together. List the fact that the object is complete on the sales sticker or tag.
2. If the original box and instruction sheet is available, place it with the object.
3. Indicate size, especially for clothing and linens, as clearly as possible. We have provided a sample page of size labels that you can photocopy, fill out, cut apart, and pin on fabrics.

4. Neatly fold or hang clothing. If possible, keep the design motif prominent.
5. Check everything electrical, from old radios and shavers to microwaves and VCRs, to make certain they work. If they do not, they are junkers. Again, we recommend you do not include these items in your sale. Their presence could cast a shadow of doubt on all your appliances. Should you insist, tag them "as is" and consider them "one to two dollar — please take them off my hands" objects.
6. If you are selling something with a defect, clearly point it out. Do not waste time hiding a defect under a fresh coat of paint or in some other fashion. The buyer may come back to haunt you.

Sell openly and honestly

Pricing

Garage Sale Manual and Price Guide is the first garage sale book to include an exhaustive price guide section. The prices are guides, not absolutes. There are no fixed prices for garage sale objects, just as there are no fixed prices for antiques and collectibles. An object that sold for one dollar at one garage sale might sell for five dollars at another. Price is very much a factor of time, place, and moment.

Value is a matter of the moment

This book is designed to get you into the ball park and up to the plate. You, and only you, determine how good a batter you will be. Consider the suggested price values, then set your own prices. The only price that counts is the one that makes you happy. Do not sell for less. There is nothing worse than ending the day feeling that you gave everything away.

You set the price

Forget nickels and dimes, whenever possible, and think in terms of quarters, half dollars, and dollars. Sell only at these increments. Nickels and dimes complicate the selling, recording, and change making process. Use only when absolutely necessary. When a garage sale is successful, goods sell quickly. Avoid anything that bogs down the selling process.

Use the following pricing structure:

$ 0.00	to	$ 2.00	Twenty–five cent increments
$ 2.00	to	$ 10.00	Fifty cent increments
$ 10.00	to	$ 20.00	One dollar increments
$ 20.00	to	$ 100.00	Five dollar increments
Above		$ 100.00	Twenty–five dollar increments

Think incremently

Over pricing is one of the biggest mistakes sellers make. It is tough to be objective and put personal feelings aside. In addition, there is a little bit of greed in us all. Get the most for something, not the least. There must be a compromise somewhere.

Avoid over pricing

There is little doubt that your initial reaction to the prices in the price guide portion of this book will be that they are low — too low. This is not true. They are based on field observations at garage sales and small town auctions. Of course, there were plenty of identical objects at garage sales with much higher prices. However, the critical question is did they sell or were they left behind at the end of the day. Bet on the latter.

A good price is one that makes the object vanish

Remember the three goals at the beginning of this book? One of them was **get rid of the stuff** — sell everything. The only way to achieve that goal is to price your goods to sell. The prices suggested are designed to achieve that goal. Consider them carefully.

Marking the price on your goods

Price everything

The price you put on an object is your offer to sell. We strongly recommend marking all objects you plan to sell. You have two goals — to mark the item with an easy–to–read price in a viable location and to avoid any price markings that may adversely affect the value of the object. These two goals are not always in harmony.

Avoid damaging your merchandise

The three most common marking methods we encounter are (1) prices marked on a piece of masking tape which has been affixed to the object, (2) prices scrawled across the surface of the object with a magic marker, and (3) stickers of assorted shapes and colors with values marked on them. Avoid the first two and use the third carefully.

Chances are you have become frustrated more than once while trying to remove a department store price sticker from an object that you planned to give as a gift. Keep this frustration in mind as you mark your objects for sale. Do not put a sticker or marking on any surface that cannot be easily removed without inflicting further damage to the object.

Here are a few marking tips:

A good tag or label is one that can be removed safely

1. Mark clothing and linens by pinning tags to them. In order to save time, divide textiles into three to six price categories. Use colored dots on the tags to denote the various prices. Post a sign indicating the values represented by the different colors.
2. Use sticker labels for ceramic, glass, metal, or wood pieces. Buy labels with a nonpermanent stick feature. Test the labels by applying one to an object and waiting a few days. If it leaves a residue behind, shop around for another brand. Do not apply stickers over surface decorations. Ceramic decoration is often above the glaze. A buyer would be rightfully upset if part of the surface decoration came up when the sticker was removed.

3. Mark all paper products, from jigsaw puzzles and board games to old letters and posters, in pencil — the softer the lead the better. Mark them on the bottom or back and avoid the use of labels of any kind.
4. Consider creating quarter, fifty cent, and one dollar boxes and tables. Again, use a color code to identify which goods are which, especially if someone other than yourself will be working the cashier's station.

Be extremely careful marking paper objects

Be alert to price tag switchers. They are part of the garage sale scene. If someone brings you an object and the price does not seem right, tell him you mispriced it, apologize, and withdraw it from the sale. Once the troublemaker is out of sight, fix the price and return the object to the selling area.

Watch out for price tag switchers

What happens if you did misprice something? It happens at every sale. Be honest. Apologize for your error but firmly explain that you are exercising your right to withdraw this object from the sale and reprice it.

PLOT YOUR GARAGE SALE

Draw a rough diagram of your garage and/or yard and plot the layout of your garage sale. This saves a tremendous amount of time in the setup process on the morning of the sale and allows you to carefully control crowd movement.

It pays to know what you are going to do

If your sale is going to be held inside your garage, you need to decide whether you are going to put tables up against the walls, use an aisle system, or combine the two concepts. If possible, we favor a setup that allows shoppers to shop from all sides of a table including the ends — the more opportunity for individuals to grab, the better.

Maximize the shopping area

The only disadvantage with an aisle arrangement is security. If your garage is small and the aisles are full, it may be difficult to keep an eye on everything. For this reason, many garage sales are set up in the shape of a "U", with tables lined up against walls and the cashier's table at one end. This layout can present its own problems. The security view of the merchandise is blocked by the shopper's back and shopping is available only from one side of the table.

Given the temporary nature of garage sales and wide variety of situations under which they occur, there is no one arrangement that will work well for everyone. You need to decide what works best for you.

Decide on what works best for you

Here are a few general suggestions:

1. If you have the space, spread out your sale.
2. It is better to display your merchandise on tables rather than on the ground.

Utilize all available space

3. If you have large items, i.e., bicycles and air conditioners, it is customary to place them in a separate section outside where people can walk around them and inspect them.
4. Position your cashier's table between the sale and the parking area.

The primary argument for doing a pre–sale plot plan is that it allows you to determine how many tables, racks, and other display units you will need the day of the sale. Just do yourself one favor. No matter what number of tables you decide upon, add three more. You will find a use for them. Trust us.

HELP

Think a minimum of three people to run your sale

How many people does it take to run a garage sale? Sounds like a joke that requires a clever answer. Here are a few hints. The answer is more than one. Two is too few. Six is too many. The ideal number is three, maybe four if you want a reserve.

Seller = Cashier

The three basic garage sale positions are cashier, the person with the answers, and the person responsible for security. The cashier totals the sales, collects the money due, and is responsible for the security of the funds. Never, ever leave the cash box unattended. The cashier also hands out any packing materials provided at the sale.

At many sales, the cashier also does the haggling, either on an individual basis or lot purchase. Given the responsibilities of keeping track of purchases and cash, a serious question must be raised about whether or not the cashier is the right person to do the bargaining.

Someone must be available to answer questions

Questions are part of the garage sale selling process — does it work, what size is it, are all the pieces there, etc. The answer can make or break a sale. We recommend that one helper be responsbile for answering all questions. We also suggest that this person does the haggling and marks any discount agreed upon on the price sticker for the cashier's benefit. This takes enormous pressure off the cashier and greatly speeds up the checkout process.

Security is an issue

Security is too important to leave to the cashier and answer person. This is why we encourage you to have a minimum of two helpers besides yourself. It is unfair to place the security burden on a young child. This job calls for an adult.

You can run a garage sale by yourself or with one other person. You also can drive your car off a cliff if you are crazy enough to do it. Think a minimum of three people. Four is nicer.

What do you pay your help? The answer is your heartfelt thanks. Presumably they are family or close friends — they are not expecting a paycheck. It is common courtesy to allow them to preshop the sale. If possible, do it the day before, not the morning of the sale. They may ask to sell some of their own belongings at your sale. Let them. It is the least you can do.

Free Help?

KIDS

One garage sale book advises sellers to send their kids somewhere else on the day of the sale. Who are they kidding? Get the pun. Kids and garage sales go together.

Kids and garage sales go together

The key is to involve your kids in the garage sale. There are a variety of ways this can be done. Children can help bag or box unbreakable items that have been purchased, run errands, or check on signs within bike riding distance. The only limiting factor is the one you put on their participation.

Some sellers allow their kids to have a separate sale of their own. They display their goods, primarily sports cards, toys, etc., apart from the main section of the sale. Their outgrown clothing generally stays with the main sale. The kids select and price what they sell and get to keep all their earnings.

Pets and garage sales do not mix

If the children are old enough, they can serve as the answer person. Parents will be astonished at how much kids know about the things around the house. If they do not know the answer, they know how to ask.

Younger children selling drinks and baked goods are a common sight. Why not? It keeps them occupied and provides a valuable service to shoppers. Normally, we would advise against selling refreshments at a garage sale. Are you running a garage sale or a restaurant? However, when kids are involved, well...that is another story.

You know your children's tolerance levels better than anyone. Is it fair to expect them to sustain a high enthusiasm level for the entire day? Probably not. Once your sale slows down, usually around noon, provide them with the option of staying, becoming TV junkies, or spending the afternoon with friends.

Enough is enough

THE DAY BEFORE

While we hope you will use and follow the Preparation Checklist that we provide, we are realists. Assuming you are like most people, the things you do the day before the sale are all the things you should have done a week ago but failed to do. This will include everything from picking

Procrastination is a fact of life

up supplies and making signs to getting cash and coordinating the help. The key is not so much when they are done, but that they get done.

Yes, it will get done

Your most important task the day before the sale is to have everything in readiness for the next morning. If your sale is inside your garage, this means virtually setting up the entire sale. It would be ideal, but is not always possible, to do this with the garage door closed. A closed door setup eliminates the opportunity for those individuals who cannot resist the temptation to try and buy early.

If your sale is outside, do as much preliminary setup as possible. Position tables, boxes of items, and other necessities so that they can be moved outside the morning of the sale quickly and efficiently. If the entire sale is going to be outside, you might consider setting up a few tables so that you can move them outside as a finished unit.

THE NIGHT BEFORE

Watch the weather

Keep an eye on the weather. Ideally, make the go or no go decision at 11:00 P.M. the night before the sale. If your sale is a no go, post a big sign stating the sale was canceled and providing the rain date. If the forecast is too unpredictable and you need to wait until morning, make your decision by 5:30 A.M. This gives your help adequate time to crawl back into bed and sleep late.

The primary reason for canceling a sale is rain. The time period you need to be most concerned about is 6:00 A.M. until noon. If rain is scheduled for that time period, postpone your sale. Seventy–five percent of sales take place within the first three to four hours of any garage sale. Better to postpone a garage sale than open it three to four hours late. Garage sale shopping is primarily a morning activity.

Those last minute chores

If everything is go and the night promises to have relatively mild temperatures and low humidity, you might want to get a jump on tomorrow's setup. Post your directional signs. If this elicits visits from unwanted early birds, remember to stand firm — the sale starts at 7:00 A.M. **tomorrow**. Depending on the character of your neighborhood, you may even be able to set up and arrange your table layout for an outdoor sale. However, don't put out any merchandise until morning — no sense tempting fate.

Finally, go to bed by 11:00 P.M. Tomorrow is a big day. You need as much rest as you can get. The excitement of coming events may keep you awake for awhile, but eventually you will drift off to sleep. The 5:00 A.M. wake–up call will arrive all too soon.

HOW TO RUN A GARAGE SALE

CHAPTER TWO

The Blessed Event

The big day has arrived. The alarm went off at 5:00 A.M. Yes, you are out of bed far earlier than you like, but there is work to be done. Your advertisements said that you would open at 7:00 A.M. Rest assured even at this early hour, there will be several early birds. You must be ready.

Up and at 'em

Assuming you followed our earlier advice, much of your work is finished. Divide remaining tasks between your helpers so that each is single task oriented during these first few critical hours. Accept the fact that it will seem impossible to get everything done in the time available. Do not panic. Things will get done.

SIGNS

Signs enable customers to find you

Some garage sale sellers like to put out their signs last thing before going to bed the night before their sale. Do it after 9:00 P.M. in order to reduce the risk of "pre-shoppers" knocking on your door.

The principal reason that we recommend waiting until the morning of the garage sale is weather. It is important that your signs look fresh and inviting. If it rains overnight or is unusually damp, your signs could be ruined. One solution is to put plastic wrap over your signs. Pull it tightly and secure with tape — if it wrinkles, your signs will be hard to read.

Sign appeal

Make twice the number of signs that you think you will need — better too many than too few. Inevitably one or two will become damaged while putting them up. As you drive around, you will notice places for signs that you missed when you first did your sign plot. Be prepared.

The best plan to ensure that your signs are accurate is to follow each of the major routes to your garage sale, posting signs as you go. Begin with the first turn from a majority artery. After the third or fourth route, you will find that the latter half of the job is already accomplished by signs that you placed earlier.

Be systematic

Most garage sale signs are placed on telephone poles. Unless you have designed your sign to wrap around the telephone pole, paste it to a piece of stiff cardboard to give it strength. It is almost impossible to read signs that droop or bend.

Ensure your signs will stay in place

Use either small nails (only hammer them in half way so that they are easy to remove) or an industrial strength staple gun to hold the signs in place. Thumbtacks, tape, or a hand stapler will not work, especially if it is windy. String has a bad habit of loosing its tension in the course of a day — make certain it is tied good and tight.

Telephone poles are not always available. Therefore, plan to mount signs with string on street sign poles or mail boxes (illegal, but done all the time). You should have half a dozen or more signs that you can pound into the ground in locations where no other opportunities exist.

Here are a few hints for placing your signs:

1. Keep them at the eye level of a driver of a car.
2. Place them at an angle that can be read easily by a driver.
3. Position signs indicating a turn far enough in advance so that the driver does not have to brake suddenly to read the sign. Give the driver enough time to spot the sign, read it, and react.
4. If the "straight ahead" distance is more than ten blocks or half a mile, consider placing another straight ahead sign to indicate to the driver that he is heading in the right direction.

Recheck signs

Finally, recheck everything around 11:00 A.M. Signs do fall down. Kids sometimes delight in stealing them or altering them as a prank. Your garage sale is an all day event. It is as important that someone be able to find your sale at 3:00 P.M. as it is at 7:00 A.M.

ON SITE

Before going outside, take a few minutes to wake up, have a cup of coffee or tea, and get your thoughts in order. Some people use checklists, others do not. Checklists help to ensure that crucial tasks are not forgotten — a definite plus. One problem with a checklist is that it often creates inflexibility and opens the door to frustation if everything is not done. Do what works best for you.

Setting up the sale

Move quickly

Set up your sale as quickly as possible. If your sale is a small one and is confined to your garage, all you need do is open the garage door. Few sellers are so lucky. If you're not one of the lucky ones, display larger, attention grabbing items outside. Garage sales yield far more income when a driveway and lawn is incorporated as part of the sale site.

Advance planning is the key. Use the site plan that you prepared. Move your large sale items and tables, display racks, and any other support equipment into place. Cover your tables with a cloth or paper. Ideally, this should take less than thirty minutes.

Position tables and props first

Start unpacking your things. Begin unpacking at the front and work towards the back. This prevents people from tripping over one another, reducing setup time considerably.

Unpack from front to back

Which is more important — keeping like things together or arranging an attractive display? The answer is — keeping like things together. Devote only a minimum amount of time to arrangement. Whatever you do will be undone within minutes after your sale opens. Garage sale shoppers will not hesitate to pick things up from one place and put them down at another. Your top priority should be to get your items out as quickly as possible to the point where they can be seen.

Position your cashier's station so that it offers a good view of the sale, yet is sufficiently removed from the action so that individuals waiting to pay do not block those wishing to shop. The ideal location is at the front of the sale, between the parking area and the first items offered for sale. This will enable the cashier to keep an eye open for individuals who may try to leave without paying.

Cashier to the front

SECURITY

You need to be concerned about security — on several fronts. The first involves theft of items that you are trying to sell. Unfortunately, a few sticky fingered garage sale shoppers spoil things for everyone. Chances are you are going to lose a few things. Make up your mind now not to let this upset you.

Thwart sticky fingered shoppers

One person should always be assigned to security. As we mentioned earlier, the ideal situation is to have three key individuals — cashier, answer person, and security person. The answer person also should help with security.

The second area of concern is your home. Keep it off limits during the sale. Make certain that all doors are locked or barricaded in such a way that it is clear that entrance is forbidden.

Your home is off limits

If someone urgently needs a restroom, be prepared with directions to a public restroom at a nearby gas station or restaurant. There is absolutely no need for you to provide a dressing room. Considering the prices you are asking for your clothing, the buyer should assume the risk that something may not fit.

Later in this book, we advise garage sale shoppers to be aggressive — to ask about things they do not see but which they would like to buy.

Fulfill requests for unseen merchandise only if time allows

When this happens and you have something that matches the request, you, and you alone, go into the house and retrieve it. There is no time for house tours while you are running a garage sale. Further, once you allow one person into your home to look around, others will follow. Put your foot down — THE HOUSE IS OFF LIMITS.

Teamwork is critical

The security person should work with the answer person to ensure that house security is maintained. Also, if there are items in the garage that are not for sale (hopefully, you removed or covered them prior to the sale), the answer person should keep an eye on them as well.

Finally, the security person has one more responsibility — keeping an eye open for the tag switchers. Inexpensive as most items are, there are individuals who cannot resist the temptation to switch tags in order to buy at an even lower cost. Having the person whose objects are being sold working as the cashier provides an extra measure of security against this practice.

Stories you absolutely should refuse to believe

The excuses invented for allowing someone to shop your sale before it opens number in the hundreds. There is no limit to human ingenuity. Here are two classic examples:

Avoid the Artful Dodgers

1. You receive a visit from someone claiming to be affiliated with the local historical society. He explains that one of the key ways the Society adds to its collection is by getting permission to shop garage sales in advance. The Society will gladly pay full price. By letting their representative shop early, you are sharing your goods with the rest of the community. Understand that this is a Society of one.

2. A woman dressed in a nurse's uniform knocks on your door at 6:00 A.M. She loves to shop garage sales, but she has to be at work by 7:00 A.M. Won't you please let her shop early?

No sales before 7:00 A.M.

Your advertisement stated that your sale starts at 7:00 A.M. Did you mean it or not? Rest assured, there will be several individuals ready to test your resolve. STAND FIRM.

Your sale begins at 7:00 A.M. — no exceptions

The only way to do this is to refuse to allow anyone to set foot on your property until 7:00 A.M. Fair is fair. If you allow them to look around, but not buy, you are asking for trouble. Treat everyone equally.

One or two shoppers will get huffy and drive away. Better to offend them than the rest of the crowd. Now that you know it is likely to happen, resolve not to let it bother you.

The initial surge

The first one to three hours of a garage sale are the most hectic. All you need to do is keep one thing in mind — YOU ARE IN CHARGE. You make the rules. Be consistent and stick to them.

The first few hours will seem like a blur

Do not allow yourself to be rushed. Deal with one person at a time. Keep your contact brief. If you cannot fulfill a request or answer a question, just say so. Most shoppers understand the pressure of the opening minutes.

Some garage sale shoppers may express impatience when standing in line. Rest assured, they are used to it. Make certain that you have added the amount due correctly. Do not be afraid to double–check. Overlooking items in the checkout process and making incorrect change are the two biggest problems faced by the cashier. If things get really hectic, have the answer person serve as a second cashier.

You control the checkout process

As a courtesy, take time to wrap and bag a customer's purchases. Hopefully, you have plenty of bags, boxes, and wrapping paper on hand. If you get extremely busy, ask the customer if he would mind doing his own packing if you provide the materials. Most will readily agree.

When do I reduce prices

If you marked your objects to sell, there may be no reason to reduce prices. Remember, the only price that counts is the one that makes you, not the buyer, happy. While price haggling is an inevitable part of the garage sale process, you need not haggle from the start.

Expect shoppers to haggle

We very much favor taking a position that you will not reduce prices in any way for the first two hours of the sale. If the person has it in his hand, he wants it. Haggling is often not about price, but winning.

Of course, there are people who just love to haggle. You may be one of them. Decide what works best for you.

Make your position clear. If you are not going to haggle, put up a sign: ALL PRICES FIRM. If things are going well, you may want to hold firm on prices past the two hour mark.

Do not yield too easily

If you are uncomfortable with haggling consider a policy of discounting the entire sale at various time intervals. For example, after the third hour, replace your ALL PRICES FIRM sign with a sign reading EVERYTHING DISCOUNTED TWENTY PERCENT. Select a discount percentage with which you can live.

How low should you go? Fifty percent is generally rock bottom for most sellers. In one instance we saw a sign at a sale in the last fifteen minutes that read: IF YOU CAN USE IT, TAKE IT. They took the goal of getting rid of the material seriously. Within a short time, the last minute scavangers had pretty nearly wiped them out.

What about left bids

Eliminate after sale headaches

Our advice is do not take them. Avoid the hassle. You want to sell. The person making the request wants to buy. Explain that you will be discounting prices during the day. If he wants to take his chances and come back later in the day and buy the object, fine. You will be glad to sell it to him if it is still there. You will be surprised, when given the option of buying or losing an item, the number of garage sale shoppers who opt to buy.

Breaks

Everyone needs a break

Do not think about taking a break until well into the afternoon. Keep a cooler of soda and other beverages on hand. A candy bar jolt about mid–morning and lunch time also is a good idea.

Eating in front of your customers is both discourteous and highly distracting. It also may result in a spill or mess on something that someone is in the process of buying. You will not starve to death if you hold off until mid–afternoon.

Stagger the helpers' breaks. The big celebration will occur when the sale ends. There will be plenty of time for evaluation and story telling as the sun sets.

CELEBRATE

Last call!

Expect your sale to run a half hour to an hour longer than advertised. There are garage shopping stragglers. Money is money.

However, when closing time comes and you have had enough, shut the sale down. Move everything that is outside into the garage and lock the door. Pack the unsold objects tomorrow morning.

The first celebration, but not the last

If your sale is held outdoors, start packing up at your advertised closing time. Some stragglers, attracted by your signs rather than the ads, may wish to shop as you are closing. Let them. Whatever they buy is money in your pocket and that much less to wrap. But don't stop packing — just concentrate on the merchandise in which they show no interest.

After securing the proceeds it's time to kick back and relax. Sit down with your co–workers and rehash the day's events. Unwind while swapping anecdotes of the sale's more interesting moments and eccentric characters. Once the party is over and your friends have departed, surrender to that overwhelming urge to count the cash and find out what you earned.

Take a long hot shower, go out for dinner, and CELEBRATE!

HOW TO RUN A GARAGE SALE

CHAPTER THREE

Is There Life After Your Garage Sale

The last of the garage sale shoppers left early last evening. You have celebrated your success. You had a good night's sleep. Time to put your garage sale behind you. Well....almost. There still are a few things that need to be done.

Don't put off until tomorrow...

Difficult though it is, attend to them today. The longer you delay, the longer they will take. Make it your mission to go to bed tonight with your garage sale totally behind you.

What am I going to do with all the stuff that is left

One of your garage sale goals was to get rid of everything. You did not do it. Do not be surprised. No garage sale is ever a sellout, even after things have been reduced to "rock bottom/giveaway" prices. Does this mean your garage sale was not successful? Far from it. Just count the cash.

Now, what are you going to do? THIS IS THE MOMENT OF TRUTH. Your mind and your heart say pack the leftovers away and sell them at your next garage sale. WHOA! STOP! WRONG!

Get rid of it, don't repack it

Remember your goal — get rid of the stuff. Your principal criteria for selecting the things you offered for sale was that they were no longer of use to you. Storing them is not going to change this. Stick to your goal.

A number of options exist from which to choose. First, you can remove price stickers and sort the items into box lots, e.g., glassware in one, clothing in another. Each box should contain one to two dozen items. Call several local auctioneers to see if any sell box lots on consignment. If you find one, arrange to drop the boxes off, provide an address to which the sales check can be sent, and drive away. Do not be surprised if the auctioneer refuses some of the lots. He may also need to combine box lots in order to get a bid.

Make box lots

Second, you may be approached by one or more individuals who specialize in buying the remains of garage sales. They take whatever is left for a small cash payment. Do not pay someone to haul your stuff away.

A little something is better than nothing

Third, consider donating what remains to a local charity. Goodwill, the Salvation Army, or a local church that holds an annual rummage sale are three possibilities. If you take this route, you will be able to take a small tax deduction. Be sure to ask for a receipt.

Try the "FREE" route

Fourth, you can give the remainder away for free. Put everything out by the curb with a sign "Free for the Taking." You will be surprised how much disappears. Whatever is left will qualify for the final alternative — the landfill. We know all about the concept of "too good to throw out." However, after it has been picked through for a day by some of the most experienced shoppers in the world, this old adage may no longer apply. Bite the bullet and trash it. Within a few days, you will not even miss it.

When all else fails, it's landfill time

Return the stuff you borrowed

Neither a borrower be

Chances are you borrowed a few things, e.g., tables, chairs, adding machine, etc., from friends and neighbors. Return them today. Avoid the embarrassment of receiving a call a month from now asking if you still have the things you borrowed.

Take down your signs

Don't be a litterbug

In some cases, local ordinances compel you to do this within twenty–four to forty–eight hours after a sale. Who cares what the law says? Do it immediately, not because you have to, but because it is common courtesy. Every experienced garage sale shopper can tell dozens of stories about hunting for sales that existed at some point in the past.

Do your accounting

Everyone likes to know what they made. Why should you be any different. Total up. Deduct expenses and take out the moneys you advanced the sale for change before figuring your total earnings.

Settle up

If you had items on consignment or participated in a multi–family sale, do the totals and disburse the funds. Be sure to deduct the pre–-arranged amount for supplies and advertising from each family's earnings.

It is amazing how little patience people have when they are owed money. Be prompt.

Celebrate a Second Time

Last night's celebration was to let off steam. Now it is time to get serious. Before your sale you set some specific monetary goals. Time to begin spending the money.

Celebrate again

Each time the proceeds pay a bill or buy a luxury item you will know your garage sale was worth the effort. Ah, the sweet taste of success!

HOW TO SHOP A GARAGE SALE

CHAPTER FOUR

Preparing For The Hunt

Shopping garage sales is serious business. If you do not take it seriously you will miss a lot of great buys. However, seriousness and fun are not mutually exclusive. Your mission, should you decide to accept it, is to retain the serious side while at the same time ensuring large amounts of fun, fun, and MORE FUN! It is not an impossible mission.

Make it fun

Be prepared — the Boy Scouts' and your marching song

Be prepared — that is the key to having fun. Take a few minutes to do a little advanced planning. It will pay off handsomely. The steps are simple. Once you have done them a few times they will become automatic. The goal is to keep focused on why you go garage sale shopping in the first place — to find great bargains.

Plan ahead

Step #1 — Allow enough time to make your garage sale shopping experience meaningful. There is no question you will feel pressured wondering what you may be missing at the next sale you plan to attend. Pace yourself. It is better to shop a few sales well, than to rush through a dozen so quickly that you miss the very things for which you are hunting.

Pace yourself

The typical garage sale shopper spends between three and four hours on the garage sale circuit. Of course, there are garage sale junkies that spend the entire day going from one sale to another. This is not for everyone. After a few garage sale shopping experiences, you will find a time frame that suits you best.

Be flexible. You probably have seen the bumper sticker that reads: "I Brake for Garage Sales." Once you have been bitten by the garage sale bug it is difficult to drive by any garage sale. Do not feel guilty. Give in to temptation every now and then. We all do.

The call of a bargain is hard to resist

Step #2 — Buy a detailed street map of the counties within an hour's drive of your home. If there are large metropolitan areas, obtain city maps. Make certain all the maps you acquire have a street index. Most garage sale shoppers believe that you cannot have too many maps. They are right.

If you are a free spirit, forget this advice. Just get in the car and go. After a few garage sale shopping adventures, you will quickly learn which neighborhoods are most likely to have the best garage sales.

Take a friend

Step #3 — Ask a friend to accompany you. Garage sale shopping with others doubles the enjoyment. Do not worry about the competition. The only "there are no friends at a garage sale" fanatics are those individuals looking for antiques and collectibles, not recyclable goods.

A friend is especially helpful when driving around trying to spot a garage sale. Sudden stops and turns are an invitation to an automobile accident. A friend can spot the signs while you keep your mind on driving and eyes on the road.

It will come as no surprise that a friend's presence will shorten the length of time between stops. Not actually, but it will seem that way. Nothing is more fun than the immediate enjoyment of talking about the bargains purchased or passed by at the last garage sale.

Find out where the sales are

Step #4 — Obtain copies of local newspapers that have garage sale classified advertising. Most daily papers run garage sale advertisements in their Thursday edition. Do not forget to pick up local pennysaver/shopper's newspapers.

Read the advertisements and circle the sales that attract your attention. Look for key words and phrases, e.g., moving, everything must go, or cleaning out grandma's attic. If the seller includes a telephone number, use it. Not everyone will follow our earlier advice and omit their telephone number from their advertisement. Find out as much about a sale in advance as you can.

A great sounding advertisement does not always mean a great sale. Experienced garage sale shoppers focus on location. Garage sales in middle and upper class neighborhoods yield the best results.

Don't be afraid to stray off the beaten path

Step #5 — Make a list of the sales you plan to attend. If you are unfamiliar with an address, check your maps. Prioritize the list, noting those sales you want to hit first. Plot a route that minimizes your driving time and maximizes your time at the sales.

Several garage sales may be off the beaten track. Don't ignore them. Remember Robert Frost's poem about the road less traveled. Some garage sale shoppers prefer more remote sales because they know the majority of shoppers are concentrating on the main line sales.

Exact change express lane

Step #6 — A day or two before you plan to go garage sale shopping, take a trip to the bank and obtain a supply of dimes, quarters, and one and five dollar bills. You will reduce the time spent at any garage sale check–out table if you can provide exact change. Fifty and one hundred dollar bills may impress a dealer at an antiques show. They will not impress anyone at a garage sale. All you will do is cause a minor crisis if the seller cannot make change. If he can, you will probably wipe out all his change.

How much cash you carry is up to you. Fifty dollars should be more than enough. Skilled shoppers generally spend between ten and twenty dollars in the course of a day. If you find a high ticket item you want, leave a deposit and head back home for the extra cash you need.

Cash only, please

CASH IS KING AT GARAGE SALES. While some sellers may relunctantly take a check, they are rarely comfortable doing so. The risk factor is too great. Do not complicate the buying experience. Think of garage sales in "cash and carry" terms.

Step #7 — Round up packing supplies and put them in your car or van. Never assume that the garage sale seller is going to provide adequate packing material. It is a plus when you find one that does.

Get your purchases home safely

Title to an object passes when money changes hands. Once you buy an object, it is your responsibility to get it home safely. Many a garage sale shopper has carelessly thrown a prized purchase in the back of his car, only to find that it broke during the trip home.

Here are some suggestions. Pick and choose as you will:

1. Three or four cardboard boxes (liquor boxes are great).
2. Several sections of bubble wrap or a roll of packing paper. You will find both at your local stationery store. Most people use old newspaper. Be aware that the ink can smear and damage some items.
3. Half a dozen to a dozen kitchen or hand towels to wrap delicate objects.
4. Small pieces of cardboard to insert between objects to prevent them from bumping together.

Recycle your packing supplies

Avoid small styrofoam peanuts or discs. Spilled, they are a disaster — something that usually happens when one is in a hurry.

Step #8 — Gas up the car or van the night before the garage sale, especially if you are one of those individuals who plans to be on his way by 6:30 A.M. We recommend putting the advertisements, maps, and packing materials in your car or van the night before — the less things to remember the morning of the garage sale hunt the better.

Get ready the night before

Consider including these additional items:

1. A few candy bars for a quick energy boost if you plan to make a day of it. It is hard to justify a stop for lunch, especially if you are on a roll.
2. Notepad and pencil to make notes of your purchases.
3. Prepackaged hand cleaning tissues — do not become a garage sale shopper if you are afraid to dirty your hands.

Chances are you'll shop right through lunch

4. Box of tissues — doubles as packing material for smalls.
5. First aid kit — hopefully you will never need it.
6. Flashlight — some garages are mighty dark.
7. Umbrella or poncho — if it begins to rain a few hours into a garage sale Saturday, a surprising number of sellers are going to find a way to stay open.

The early bird catches the worm

Step #9 — Get a good night's sleep. Hit the garage sale circuit early. Veteran shoppers agree that the best buys are made either early in the morning before the bargains have been picked clean or late in the day when sellers are wearily eyeing the piles of merchandise waiting to be repacked. Even if you only spend a few hours garage sale shopping, it is likely that these hours will be highly intense. You will feel less pressured and more energetic if you are well rested.

There are no bathrooms on the garage sale circuit

Step #10 — Limit how much you eat and drink before heading out garage sale shopping. If you have weak kidneys, do not drink two to three cups of coffee.

Assume that the only available restrooms will be at gas stations and restaurants along the way. Sellers will strongly resist requests to use their restrooms. Their most likely response will be to provide you with directions to the nearest public facility. I have yet to attend a garage sale, even a neighborhood one, that made arrangements to have a portable restroom on site. The expense at a small sale would be prohibitive.

Overkill

How much of the above is overkill? While the correct answer is none of it, the more realistic answer is much of it. Your personality will determine how many of these steps you implement.

Count on a man to take the pleasure out of garage sale shopping

The obsessive compulsive individual, i.e., the plotter and planner, will follow all these suggestions and even add a few of his own. This is a shopper who is taking the process entirely too seriously. Garage sale shopping for him is equivalent to staging a military campaign. Battle strategies must be planned and executed. Victory or defeat is determined by the purchases of the day. If you take garage sale shopping this seriously, we recommend you find another outlet for your energies.

Our intention throughout this book is to encourage you to pick and choose those things that you want to do and ignore the rest. There is no one right way to go garage sale shopping. There are hundreds of right ways. Which way is best? The one that works for you.

HOW TO SHOP A GARAGE SALE

CHAPTER FIVE

Big Game Ahead

Today is the big day. You are going garage sale shopping. The weather is perfect — the sun is out and the humidity is low. Your best friend is going with you. All is right with the world.

Heigh Ho, Heigh Ho!

Your advance planning has worked like a charm. It has only been a matter of minutes and you are already drawing near to your first garage sale of the day. Anticipation is running high. As you round the corner, you immediately notice more than a dozen cars already parked at the site. Suddenly your heart beats faster than normal. Your mind entertains thoughts such as "I didn't arrive early enough; all the bargains are gone."

STOP. Slow down. Take a few deep breaths. There is plenty for everyone at a good garage sale. Many garage sale shoppers will tell you that they made some of their greatest purchases late in the day.

You will find your share

One experienced garage sale shopper shared his philosophy with us. It made so much sense, we decided to pass it along. This shopper used to rush through a garage sale in order to get to the next one as quickly as possible. He was afraid of missing bargains, afraid someone already had bought the thing he would most love to own. The thrill of the chase was overpowering. Instead of coming home from his garage sale shopping tired, yet content, he arrived home tense and frustrated. He loved garage sale shopping, but not what it was doing to him.

His solution was to adopt the following philosophy: "If God meant for me to own it, it will be at a garage sale when I get there and at or below a price that I am willing to pay." The dark garage sale shopping clouds disappeared overnight. He not only found garage sale shopping to be a much more enjoyable experience, he actually bought more items, rather than less.

Just waiting for me to buy it

This is not surprising. The garage sale shopper now had the time to poke around. He noticed five times as many desirable items as he did before. "How many great things can I buy in a day" is now the record toward which he aspires, not "how many garage sales can I visit in a day."

If you are meant to own it, it will be there. The great news is there are hundreds of items with your name on them. The same holds true for everyone. Imagine those unfortunate souls who never go garage sale shopping to see what items are inscribed with their name.

It had my name on it

MAKE IT AN ADVENTURE

Stalking the prey

It is easy to draw an analogy between garage sale shopping and big game hunting. The jungle is thick (dozens of sales) and dense (five in the same block). You have to work to find the game (object) that you seek. There are hundreds of distractions (stuff in which you have no interest) and a few pitfalls (everyone gets lost sooner or later). Not every animal (object) you see is a keeper. Some will be too old (damaged or heavily worn) to be of interest, others too young (you just bought a new one). When you do not have a clear shot at the animal (you are not quite willing to pay the price asked), you will have to maneuver (haggle). Sometimes this pays off (you buy the object), other times it does not (you leave empty handed). Enough! You get the picture.

Success is determined by the fun you had, not by what you did or did not buy

Garage sale shopping is an adventure. First, there is the thrill of the hunt. For many shoppers, this is all that is necessary. They do not really care how many great buys they make. Their joy comes from the act of doing. Second, there is the excitement of bagging the game, especially when you make an incredible buy that provides you with bragging rights for the rest of your life. Not every purchase is of trophy proportion. Who cares so long as the object is usable and cheap?

You already know from reading earlier portions of this book two of the key tips to garage sale shopping: cash is king and bring your own packing materials. Here are five more tips for you to consider:

To haggle or not to haggle — that is the question

Do not argue over small change

Let's put the matter of haggling quickly behind us. There are born hagglers and there are persons who detest it. Unfortunately, some garage sale shoppers think it is the only way to buy something. This is not true. We suggest you keep haggling to a minimum. There really is no sense in arguing over nickels, dimes, and quarters.

Make the seller do the pricing

Garage sale objects should be priced. Ideally, this means a price marked on each item. It is the responsibility of the seller to make the initial offer. When you find a garage sale with unpriced goods, do not hesitate to inquire "how much do you want?" Most sellers will respond with a set price. Occasionally you may encounter a seller who replies "how much will you give?" Put the object down and walk away. It is not your job to price a person's merchandise for them. Do not let any transaction become a contest to "see how much you will pay." Remember, you are bargain hunting.

Assuming an object is priced, only one of three possibilities now exists — the object is priced below what you are willing to pay, near what you are willing to pay, or so much above what you are willing to pay that a counteroffer would be ridiculous.

Don't kick a guy when he's down

If the object is priced below what you are willing to pay, buy it. Do not haggle. You would not like being kicked when you made a pricing mistake. Why do it to someone else?

If the object is priced far above what you are willing to pay, save yourself and the seller the hassle and walk away. If you make a really low counteroffer, the seller is either going to think you are incredibly cheap, insulting his intelligence, or both. Do not look for trouble.

Pick battles you can win

All that remains are those objects that are priced slightly higher than you are willing to pay. The seller has made his offer. It is up to you to make a counteroffer.

Minimize haggling

NOW FOR THE BEST ADVICE IN GARAGE SALE SHOPPING — MAKE YOUR COUNTEROFFER A ONCE AND DONE DEAL. Yep, do not haggle. Give it your best and only shot. If the offer is taken, the deal is done. If not, walk away. The end result will save you and the seller a tremendous amount of time.

Be prepared to decide instantly

Most garage sale sellers do not want to be bothered by left bids. Who can blame them? No seller wants a sale to linger into the night or next day because they have to make numerous telephone calls and appointments regarding earlier offers .

Buy now

Make your decision to buy or not to buy instantly. Garage sale shopping requires decisive actions. Oh, you could take a stroll around the yard or block to think about it. Why waste the time?

Follow this simple rule. If you have to think more than twice about an object, do not buy it. Do not fight what your mind is trying to tell you. It is time to move on to something else.

Check for completeness

Buy only if something is complete

When you buy at garage sales, you buy at your own risk. Caveat emptor — let the buyer beware. ALL SALES ARE FINAL. Only a fool does not take time to check and double-check an object's completeness. For example, count the parts of a boxed board game or the pieces in a silver flatware service. If you are unsure everything is there, put the object down and walk away — no matter how tempting the price.

How important are the original box and/or instructions? If you know how something works, they are not very important. If you do not, or the thing you are considering buying requires assembly, they are.

$^1/_2 + {}^1/_2 = {}^3/_4$

Do not delude yourself into thinking that if you buy an incomplete unit, you easily will find another incomplete unit and assemble one good unit out of two incomplete ones. Yeah, right! Resist this tempation unless working from a specific list of parts needed.

When an object is incomplete, take time to check the surrounding area. The missing parts or accessories may be with another object or in another box. The seller may have simply forgotten to put them out. Ask the seller if he knows where they are located. You will be surprised at the number of affirmitive answers you will receive. However, be prepared for the occasional "are you kidding?" response.

Be aggressive, but not obnoxious

Ask the seller to hold the objects you want to buy

When you see something you want at a garage sale, grab it and hang on to it. If you put it down, you might lose it. We have had this happen more times that we care to remember. If you see a number of items you would like, ask the seller to set your selections aside for you. Be fair to both the seller and other buyers. Be discriminating. We have seen individuals make a large stash and then, after shopping the entire sale, re-examine their choices and return a large percentage to the tables. This is not only rude, it can be costly to the seller. Items you are holding in reserve are unavailable to other buyers. Keeping this in mind, if you should experience a change of heart, we have yet to attend a garage sale where a sign said: "Sold The Moment You Pick It Up!"

Respect "Off Limits" requests

Do not be afraid to tell the seller your wants

Most individuals will post their home as off limits. The same may be true about a portion of the garage. While it is important to respect any "Not For Sale" signs, nothing prevents you from asking the seller if he has specific objects for sale that you want but did not see. Often a suggestion may remind him of something he forgot to put out or an item for which he thought there would be no interest. If the seller responds in the positive and the sale pace is hectic, offer to return at another time. Besides, you do not want to alert other shoppers to the possibility of another gold mine to be explored.

Do not waste time asking for a receipt

Garage sale finances: nobody's business but your own

Do not ask for a receipt. You will not get one. Although we provide a sample sales receipt, we have yet to attend a garage sale where a seller was prepared to give a receipt. Receipts take time to write, something that is a scarce commodity at a highly successful garage sale. Even if you offer to provide a receipt that they can use, most sellers will refuse. Garage sale earnings are rarely claimed as income. Most sellers are reluctant to provide a written record of these unreported transactions.

Likewise, if a garage sale seller tries to charge sales tax, tell him to take a hike. The seller is attempting to pocket extra cash. Rest assured, virtually no garage sale income is ever reported to the authorities, no matter what the law.

CELEBRATE

Our advice to garage sale shoppers is the same as it is for garage sale sellers. At the end of a successful day, set aside a few minutes to celebrate. Sit back and survey the fruits of your labor. However, before you call it a day, take time to do the following:

1. Unload the car and unpack the goodies. Make certain everything arrived home safely. Set those objects aside that need cleaning or those designated as gifts for friends, the kids, or grandchildren. Store the rest away until you need them.
2. Check your notes and complete a final log of your acquisitions. If you do not care what you spent and on what purchases, skip this step.
3. Convince your spouse to take you out to dinner. It will not work all the time, but it will some of the time. Some is better than none.

Enjoy your treasures

That is all there is to do. Give yourself a pat on the back. Slap a high five. It takes awhile for the adrenalin rush of a successful garage sale shopping day to end. This is as it should be.

May all your finds be treasures.

PRICE GUIDE TIPS

Welcome to the first detailed price guide for items sold primarily at garage sales. Its purpose is to take as much guesswork as possible out of the "how much should I charge for this?" question. There are a number of things we ask you to keep in mind when using it:

1. There are no fixed prices for garage sale objects. These are guides, not absolute prices. You make the final decision about how much to ask. The only price that really counts is the one that makes you happy. This applies to garage sale shoppers as well as sellers.

2. These prices are identical to those found on similar goods which we have seen sold at garage sales, small town and rural auctions, church bazaars, and swap meets. They reflect what a bargain conscious garage sale shopper is willing to pay provided he needs the object in question.

   It is hard to price objectively when you are the seller. Everyone thinks his objects must be worth more, if for no other reason than that they belong to him and he has taken good care of them. Time for a reality check.

3. We realize that these values may appear low to some sellers. We ask you to remember that one of the principal goals of your garage sale is to sell everything. Our suggested prices are reasonably set, but bargain driven. We want you to sell fast. When the price is a bargain at the onset, counteroffers are reduced. Word will spread like wildfire among garage sale shoppers at other sales that there are bargains to be had at your sale.

4. Pricing is based on the concept that these pieces are ready to use or display. Everything is complete and/or works. No major or minor repairs need to be done to the piece to make it usable.

5. If an object is still in production, mark it with a price that is ten to twenty percent of its current retail value. Attempting to recover fifty cents on the dollar for small ticket items is far too ambitious. Garage sale shoppers will not pay this amount.

6. Our prices are designed to cover broad general categories of objects. You will only find a few specific manufacturers and/or models listed. Questions such as does it work, is it complete, and how old is it, are more important at a garage sale than who made it.

7. Take time to read the introductions. They are loaded with great hints and pricing tips relevant to each category.

8. If you mark an object with the price we suggest, does this mean it is guaranteed to sell? We wish it did, but it does not. Price is momentary. Every sale is contingent upon there being a buyer who needs or wants the object — regardless of its price. We do hope that if you follow our suggested pricing, there will be far more right than wrong moments.

ADDING MACHINES

Although manual (nonelectric) adding machines have an obvious advantage during power outages and for use at remote sites with no electric service, most people are more comfortable using modern electric adding machines. The older manual styles are not only cumbersome to carry, they are also exhausting to use, as the operator must crank the registering arm following each entry.

Be sure to include your extra rolls of adding machine tape with your adding machine. A potential buyer would also be impressed with a machine whose printing is sufficiently dark to read. Install a new ribbon or cartridge if necessary.

Adding Machine, Texas Instruments, TI-5045 II, twelve digits, two-color printing, $10.00.

Electric	10.00
Manual	4.00

AFGHANS

Every home has at least one knitted or crocheted afghan. Customarily given as wedding and shower gifts, many homeowners have several – some never used! The best sellers are freshly laundered afghans made in neutral or currently popular complementary decorator colors. Generally, bigger *is* better.

Baby Size	4.00
Couch Size	8.00
Doll Size	.50
Double Bed Size	12.00
Lap Size	5.00

AIR CLEANERS

Today's air cleaners are deluxe versions of their earlier, simpler counterparts. Older cleaners (5 years and older) were electric table top models with charcoal filters that required frequent replacement. The newer purifiers are larger and more efficient. Some are equipped with filter change indicators and filters that can last from three months to three years. Before buying an older model, be sure replacement filters are still available.

Less Than 5 Years Old	
multiple speed, filter indicator	25.00
single speed, filter indicator	15.00
More Than 5 Years Old	2.00

AIR CONDITIONERS

When selling an air conditioner, the higher the BTU value, the higher the price tag. An exception to this rule is commercial or other oversized models. If it is too big to fit in the average home's window, chances are you will have a hard time selling it, and should discount its price accordingly. Age is also a factor. Newer air conditioners compact a higher BTU rating into a smaller unit, are lighter weight, and should have seen less use.

If you are shopping for an air conditioner at a garage sale, be sure to measure the size of your window opening before you buy. Nothing could be worst than buying an air conditioner, lugging it home, and finding it is too big for your window.

Hotpoint Porta-Cool, 4,000 BTU, window unit, $35.00.

4000 – 6000 BTU
- less than 5 years old 60.00
- more than 5 years old 35.00

8000 – 10,000 BTU
- less than 5 years old 80.00
- more than 5 years old 50.00

12,000 – 18,000 BTU
- less than 5 years old 150.00
- more than 5 years old 100.00

Over 18,000 BTU
- less than 5 years old 200.00
- more than 5 years old 150.00
- oversized 150.00

APPLIANCES, KITCHEN

The two most important factors in selling electrical appliances are that they work and all parts and accessories are intact. Be prepared to plug in appliances to demonstrate that they are in working order. Having the original manuals and instructions is also a plus – display them with the appliances. Finally, cleaning and shining your appliances can make the difference between selling them at a reasonable price and not selling them at all.

Bag Sealer, electric 4.00

Blender
- single speed 5.00
- multiple speeds 10.00

Blender, Osterizer Imperial, Dual Range Pulse Matic 12, $10.00.

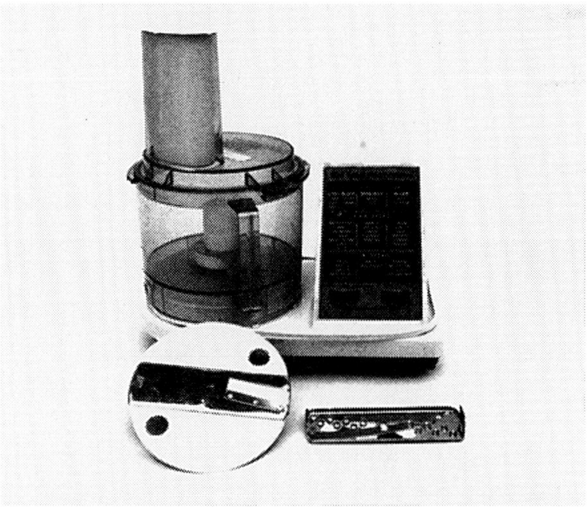

Food Processor, Hamilton Beach Scovill, Dual Speed, $10.00.

Bread Machine 35.00

Can Opener, electric 2.00

Cappuccino Machine 20.00

Coffee Grinder
- electric 3.00
- manual 2.00

Coffee Maker, electric
- drip
  - no features, on/off switch only 3.00
  - programmable, digital 12.00
- percolator, glass or metal 2.00

Convection Oven 25.00

Crock Pot
- 1 gallon
  - one piece 3.00
  - removable crock 5.00
- 1½ gallon
  - one piece 5.00
  - removable crock 8.00

Deep Fryer
- fry baby 3.00
- full size 5.00

Dehydrator 20.00

Egg Whip, electric 2.00

Espresso Machine 20.00

Fondue
- electric 3.00
- sterno 1.00

Food Chopper, electric 2.00

Food Processor
- full size 10.00
- miniature 7.50

Food Steamer 5.00

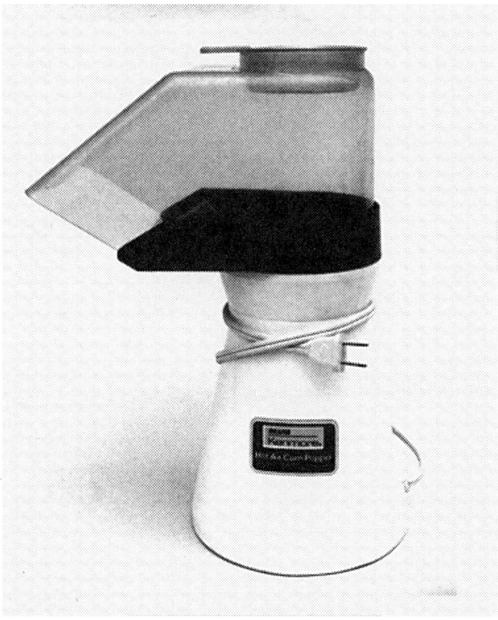

Popcorn Popper, Sears Kenmore, Hot Air Corn Popper, $4.00.

Frying Pan, electric
- Teflon or Silverstone 5.00
- uncoated 3.00

Hamburger Griller, individual 2.00
Hot Dog Cooker, cooks six hot dogs, electric 2.00
Hot Plate 5.00
Hot Shot 3.00
Ice Cream Freezer 5.00
Ice Crusher 3.00
Juicer
- electric 5.00
- manual 3.00

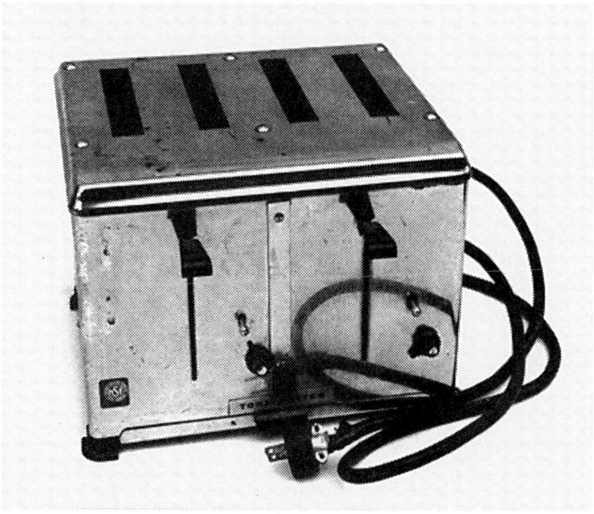

Toaster, Toastmaster, 4 slice, $4.00.

Knife, electric 3.00
Knife Sharpener 2.00
Meat Slicer, electric 15.00
Microwave Oven
- less than 1 cubic foot capacity, two power levels 25.00
- more than 1 cubic foot capacity, programmable, multiple power levels 35.00

Mixer
- counter top
  - two bowls, juicer, dough hook, and wire whip. 25.00
  - two bowls, no attachments 15.00
- hand held 5.00

Pasta Maker 12.00
Popcorn Popper
- hot air 4.00
- oil 2.00

Roaster, electric, floor model 20.00
Rotisserie 15.00
Sandwich Grill 3.00
Toaster
- 2 slice 2.00
- 4 slice 4.00

Toaster Oven 8.00
Waffle Iron, electric 5.00
Wok, electric 2.00

ARTIFICIAL FLOWERS

Beauty is purely in the eyes of the beholder. In the case of artificial flowers, a floral arrangement that brightened your home may clash with your neighbors' decor. Be conservative when pricing. While retail prices for home decorating accessories are high, resale value is relatively low. Also, keep in mind that the container holding the arrangement may be worth more than the arrangement itself. Take a closer look at that planter, basket, or vase.

Realistic silk flowers are currently favored over the plastic variety, the latter having been relegated to cemetery logs and memorials. A final note: wash your plastic flowers in soap and water, you'll be amazed at the difference it makes.

Plastic
- arrangement 1.00
- cemetery basket or log 3.00
- holly garland 1.00
- individual, price per dozen 25

Silk
- arrangement 4.00
- individual, price per dozen 1.00
- wreath 4.00

ASHTRAYS

As more people kick the habit, the need for ashtrays has declined. Advertising ashtrays, especially the tire variety with a glass insert, are avidly sought by collectors and should be properly researched before being priced. An exception is common ashtrays from hotels, motels, and restaurants. They are generally inexpensive and plentiful and frequently wind up in the homes of travelers.

Be on the lookout for ashtrays with airliner logos. As more airports and airline companies enforce a no-smoking ban, these should become relatively scarce. Old floor standing ashtrays are also highly collectible, the more ornate, the higher the price. Common glass, metal, ceramic, and plastic examples should be moderately priced.

Common ashtrays, ceramic and glass, $.50 each.

Advertising
- hotel or motel 2.00
- restaurant 2.00
- souvenir, vacation site 2.00
- tires, rubber tire with glass insert 35.00

Common
- ceramic 50
- glass 50
- metal 25
- plastic 25

Personal, brass, lidded 50
Sand Weighted, automobile 2.00
Smokeless, battery operated 3.00
Standing, wood or metal, glass insert
- ornate 50.00
- plain 25.00

ATTACHÉ CASES

Attaché cases run the gamut from inexpensive vinyl to VIP quality top-grain leather. Combination locks, file compartments, fitted pockets, and padded handles are extras found on many cases. If your case locks, do the buyer a favor and provide the combination or key. One sign of luxury which will hamper a sale is the addition of a monogram. Unless the prospective buyer shares your initials, chances of a sale are minimal.

Attaché Case, black leather, combination locks, fitted interior, $10.00.

Leather, fitted interior, locking 10.00
Vinyl
- fitted interior 5.00
- plain 2.00

AUTOMOTIVE ACCESSORIES

When selling auto accessories like racks and carriers, having the necessary hardware certainly helps. Battery chargers, air compressors, and other electrical equipment should be in working order, preferably with original instruction books present. The sale of other accessories such as tires, jacks, and hubcaps, will depend entirely upon the buyer owning a vehicle with identical specifications.

Have you priced auto parts and accessories lately? If you can find them at a garage sale, they can be a great bargain. If they don't fit, or are not compatible with your car, they are useless. Before you buy, be sure it is something you can use.

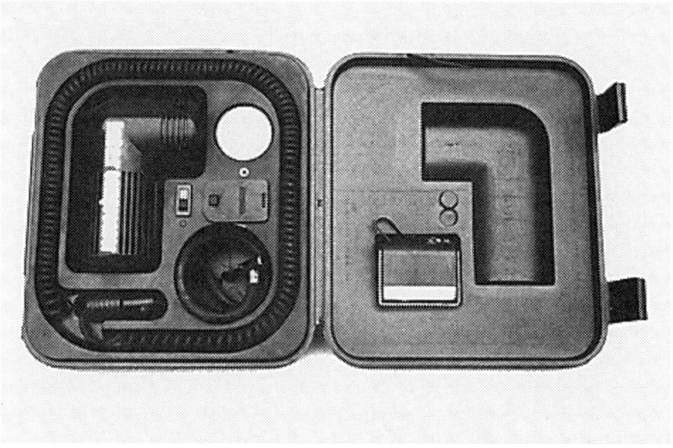

Air Compressor, Inter Compressor, 275 psi, 12 volt, plugs into car lighter, 15' electric cord, 36" air hose, pressure gauge, work light, molded plastic storage case, $20.00.

Air Compressor	20.00
Battery Charger	15.00
Bike Rack	10.00
Car-Top Carrier (turtle shell), plastic, complete with straps and hardware	25.00
Console Organizer	1.00

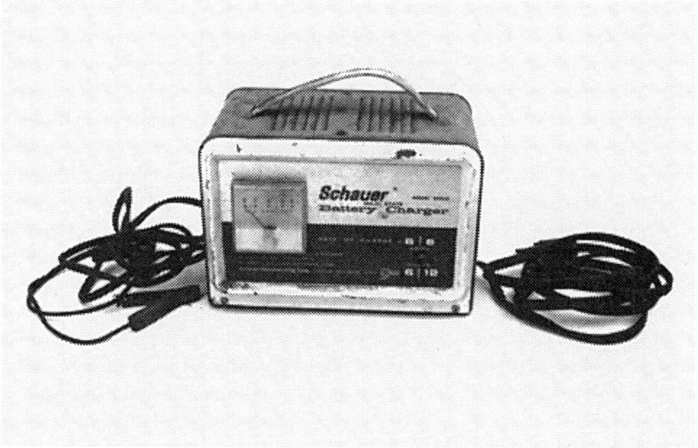

Battery Charger, Schauer, Cincinnati, OH, model B6612, 6° volts, 6 amps, $15.00.

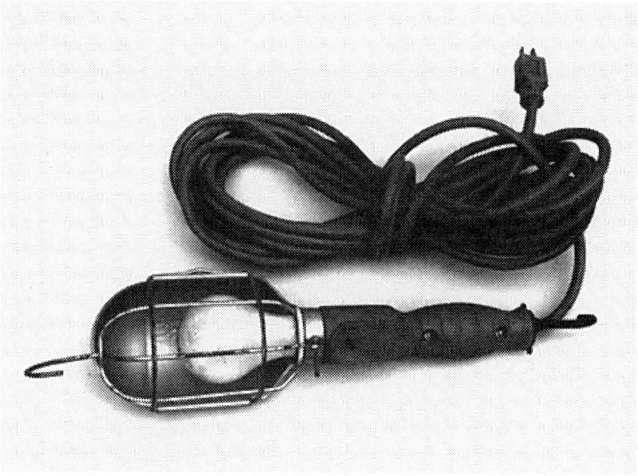

Trouble Light, 50' cord, grounded plug, $5.00.

Cup Holder	.50
Floor Mats, set of four	5.00
Hubcap	5.00
Jack	
hydraulic	10.00
scissor	5.00
tripod	5.00
Lug Wrench	3.00
Radar Detector	15.00
Roof Rack, universal type	15.00
Seat Covers	4.00
Side View Mirrors, extended for towing, pair	5.00
Tire, used	5.00
Tire Chains, pair	5.00
Trailer Hitch	12.00
Trouble Light	5.00
Wheel	
locking, set of 4	75.00
regular	8.00
Windshield Sun Shade, cardboard	1.00

BABY ITEMS

Used baby furniture, clothing, toys, and other paraphernalia are among the most common items found at garage sales. Eventually, they are outgrown and no longer needed.

If you plan on selling that cradle or highchair that's been passed around your family, wait! Is it made from wood? If so, how old is it? Is it an antique? It could be valuable so take the time to check it out.

For the buyer, cleanliness is of utmost importance. It must be clean enough to eat from because, sooner or later, everything ends up in baby's mouth. Furniture and items such as carriers, gates, walkers, etc., should be sturdy and free of cracks or other sharp edges. Monitors and swings must be in working order. Finally, car seats, cribs, and playpens should conform to today's safety specifications.

Activity Center	2.00
Baby Book, unused	2.00
Backpack Carrier	8.00
Bassinet, wicker	20.00
Bath Seat, plastic ring, suction cup feet	1.00
Bath Set, hooded towel and wash cloth	3.00
Bathtub, molded plastic	2.00
Bedding	
bumper set	5.00
mattress	10.00
mattress pad	2.00
sheet set	3.00
Booster Seat	5.00
Bottle	.50
Bottle Sterilizer, holds 9 bottles	5.00
Bouncer	2.00
Car Seat	15.00
Carriage	5.00
Carrier, positions for feeding and reclining	8.00
Cradle, modern	20.00
Crib	25.00
Crib Wedge	2.00
Diaper Bag	2.00
Diaper Genie	4.00
Diaper Pail	1.00
Feeding Dish, plastic, hot water compartment	2.00
High Chair, modern, plastic and metal	15.00
Infant Scale	3.00

Wall Hanging, soft sculpture, fabric, $1.00.

Lamp, nursery theme	4.00
Layette or Changing Table	10.00
Monitor	8.00
Music Box	1.00
Nursery Decorations	
lamp	4.00
mobile	1.00
wall plaque	.50
Playpen	
modern, metal tubing, nylon netting	12.00
old, wood slats	5.00
portable, folds into compact carrying bag	15.00
Potty, plastic	2.00
Receiving Blanket	1.00
Safety Gate	4.00
Stroller	
full size	15.00
umbrella type	5.00
Swing, windup	15.00
Walker	8.00

BAKING ITEMS

Be careful when pricing old kitchen goodies. Many older items are extremely collectible. If your rolling pin is made of glass, or is wood and has colored or fancy turned handles, it could be worth more than the $2 price tag placed on an average example.

Old tin cookie cutters also fetch high prices compared to the aluminum and plastic varieties made today. A general rule of thumb for determining age is the more tin, the older the cookie cutter. Early cutters were shaped tin strips soldered to a rectangular tin back. As time went on and tin became more expensive, the backing piece was gradually pared down, until eventually there was no backing at all. Do some research before pricing your old cutters.

Take a look at the back of your ceramic pie plates. Is there a mark showing the maker? Many American dinnerware manufacturers included a pie baker as a serving piece in their dinnerware lines. Companies such as Hall and Homer Laughlin, to name just two, are currently experiencing strong popularity on the flea market circuit. Look them up before you price.

Baking Board, wood, 36" wide	10.00
Bread Loaf Pan	
glass	2.00
glass, decorative metal or wicker stand	4.00
metal	1.00

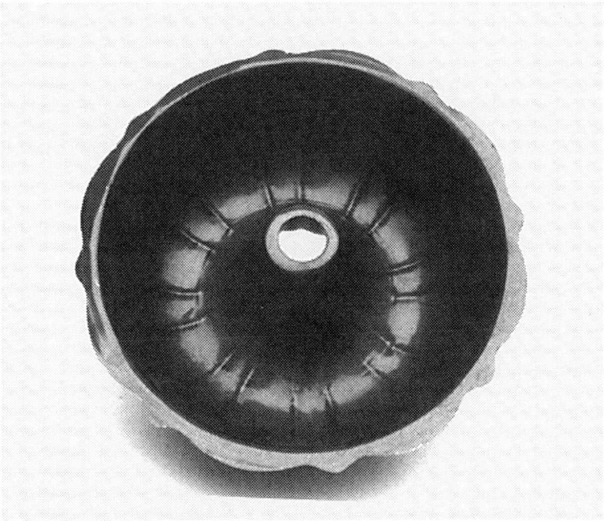

Bundt Pan, Teflon coated interior, blue enameled exterior, $2.00.

Bundt Pan	2.00
Cake Decorator, aluminum	2.00
Cake Pan	
jelly roll	2.00
round or square	1.00
9" x 13", covered	2.00
Cake Racks, cooling, price for pair	2.00
Candle Holders, birthday, plastic, set of 10	
animals or cartoon characters	2.00
flowers	.50
Cookie Cutter	
advertising, tin	3.00
aluminum, modern	.50
plastic, modern	.25
Cookie Sheet	2.00

Cookie Cutters, modern, left: star, aluminum, green wood handle, $.50; center: Kermit the Frog, green plastic, $.25; right: candy cane, red plastic, $.25.

Cupcake Tin	3.00
Muffin Tin	3.00
Nut Tocci Pan	2.00
Petit Four Set, miniature cutters, 10 shapes in original tin can	2.00
Pie Plate	
ceramic, decorated	3.00
china, dinnerware pattern	10.00
glass	2.00
metal	1.00
Rolling Pin, wooden, plain	2.00
Spring Form Pan	3.00
Tube Pan	2.00

BAR SUPPLIES

Many homeowners, when building a rec room, automatically include plans for a bar. Supplies such as those listed below are readily found at garage sales. Cocktail shakers and ice buckets from the 1950s with an Art Deco design command higher prices than other examples. Old beer trays can range in price from $10 to hundreds of dollars. It pays to do some research before pricing these items.

Traveling liquor cabinets enjoyed immense popularity during the 1960s and early 1970s. Resembling a small leather or vinyl suitcase, they carried everything needed for a party away from home. Fitted interiors contained essentials such as shot glasses, cocktail shaker, strainer, stirrer, combination bottle/can opener and corkscrew, four cups, and pockets to hold two or three bottles.

Bar Stool	
metal frame, padded seat and back	10.00
wood	
swiveling	15.00
fixed position	12.00
Beer Mug	
ceramic, stein type	5.00
glass	1.00
pewter	2.00
Clock, beer advertisement, electric	20.00
Coasters	
cardboard, beer advertisement	.10
glass, plastic, or wood, set of 6	2.00
Cocktail Shaker, glass and stainless steel	3.00
Ice Bucket	
glass	5.00
metal	8.00
plastic	3.00

Beer Tray, Schaefer Beer, common, $10.00.

Tupperware	2.00
Mirror, beer advertisement	5.00
Portable Bar	75.00
Serving Tray, beer advertisement, common example	10.00
Shot Glass	
single shot	.25
double shot, bar advertisement	.50
Stirrers	
glass, set of 6	2.00
plastic, advertising	.10
Traveling Liquor Cabinet, complete	20.00

BARBECUE GRILLS & ACCESSORIES

The art of barbecuing has evolved considerably over the last ten years. Everyone remembers the inconvenience of waiting (and waiting) for the charcoal briquets to reach the proper temperature before loading the grill. How often did you go to start the grill only to learn you were either short of charcoal, or couldn't find the lighter fluid? Today's gas grills offer a number of advantages over their predecessors: propane tanks need replacement far less often than bags of charcoal, lighter fluid is no longer needed, temperature can be regulated and, best of all, lava rocks heat up much more quickly.

The hibachi also has its gas counterpart, fueled by the same propane tanks used for Coleman lanterns and camp stoves. It's no wonder there is little demand for the old charcoal grills.

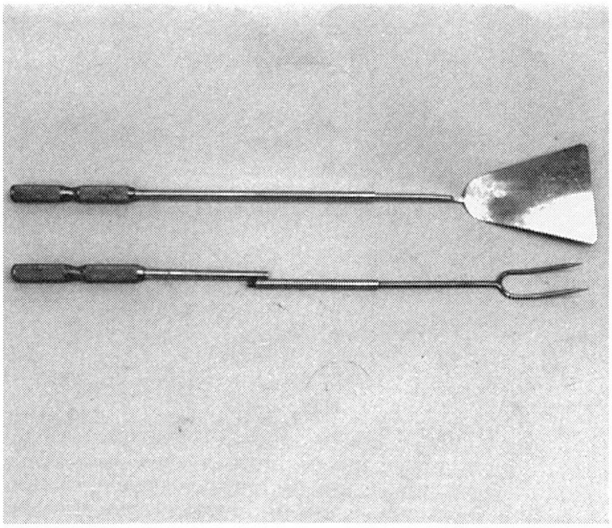

Fork and Spatula, aluminum and stainless steel, unscrew at centers for easy storage, $5.00.

Chef's Apron, cloth, bibbed	2.00
Grill	
charcoal	
full size	1.00
hibachi	2.00
table top	.50
gas	
full size	75.00
table top	15.00
Grill Cover	3.50
Mitts, pair	1.00
Propane Tank	
disposable, 16.4 oz, full	1.00
refillable, 20 lb	
empty	5.00
full	18.00
Rotisserie, electric	5.00
Utensils, long handles, fork, spatula, tongs	5.00

BATTERY CHARGERS & RECHARGEABLE BATTERIES

Anyone who has kids knows the value of rechargeable batteries. Most toys made today require batteries. What could be better than rechargeables? No more searching the junk drawer, only to find weak or dead batteries. Just pop a battery in the charger and you're set.

Although rechargeable batteries do wear down eventually, you probably won't find dead batteries at a garage sale. Most people throw them away once they've outlived their usefulness. Most batteries are interchangeable and can be used in any charger, so name brand is of little importance.

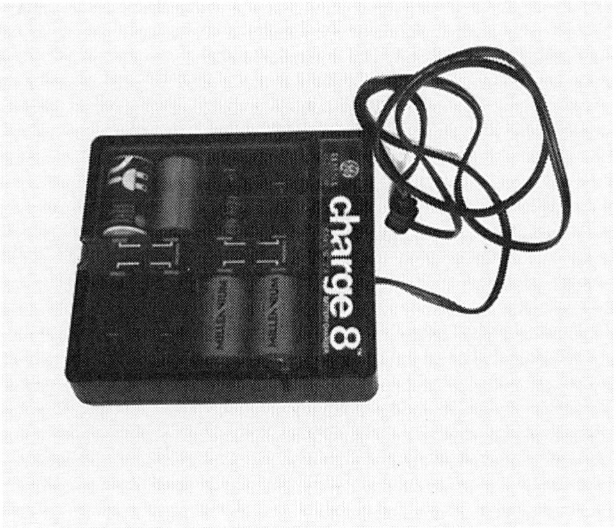

Battery Charger, General Electric Charge 8, $6.00.

Battery	
9 volt, with adaptor	1.00
AAA	.50
AA	.50
C	.50
D	.50
Charger	
4 battery capacity	4.00
8 battery capacity	6.00

BICYCLES

Classic bicycles, such as the Schwinn Phantom and Cleveland Welding Company's Roadmaster command high prices in today's collectibles market. If your bike dates from the 1940s through early 1960s and has fenders, balloon tires, and/or flashy chrome trim, it could be worth hundreds or thousands of dollars, depending on its condition.

Most bicycles found at garage sales will be less than ten years old, castoffs resulting from being outgrown. Usually tagged at a fraction of their original retail price, bicycles make great garage sale buys.

Before you sell your used bike, take the time to clean it up. A bright, shiny bike will sell quicker and for a higher price. Fill the tires with air so prospective buyers can take it for a road test.

Accessories	
baby seat, hardware included	10.00
basket	1.00
bell	2.00
car rack	10.00
chain lock, combination	2.00
handlebar streamers	.50
helmet	5.00
horn	2.00
pedals, pair	2.00
siren	3.00
training wheels	4.00
water bottle and holder	1.50
Bicycle	
12", training wheels	15.00
16", coaster brakes	15.00
20"	
coaster brakes	15.00
hand brakes, multispeed	20.00
24"	
coaster brakes	20.00
hand brakes, multispeed	30.00
26"	
coaster brakes	25.00
hand brakes, multispeed	35.00
Big Wheel, plastic, three wheels	3.00
Power Wheel, 12 volt, accelerator and brake pedals, rechargeable batteries	
full size, holds up to 90 lbs, 2 forward speeds and reverse, jeep, car, or quad racer	45.00
small size, holds up to 40 lbs	20.00

Bicycle, Huffy Westpoint, lady's, 26", hand brakes, 3 speed, $35.00.

Scooter, two wheels	10.00
Tandem Bicycle	50.00
Tricycle	
adult size	25.00
child size	8.00
Unicycle	20.00

BINOCULARS

When comparing binoculars, keep three things in mind: power, lens diameter, and zoom. Power refers to the degree of magnification; the higher the power, the closer the view. Lens diameter is measured in millimeters and determines the binocular's brightness; the larger the diameter the brighter the view. Finally, zoom binoculars allow you to get a closer or more distant view through the use of a lever rather than the traditional focusing dials. A good pair of binoculars will have a power range of 7 to 20 and a lens diameter of at least 35 mm. Having a zoom lever is an added bonus, but not essential. Unless they have been lost, binoculars will also be equipped with four lens covers and a carrying case. The better the set of binoculars, the more expensive the case.

Binoculars, Bushnell Custom, 7 to 21 power x 35 mm, full size, insta-focus, "Squintpruf" lenses, leather case, $15.00.

Compact, 7 to 15 power x 35 mm, case	10.00
Full Size, carrying case and strap	
7 to 15 power x 35 mm	15.00
8 to 20 power x 50 mm	20.00
Miniature, folding sports type	3.00

BIRDBATHS

Birdbaths are quaint additions to any garden. Made of concrete or plastic, they are durable and require little maintenance. During the winter months, the bowl is often removed and replaced with a weighted glass ball. This prevents the bowl from cracking due to ice expansion and adds a festive touch of color during the Christmas season.

Due to its delicate nature, a used glass ball is a rare find. Before you buy, check the bowl for cracks – if it won't hold water its useless.

Birdbath, bowl and pedestal	
concrete	10.00
molded plastic	5.00
Glass Ball Ornament	
8" diameter	5.00
10" diameter	8.00

BOOKENDS

Bookends have been made from almost every material imaginable. A pair of cast iron bookends dating from the late 1920s to the early 1940s can range in price from $60 to over $100. Check for maker's marks on bookends made of metal or ceramics and do your homework. Look for similar examples in general antiques and collectibles price guides. Don't give away valuable Hubley or Roseville bookends for a song.

Metal, institutional type, pair	1.00
Plaster, souvenir, pair	3.00
Plastic, child's, cartoon character, rack type	.50
Pressed Wood, figural, pair	5.00

BOOKS

The value of a book is rarely defined by its age. It is a common fallacy that just because something is old, it must be valuable. While this may often be the case, books are a major exception. Two important factors in determining a book's value are condition and rarity.

Books that are torn or otherwise marred have little value except as reading material. Generally, the first edition of a title is the only edition that may be of value, although even these are often worthless.

Remember the Bible that Grandma had in her parlor? The real big one with heavy embossed covers, lots of color pictures, and the family's history written inside? Here is a great example of the importance of rarity in determining value. These Bibles were well cared for and treasured. Because of this, many, many copies have survived. Its only value is that of sentimentality. It may be beautiful and it may be big but it's still worth only about $40.

Children's books, because of the current interest in famous illustrators, bring fairly good prices. Big Little Books and others of that ilk have been popular for quite some time, with prices remaining relatively stable for the last 15 years. As collector interest in Little Golden Books has increased, so have prices.

Library and book club editions of books, in addition to paperbacks, are of minimal value. The sole purpose of these books is to be read, enjoyed, and passed on.

Bible	
New Testament, pocket size	1.00
pre–1900, oversized	35.00
others	2.00
Children's	
Big Little Book	40.00
coloring books, modern, unused	.50
famous illustrators, post–1900	20.00
Little Golden Book	
1940s	15.00
1950s	10.00
1960s	5.00
others	.50
Hardcover, adult fiction	1.00
Paperback	
adult fiction	.50
children's stories	.25
others	.25
Reference Books	
hardcover	
dictionary	3.00
textbooks	1.00
thesaurus	1.00
paperback	
dictionary	1.50
textbooks	.50
thesaurus	.50

Webster's New World Dictionary of the American Language, Second College Edition, c1980, $3.00.

BREAD BOXES

Bread boxes were once a standard accessory in every kitchen. With the demise of the Hoosier kitchen cabinet and its built-in bread drawer, the need arose for counter top bread boxes. Dinnerware manufacturers such as Hall often had tin and glass accessories made to match their more popular patterns. An Autumn Leaf bread box will bring a higher price than a generic example. Wood boxes with tambour sliding doors were also popular during the 1960s.

Metal	
dinnerware pattern	15.00
generic	8.00
Plastic	3.00
Wood	10.00

BUG ZAPPERS

As recently as five years ago, the crackling and popping of electric bug zappers could be heard in back yards across America. These black light exterminators are no longer the fad they once were. Be wary of buying a used bug zapper, most were used until they malfunctioned, usually due to burned-out bulbs. If you plan on selling your unwanted zapper, be prepared to plug it in.

15 Watt	4.00
40 Watt	6.00
80 Watt, 1½ acre coverage	8.00

BUILDING MATERIALS

Home remodeling often results in the homeowner winding up with a garage full of unwanted building materials. Items that don't make it to the dumpster may include outdated doors, kitchen cabinetry, and hardware. While the homeowner will usually save excess paint and floor and ceiling tiles for future touch-ups and repairs, the remainder may be sold to help recoup expenses. Outdated kitchen cabinets can be recycled for use as laundry room and garage storage. Old paneled doors and shutters are sought by contractors and handymen for old home restorations.

Brick	.20
Concrete Block	.35
Door	
hollow core	5.00
screen, wood	5.00
solid, paneled, old	15.00
Fencing, cast iron, ornate, price per section	40.00
Kitchen Cabinets, price per section	15.00
Screen, louvered, sliding adjustable width	.50
Shutters, pair	
molded plastic	10.00
wood, paneled or louvered, old	20.00

CALCULATORS

Calculator, Royal LD 40, 8 digit, solar and battery powered, EZ Vue tilting lens, sliding cover, $4.00.

Since their inception during the 1970s, pocket calculators have become increasingly affordable and, not surprisingly, commonplace. Originally costing upwards of $50 and $100, they can now be purchased new for as little as $10. It stands to reason that a used example must be very moderately priced in order to sell.

Financial	8.00
Graphics	20.00
Mathematical Functions	
solar and battery powered	4.00
solar powered	2.00

CAMERAS & ACCESSORIES

Camera equipment has been revolutionized since the days of Super 8 movies and Kodak Instamatics. With the onslaught of camcorders and 35 mm autofocus cameras, those earlier relics have become obsolete.

When buying or selling a camcorder at a garage sale, it is virtually impossible to prove the workability of every feature. The best one can do is demonstrate the major functions such as automatic focus, zoom, record, rewind, and fast forward. Be sure to test the battery. A new battery averages about $60.

For the amateur photographer, a 35 mm camera with autofocus is the best buy. Polaroid cameras, with their instant film developing, will appeal to the impatient photographer, provided he is willing to sacrifice quality for speed.

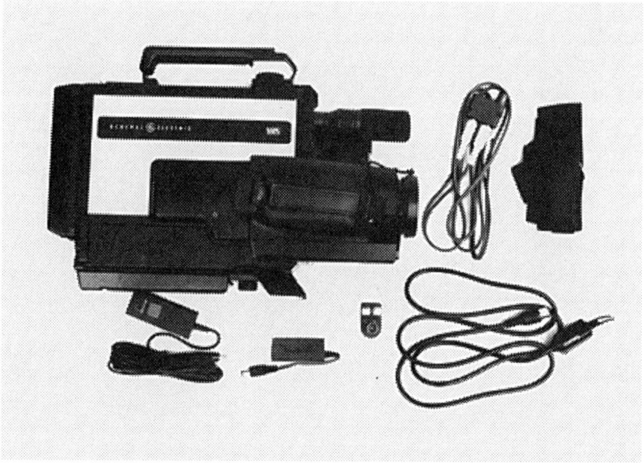

Camcorder, General Electric, VHS, 1980s, $125.00.

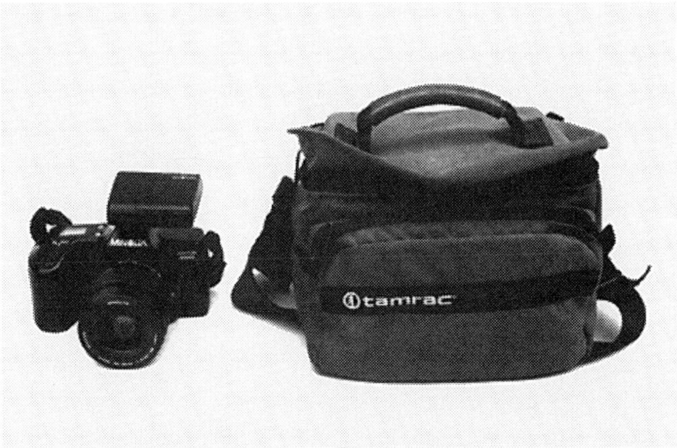

Camera, Minolta Maxxum 3000i, 35 mm, autofocus, autowind, Tamrac camera case, $60.00.

Accessories
- battery pack, camcorder 10.00
- camcorder monitor 20.00
- carrying case
  - fabric, padded
    - camcorder 10.00
    - camera 5.00
  - plastic, camera 1.00
- lenses 15.00
- light meter 4.00
- projection screen 5.00
- projector
  - movie, 8 mm, super 8, or 16 mm .. 3.00
  - slide 10.00
- tripod 12.00
- tripod case, nylon 2.00

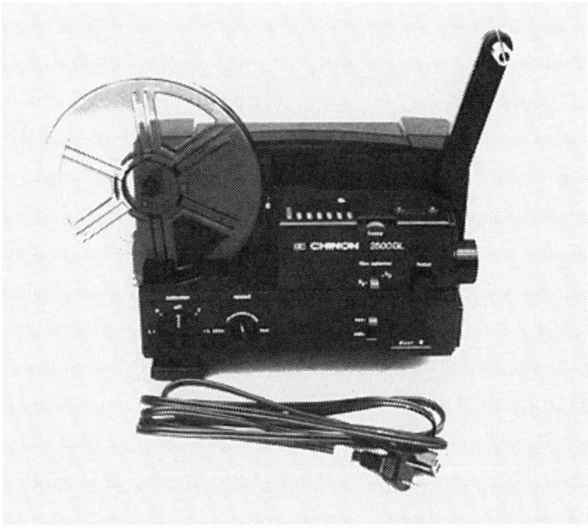

Movie Projector, 8 mm/Super 8, $2.00.

Camcorder, with AC adaptor, battery charger, and battery pack
- 8 mm 125.00
- VHS 125.00
- VHS-C 100.00

Camera
- disc .... .50
- instamatic .... .50
- Polaroid 5.00
- 35 mm
  - autofocus 50.00
  - auto/manual focus combination ... 75.00
  - fixed focus 25.00
  - manual focus 75.00

Movie Camera, 8 mm, 16 mm, or Super 8 . 2.00

CAMPING EQUIPMENT

Camping gear has proven itself to be a good seller at garage sales. With the exception of air mattresses and styrofoam coolers, most camping items are made to last. They are sturdy and durable and realize good prices when resold.

Air mattresses always seem to spring a leak. Be prepared to patch a hole in any used mattress you buy. Coolers range in size from the small 6 pack style to the full size 100 quart variety with drain plug. Some are electric and run from either a 12 volt source or can be converted to AC current.

Cook stoves and lanterns are fueled with either white gas or bottled propane gas. While the propane type is more convenient to use, it costs slightly more to run due to the higher cost of bottled gas canisters. Missing and broken mantles on lanterns are not a problem – they are inexpensive and easily replaced.

Examine zippers on tents and sleeping bags for broken teeth and tears. Check tents for mildew, torn stake loops, and rotted seams, especially on the flooring. Be sure all poles and tent stakes are present. Finally, having the original setup instructions can be extremely useful to the new owner.

Air Mattress
- single 3.00
- double 8.00
- queen 10.00

Air Pump
- foot pump 5.00
- hand pump 2.00
- 12 volt 4.00

Camp Stool 2.00

Canteen, metal, wool covering, canvas strap, $2.00.

Camp Stove	
propane	
1 burner	2.00
2 burners	20.00
white gas	10.00
Canteen	2.00
Compass	1.00
Cooler/Ice Chest	
electric	25.00
insulated, plastic or metal	
6 pack size	5.00
55 quart	10.00
100 quart, drain plug	15.00
styrofoam, any size	1.00
vinyl or nylon, zippered	
tubular, holds five beverage cans	1.50
24 quart, collapsible	3.00
Cot, folding, metal frame, canvas cover	
52" long	3.00
72" long	5.00
84" long	7.50
Duffel Bag, canvas	5.00
Hatchet	1.00
Ice Pack, refreezable	.50
Lamp, 6 volt battery and bulb	3.00
Lantern	
fluorescent, rechargeable	5.00
propane	15.00
white gas	8.00
Mess Kit, stainless steel, 4 pieces	3.00
Porta Potty	20.00
Sleeping Bag	10.00
Sleeping Bag Pad, foam, 20" x 72"	2.50
Swiss Army Knife	2.00
Tarpaulin, canvas or vinyl coated nylon	
8' x 10'	3.00
10' x 20'	5.00
20' x 40'	10.00
Tent	
cabin or dome, 8' x 10', sleeps 4 to 6	25.00
pup, sleeps 2	5.00
two room, cabin, sleeps 8 or more	35.00
Tie-downs, bungie cords	1.00
Water Cooler, metal, insulated, 10 gallon	5.00
Water Jug, plastic, 5 gallon, collapsible	3.00

Cooler, Coleman, plastic, locking, drain plug, blue and white, $15.00.

Lantern, Coleman, white gas, double mantle, $8.00.

CANISTER SETS

Canister sets have been made from various materials, including glass, wood, metal, and ceramics. Preferences are strictly personal, according to the color scheme and/or decorative theme used in your kitchen.

Four piece canister sets, like bread boxes, were also made to complement some popular dinnerware lines. Made of tin, they have floral decals that match the dinnerware's pattern. These will bring slightly higher prices from the right buyer. Glass canisters are plentiful and should be priced low. Plastic examples, on the other hand, are less common but still bring low prices due to their lack of decorative interest. Wooden canisters with decals and/or decoupage decoration have never been particularly popular. Consequently, they are relatively hard to find, although still moderately priced. Prices listed are for four–piece sets.

Ceramic	
cylindrical	8.00
figural	12.00
Glass, wooden lids	5.00
Metal	
dinnerware pattern	18.00
generic design	5.00
plain, silver or copper colored	4.00
Plastic, Tupperware, Rubbermaid, or other similar types	4.00
Wood	5.00

Canister Set, tin, country store theme, purchased with S & H Green Stamps, $5.00.

CANNING EQUIPMENT

With the advent of two–income households, many time consuming chores have fallen by the wayside. Full-time wage earners no longer have the time needed to spend on gardening and canning. Additionally, low supermarket prices and the availability of fresh produce year round has eliminated the need for preserving.

Canners and jars have changed little over the years. The most common canner is enameled dark blue with tiny white specks. A complete canning setup includes a lidded canner, several jars with lids and rings, a jar rack, a jar lifter, and a wide mouthed funnel. You will need to invest in new jar rubbers. Over time they crack and dry out. Rubbers are inexpensive and readily found in most supermarkets.

Canner and Lid	5.00
Funnel, wide mouth, glass, tin, or plastic	.50
Jar, pint or quart, with ring and lid	.25
Jar Lifter	1.00
Jar Rack	1.00

CD PLAYERS & DISCS

The compact disc player is the latest piece of audio equipment to hit the market. Compact discs are superior to their predecessors, the phonograph records, in several ways. Enhanced sound quality, easy care, and competitive prices have all helped to boost CD players and CDs to the top of the sound system heap.

Discs sell best when housed in their original cases. Although discs are reasonably durable, they can be damaged by improper handling. Before buying, carefully examine discs for fingerprints and scratches.

CD players come equipped with numerous options including multi-disc carousels, random and shuffle play, AM/FM stereo, dual cassette decks, and wireless remote control. If it is imperative that your CD player have all these features, you may need to do your shopping at Circuit City.

Disc	4.00
Player	
automotive	35.00
personal	20.00
portable (boombox), single disc	50.00
stereo component, single disc	50.00

CLEANING SUPPLIES

Every household has its share of unwanted cleaning implements. For various reasons, we sometimes end up with duplicate items or machines that we no longer want or need.

Floor polishers and carpet cleaners are tools attractive only to homeowners with plenty of closet space. Many people prefer to rent these machines when needed rather than find a place to store them. Rechargeable vacuum cleaners take up little space and are extremely convenient – provided they still hold a charge. Check to see that attachments are included with vacuum cleaners and be sure to test all electrical appliances before buying.

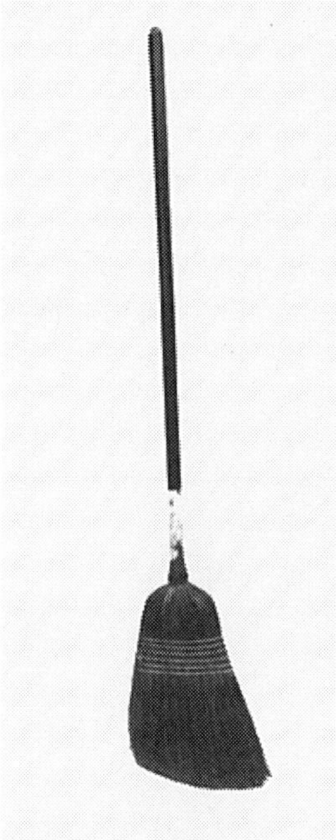

Broom, Hercules, Hamburg Broom Company, Hamburg, PA, $3.00.

Broom	3.00
Bucket	
galvanized	2.50
plastic	1.00
Carpet Cleaner/Steamer	10.00
Dry Mop	1.00
Dust Pan & Brush	1.00
Electric Broom	8.00
Feather Duster	1.00
Floor Polisher, buffer	8.00
Rug Beater	10.00
Scrub Brush	.50

Feather Duster, ostrich feathers, telescoping plastic handle, $1.00.

Sponge Mop	2.00
Vacuum Cleaner	
auto	5.00
canister, with attachments	
no power head	10.00
power head	15.00
hand held (Dust Buster, Little Devil, etc.)	5.00
shop vac	15.00
upright	
with attachments	20.00
without attachments	15.00

CLOCKS

Clocks can be found in all shapes and sizes and to suit every room in the house. Electric clocks are probably the most reliable. Whether they're used in the kitchen or bedroom, chances are, if they run they keep the correct time. Windup alarm clocks and travel alarms tend to be less accurate but will serve adequately for limited periods of time.

Cuckoo clocks are not as popular as they were fifteen years ago, but they still appeal to many people. Be sure that the clock's chains and weights are intact. Also, examine the clock's decorative trim carefully. Small pieces such as deer antlers and leaves are often broken or missing.

Wall Clock, Westclox Electric, plastic, silver rim, 14" diameter, $5.00.

Alarm	
electric	5.00
windup	3.00
Anniversary, glass dome	5.00
Bar, beer advertisement, electric	20.00
Clock Radio	8.00
Cuckoo	15.00
Kitchen, battery operated or electric	5.00
Mantel, tambour, Westminster chimes	8.00
Regulator, oak, modern	10.00
Travel Alarm	
quartz	3.00
windup	2.50
Wall, electric	5.00
Wall Set, clock and 2 sconces	5.00

CLOTHES HAMPERS

Every home needs somewhere to stash dirty wash until washday. Metal hampers with painted floral designs were the norm in homes of the 1950s and 1960s and have held up well over time. Woven cane and rattan hampers with plastic or vinyl covered lids have not fared so well, their caning is usually weakened and sagging. Today, most people prefer hampers resembling wicker baskets or the easy care of those made from plastic.

Metal, floral design	5.00
Plastic	2.00
Wicker Basket	8.00
Woven Cane, painted white	4.00

CLOTHING

What garage sale would be complete without tables and wash lines loaded with an assortment of used clothing? Outgrown children's clothing is probably the mainstay of most yard sales today. Many articles of children's clothing are outgrown long before they become outdated or worn out. What's more, they are priced at a fraction of their original cost, making them the best bargain to be had.

Display clothing in an attractive manner. Make it easy for buyers to find what they are looking for. Hang dress shirts, suits, coats, jackets, and dresses neatly on hangers on a clothesline arranged by size. T-shirts, shorts, pajamas, and other clothing normally stored in dresser drawers should be neatly folded and arranged according to sex and size.

When tagging clothing for sale, a general rule is to price an article at roughly $^1/_7$th of its original cost. Start by sorting clean clothes into three piles. Be objective. The first pile should contain clothing in new or like-new condition. These should be priced slightly higher than the second pile. Clothing that shows signs of wear but is clean and serviceable belongs on the second pile. Finally, anything with stains or tears goes on the last pile. Do yourself a favor and keep this pile to use as cleaning rags. If they are too worn for your family to wear, chances are nobody else will buy them either, no matter how reasonably priced.

Boys'	
belt	.25
boots	1.00
coat	5.00
dress suit	8.00
gloves	.50
hat	.50
jacket	3.00
jeans	1.00
mittens	.50
pajamas	.50
robe	.75
shoes	2.00
shorts	.50
slacks	1.00
slippers	.50
snowpants	2.00
snowsuit	3.00
sport coat	5.00
sport shirt	1.00
sweater	1.50

Girls' Clothing, sizes 10 – 12, various prices.

- sweatpants .50
- sweatshirt 1.00
- tie .50
- T-shirt .25

Girls'
- belt .25
- blouse 1.00
- boots 1.00
- coat 5.00
- dress 3.00
- gloves .50
- hat .50
- jacket 3.00
- jeans 1.00
- jumper 2.00
- pajamas .50
- robe .75
- shoes 2.00
- shorts .50
- skirt 1.00
- slacks 1.00
- slip .25
- slippers .50
- snowpants 2.00
- snowsuit 3.00
- sweater 1.50
- sweatpants .50
- sweatshirt 1.00
- T-shirt .25

Infants'
- bib .25
- bonnet .75
- booties .25
- bunting 3.00
- hat .50
- onesie .25
- pants .75
- rubber pants .10
- sleeper .50
- snowsuit 2.00
- T-shirt .25

Men's
- belt 1.00
- coat
  - camel hair 15.00
  - leather 25.00
- dress suit 20.00
- gloves 1.00
- hat .50
- jacket
  - fabric 5.00
  - leather 15.00
- jeans 2.50
- pajamas 1.00
- raincoat 8.00
- robe 2.00
- shoes 5.00
- shorts 1.50
- slacks 3.00
- sneakers 3.50
- sport coat 10.00
- sport shirt 2.00
- sweatpants 2.00
- sweatshirt 2.00
- tie .75
- T-shirt 1.00

Women's
- apron .50
- belt 1.00
- blouse 2.00
- coat
  - leather, suede 25.00
  - wool 15.00
- dress 5.00
- gloves 1.00
- hat .50
- jacket
  - fabric 5.00
  - leather 15.00
  - rabbit fur 8.00
- jeans 2.50
- mittens .50
- pajamas 1.00

Apron, handmade, c1950, $.50.

raincoat	
full length, trench coat type	8.00
slicker, stadium length	2.00
robe	2.00
shoes	3.00
shorts	1.50
skirt	2.50
slacks	3.00
slip	.25
sneakers	3.50
suit	8.00
sweatpants	2.00
sweatshirt	2.00
T-shirt	1.00

COMPUTER EQUIPMENT

One year is all it takes for computer equipment to become outdated and obsolete. Yesterday's state-of-the-art system is a dinosaur by today's standards. If you are lucky enough to find a buyer for your old computer, expect to realize only pennies on the dollar. If it's more than five years old, and/or not MacIntosh or IBM compatible, it probably won't sell at any price.

Caveat Emptor – Let The Buyer Beware! This is especially true when buying used computer equipment. A promise that it worked the last time means little if it doesn't work now. Repairs and replacement parts can cost hundreds of dollars.

CD-ROM, external	
double	20.00
single	5.00
Computer	
8088	25.00
286	35.00
386	100.00
486	200.00
portable lap top	40.00
Keyboard, 101	10.00
Master Switch/Surge Protector	5.00
Monitor	
color	25.00
monochromatic	2.00
Printer	
bubble jet	20.00
daisy wheel	15.00
dot matrix	5.00
laser jet	50.00
thermal printer	10.00
Software	
adult programs (accounting, genealogy, word processing, etc.)	2.00
children's, games or educational	1.00
Spike Bar/Surge Protector	1.00

COOKBOOKS

Some of the best recipes can be found in cookbooks published by local churches, schools, and ladies' auxiliaries. Everyone has at least a few stored on a kitchen shelf. These books sell best in their home locale. A native resident of Coopersburg, PA will find a cookbook published by Liberty Bell Elementary School more appealing than will someone unfamiliar with the area.

Old cookbooks distributed by food companies often contain ads that make them desirable to collectors of advertising memorabilia. Some titles published before 1900 are valuable and should be researched before being priced.

Hardcover, miscellaneous titles	3.00
Locally Published, spiral bound (fire company auxiliaries, churches, school groups, etc.)	2.00
Paperback, advertising	5.00

COOKIE JARS

The ceramic cookie jar market has been hot for several years. Prices can range from $5 to $1,000, depending on the manufacturer and condition. Become familiar with names such as American Bisque

Company, Brush–McCoy, Metlox, Regal, and Robinson–Ransbottom. These are just a few companies whose cookie jars are highly collectible. If your cookie jar is more than ten years old, take a trip to the library and see if it is listed in any of the cookie jar reference books in the antiques and collectibles section.

Not all old jars are expensive and not all jars made by the same company are equal. An apple cookie jar made by McCoy can be bought for about $35, while a Raggedy Ann jar by the same company goes for double the price. It pays to do your homework.

Ceramic, less than ten years old	
canister type	4.00
figural, animal or other shape	8.00
Metal or Plastic, canister type	2.00

COPY MACHINES

It's not often that you'll come across large business machines at a garage sale, but with the number of people working out of home offices, table top copy machines do surface occasionally. The only way to tell if the machine works is to ask for a demonstration. If the copies are light or unevenly printed, don't rule out buying yet – it probably just needs a new ink cartridge. When deciding on a price, keep in mind a new cartridge can cost from $40 to over $100.

Table Top Model	75.00

CORNINGWARE

Corningware is probably the most versatile cookware on the market. It can be used to store leftovers, as serving dishes, or as cookware for the range, oven, or microwave. Lids often get broken or misplaced but this may not be a problem if you have similar pieces at home. Many lids are interchangeable. When pricing Corningware, charge only half the price listed below if the lid is missing.

Bacon Crisper, microwave	1.00
Casserole, covered	
1 quart	2.00
$1^1/_2$ quart	3.00
2 quart	4.00
Lasagne Pan	5.00
Soup Bowl, lug handle, covered	1.00

Corningware, casserole, covered, Cornflower pattern, 1 quart, $2.00.

CRUTCHES

Sooner or later, every family ends up with a pair of crutches stored in the attic. Although they are extremely useful when needed, nobody likes to tempt fate and buy them when they're not. Additionally, with today's attitudes regarding insurance, most people will let their insurance company pick up the tab for a new pair whenever an accident occurs. If you do decide to buy a pair, do your hands and armpits a favor and buy crutches only if the rubber pads are still present.

Metal	2.50
Wood	1.00

CURLERS

Does anybody still use curlers? Before the 1980s, they were the preferred method for curling straight hair. Anybody who spent a sleepless night being jabbed by curlers and bobby pins knows why they have been replaced by curling irons and perms. The market for curlers, electric or otherwise, is practically nonexistent. If you're lucky, a little girl aspiring to be a beautician may buy your unwanted curlers to practice on her dolls.

Electric	
dry	2.00
steam	3.00
Nonelectric, bag of 20	.50

CURLING IRONS

Modern curling irons are a welcome relief from the days of wearing your hair in rollers for hours in order to achieve just the right do. Iron variations include models with steam, multiple heat settings, and interchangeable rod sizes and brushes. Deluxe versions come in fitted vinyl cases. As always, plug the iron in to be sure it heats properly.

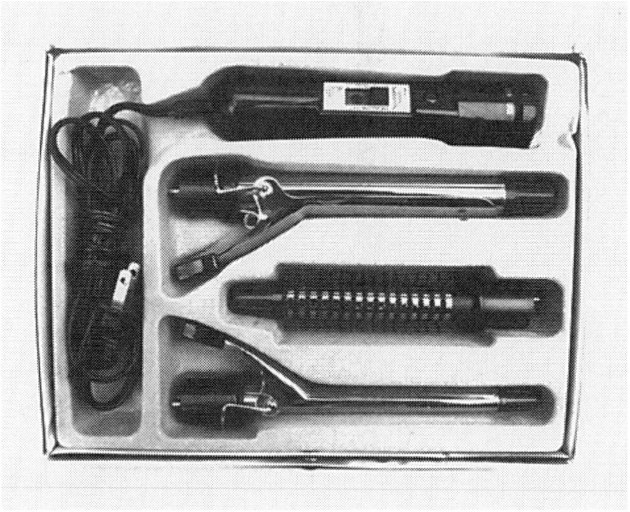

Curling Kit, Vidal Sassoon, two rods, one brush, two heat settings, fitted vinyl case, $5.00.

Curling Brush, single heat setting	2.00
Curling Iron	
butane, with canister	5.00
electric	2.00
Curling Kit, interchangeable brush and 2 rods, multiple heat settings, fitted vinyl case	5.00

CURTAIN RODS

Three types of hardware made for hanging curtains are curtain rods, traverse rods, and tension rods. Through use and abuse tension rod springs are often broken. Traverse rod cords can also present a problem. Test them both to see they that still work properly. In order to avoid losing the hardware pieces needed for attaching the rods to walls, tape them to the rods. When shopping, know the width of your windows to be sure the rods are of adequate length.

When cleaning the attic, if you come across an adjustable wooden contraption with hundreds of protruding wire tacks, discard it. It's a curtain stretcher, it's obsolete, and so far no one has come up with a reason to save them.

Curtain Hook, wire, 12 pieces	1.00
Curtain Rod	.50
Tension Rod	.75
Traverse Rod	
30" to 45" long	2.00
60" and longer	5.00

CURTAINS, DRAPES & BLINDS

Measure your windows before you shop. Unless your house is fitted with standard size window, it can be extremely difficult to find curtains at a garage sale. Keep in mind they not only need to match the style and color scheme of your room, but also the length of your windows. While excess width can be adjusted through fullness, the curtain's length is crucial. If they're too long and you're handy with needle and thread, it's a simple matter to hem them shorter. Unfortunately, nothing can be done to make them longer. If blinds are more to your liking, be especially exact with your measurements. Only the length can be adjusted on horizontal mini blinds.

Curtains or Drapes, price per pair	
patio door size	10.00
standard window sizes	
insulated	3.00
lined	2.00
unlined	1.00
Venetian Blinds	
mini blinds	
metal	4.00
vinyl	3.00

Unlined Curtains, wire curtain hooks, pair, $1.00.

wide slats
- metal 2.00
- vinyl 1.00

Vertical Blinds
- patio door size 15.00
- standard window sizes 5.00

CUTLERY

Cutlery and carving sets are standard fare for wedding and shower gifts. Many a bride receives duplicate sets. After being stored in the attic for years they often end up being sold at garage sales. With proper care, a good set of knives can last a lifetime.

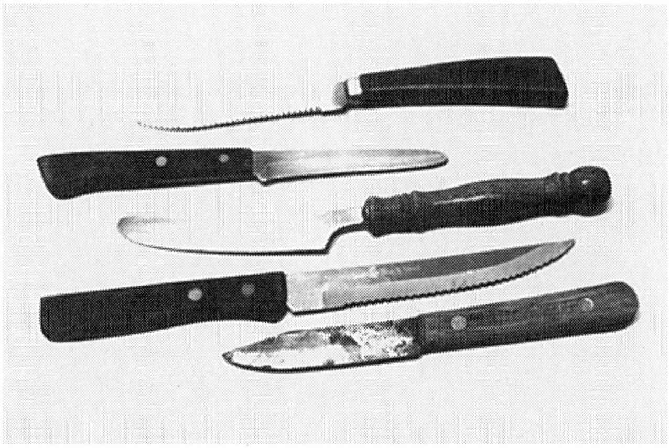

Steak, butter, and paring knives, various prices.

Bread Knife, serrated blade	1.00
Butcher Knife	2.00
Butter Knife	.50
Carving Set, knife and fork, boxed	3.00
Cutlery Set, 6 knives and rack or block	7.50
Paring Knife	.50
Steak Knives, serrated blades, set of 8 in rack or block	5.00

CUTTING BOARDS

Cutting boards come in all shapes and sizes, from small round boards used for cheese to larger rectangular ones for the Sunday roast. Boards made in the shape of a pig are often sought by collectors. Wooden boards are often scarred from years of hard use. Don't sand an old board to remove these blemishes, many buyers prefer a worn look. Because acrylic does not absorb juices like wood, these modern cutting boards are more sanitary and sometimes preferred.

Cutting Board, school shop project, wood, $3.00.

Acrylic
- large 5.00
- small 3.00

Wood
- pig shaped 8.00
- rectangular, square, or round 3.00

DART BOARDS & DARTS

Bull's Eye! Dart boards are often great sellers at garage sales. Their bright colors appeal to many buyers. Make sure you have the complete set of darts. Feather darts will bring more than their plastic counterparts and the more decorative the board and vivid the colors the higher the value will climb. Damage, heavy use, or missing darts or feathers will result in lower prices. Remember – keep sharp darts out of reach of young garage salers – their aim could lead to disaster!

Dart Board
- full size
  - cork 5.00
  - paper, barroom quality 8.00
- miniature, "executive" set 2.00

Darts, set of 6
- metal shaft, plastic "feathers" 2.00
- wood shaft, feathers 5.00

Dart Board, miniature, cork board, set of 6 metal darts with plastic feathers, $2.00.

DEHUMIDIFIERS

If you are lucky enough to spot a dehumidifier at a garage sale, examine it for signs of neglect or rust. Compare moisture removal rates. A 50 pint model will achieve an ideal humidity level in half the time it takes for a 25 pint unit to do the job.

15 Pint	25.00
30 Pint	35.00
50 Pint	45.00

DINNERWARE

Extra serving dishes, mismatched china, and odd place settings are garage sale staples. Buyers look for china to replace their broken pieces and complete their pattern. Wash the dishes and make them sparkle. If priced reasonably, they should sell quickly.

Have plenty of boxes and newspaper available for packing. Large serving pieces and place settings could be displayed on the ground in boxes. Don't bother wrapping the individual pieces of a dinnerware service – most buyers will want to examine each piece for chips or cracks.

Check for makers' marks on the backs and display dishes with like marks together. A little time spent researching a maker or pattern could yield a higher dollar value. Seasoned garage sale pickers will be out early scouting for inexpensively priced pieces of Fiesta or Autumn Leaf china.

Cake Plate	2.00
Cereal Bowl	.50
Coffee Cup	.25
Coffee Mug	.50
Creamer and Sugar	2.50
Gravy Boat	2.00
Plate	
dessert, 7" diameter	.50
dinner, 10" diameter	1.00
Platter	2.00
Salt & Pepper Shakers, pair	2.00
Saucer	.25
Serving Bowl, vegetable	1.00
Soup Plate, flat	.50
Teacup	.25
Sets	
service for 4, 4 each dinner plates, dessert plates, cereal bowls, cups, and saucers	25.00
service for 8, 8 each dinner plates, dessert plates, cereal bowls, cups, and saucers	50.00

Dish, multicolored flowers, $1.00.

DISH DRAINERS

These handy kitchen helpers are a great way to display odd dishes you wish to sell. However, don't forget to put a price sticker on the dish drainer, too! While plastic is colorful and easy to care for, older dish drainers made from coated wire are sturdier.

Wooden examples add a touch of nostalgia and are a welcome addition to modern kitchens.

Plastic	
large	1.50
small	1.00
Vinyl Coated Wire	
large	2.00
small	1.50
Wood	4.00

DISHWASHERS, PORTABLE

Portable dishwashers found at garage sales should be inspected for cracked cords and hoses and rusted and pitted racks. Other components such as the pump and timer cannot be tested until you get it home. Ask the owner if it works. When was the last time it was used? Is the instruction manual included? White dishwashers sell more quickly than outdated decorator colors such as avocado or harvest gold. If you're shopping for any large appliance be sure to have help getting it loaded – older models can be quite heavy.

Butcher Block Top, white	60.00
Counter Top, white	50.00

DRESS FORMS

Dress forms have been around for years, mostly stored in attics. When buying a dress form, check to see if it is adjustable. The covering should be clean and free from holes, dust, and tailor's chalk. If you're selling a form, try dressing it to attract attention. Dress forms are often recycled and used by antiques shop owners to display vintage clothing.

Dress Form	10.00

DRYERS

Automatic clothes dryers are a necessity in the 1990s. Insufficient wash line space and hectic work schedules often make it impossible to hang wash outside to dry. Dryers are made in both gas and electric models, be sure you know which hookup is right for you. Does it work? Is the manual available?

No matter how little time one has, some things must be hung to dry. Keep your eyes open for free-standing drying racks. Vinyl coated wire racks are easy to keep clean and take up little room when folded for storage. Older wooden racks are great for displaying old quilts and linens. Expect to find these priced slightly higher.

Automatic Dryer	
full size	
electric	
extra large capacity	75.00
standard size drum	65.00
gas	100.00
portable, apartment size	50.00
stacking unit	75.00
Drying Rack	
vinyl coated wire	2.00
wood	4.00

DUTCH OVENS

Heavy, cast iron, and lidded, Dutch ovens were once a fireplace cooking necessity. Today, they are more often used only on camping trips. Dutch ovens range in size from two to twelve quarts and weigh from ten to thirty-two pounds. Some have lids fitted to hold hot coals. If you plan to buy, examine the oven for excessive rust and pitting. The interior surface should be smooth for best heating results.

Dutch Oven	5.00

ELECTRIC TOOTHBRUSHES

The electric toothbrush craze may be over for adults, but there is still a market among children. Brushing time is more enjoyable when accompanied by the child's favorite cartoon character. Check for completeness when buying at a garage sale. Don't be surprised to find one in its original box, unused. Buy only models with replacement brushes still on the market. Generic models may be difficult to sell but battery operated cartoon character versions sell quickly to both kids and collectors.

Electric Toothbrush	
character related	5.00
generic	2.50
Water Pik	8.00

EMBROIDERY HOOPS

Embroidery hoops have more uses today than just holding your needlework secure. They serve double duty as frames for holiday crafts or for thwarting the family cat by holding a screen in place over the fishbowl. They are made of plastic, metal, and wood with various devices for holding tension. Check hoops for splits and excessive wear. Be sure they are correctly mated. Examine older metal hoops for signs of rust which could stain your fabric. The spring used in many of these hoops loses its tension over time. Hoops with a threaded screw closure hold up better.

6" to 12" diameter, metal, plastic, or wood	1.00
36" diameter, wood	8.00

ENCYCLOPEDIA

World Book, Britannica, and *Collier's* have always been popular household encyclopedia names. When the kids have grown and the encyclopedia set is either unneeded or outdated put it out for the garage sale. Be realistic with your pricing. The fact that it cost hundreds of dollars when purchased new from the salesman is irrelevant. In today's computer age of software encyclopedia, the hard-bound versions are becoming less and less popular. Don't forget to include those yearbooks and special volumes. They may enhance the value slightly.

World Book Encyclopedia, © 1963, full set plus yearbooks 1966 through 1973, $5.00.

Books, hardcover	
pre–1970, price for set	5.00
1970 – 1980, price for set	10.00
1980 – 1990, price for set	15.00
1990 – to the present, price for set	20.00
CD-ROM	20.00

EXERCISE EQUIPMENT

Whether you are a fitness enthusiast or someone who believes exercise equipment is the 1990's equivalent of the iron maiden, you've undoubtedly seen plenty of it at garage sales. Often hardly used and in great condition, it should be priced to move. Weights and weight lifting benches are especially common garage sale finds. More complex equipment like total gyms should include original manuals explaining assembly and use.

Bicycle	20.00
Gravity Rider	10.00
Home Gym	100.00
Medicine Ball	5.00
Miscellaneous Devices	
abdominal toner	3.00
ankle weights, pair	2.00
chest developer, springs	3.00
grip strengthener, spring tension	1.00
Thigh Master	4.00
Nordic Track	75.00
Punching Bag	
large	12.00
small	5.00

Weight Set, Challenger Orbatron, 110 lbs of sand–filled plastic weights, 2 dumbbells, and barbell, $7.50.

Rowing Machine	50.00

Skier	15.00
Slant Board	6.00
Step Machine	50.00
Stepper	7.50
Trampoline	
full size, 13' diameter	75.00
miniature, 36" diameter	5.00
Treadmill	
manual	20.00
1¼ hp DC motor	50.00
Weight Lifting Bench	
adjustable bench, leg exerciser	15.00
flat bench with uprights to hold barbells	7.50
Weight Set, barbell, dumbbell, 110 lbs	7.50
Workout Videos	3.00

EXTENSION CORDS

Also known as "trouble cords," extension cords are a necessity of modern life. New types with surge protectors are great for use with today's electronic equipment and toys but beware, the built-in devices wear out. Examine cords for bare spots and cracked plugs. Test the cord to be sure it carries a current.

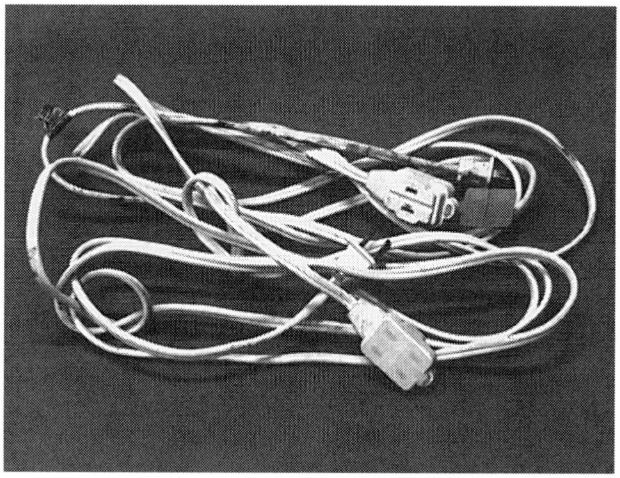

Extension Cords, 10' long, price each, $1.00.

Indoor	1.00
Outdoor, grounded, orange	
25' long	5.00
50' long	8.00
100' long	12.00

FANS

Have you noticed there is a direct correlation between the temperature outdoors and the availability and price of cooling devices? As temperatures climb higher and higher, the availability of fans and air conditioners decreases while their prices escalate. Garage sales can be a cheap alternative source. Fans generally sell at a fraction of their retail cost. Ask the owner to plug in the fan. If it works – listen to see that it runs quietly. There's nothing worst than a noisy fan on a hot summer night.

Box, window unit	
3 speed	5.00
3 speed, reversible	7.50
Ceiling	
multiple speed, with light fixture	15.00
single speed, no light fixture	10.00
Dashboard	2.00
Desk, personal, 2 speed	3.00
Exhaust	
9" diameter, 2 speed	5.00
16" diameter, 3 speed	10.00
20" diameter, 3 speed, thermostat	15.00
Hand Held, battery operated	1.00
Hassock, floor unit, 3 speed	5.00
Oscillating	
floor model, 3 speed	15.00
table model	
12" diameter	10.00
16" diameter	15.00

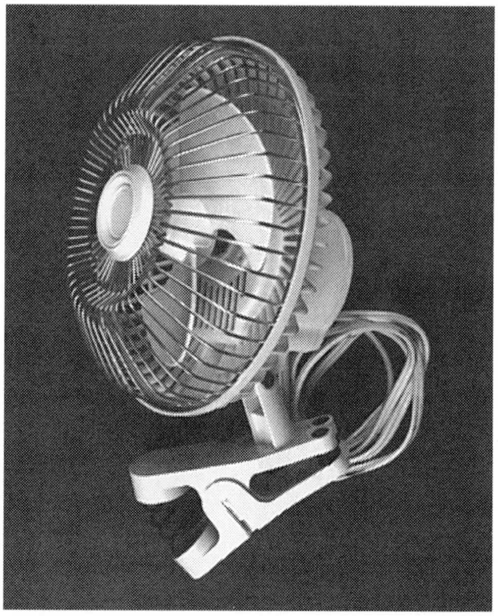

Fan, portable, clamps on furniture, $3.00.

FAX MACHINES

As fax machines become more advanced and an essential business communications device, you can expect to find more used machines at garage sales. These earlier models are often simpler to operate than their more modern counterparts. Ask the owner how difficult it is to use and whether it requires a separate phone line or uses special paper. The original manual is extremely helpful. Remember, like all electronic equipment, it's only a bargain if it works. Repair bills can far exceed the machine's value.

Plain Paper Model	75.00
Special Paper Required	50.00

FILING CABINETS

Buying a filing cabinet at a garage sale may be difficult, especially if you have your heart set on an old wooden cabinet like the kind found in old office buildings. Oak filing cabinets are getting harder to find and their prices are increasing proportionally.

Metal cabinets are much more affordable and just as serviceable. Test drawers to see that their tracks work properly. Some metal cabinets are fireproof and quite heavy. Take this into consideration if you live in a second floor apartment. Finally, if you're selling a locking cabinet, find the key and give it to the buyer.

Metal	
2 drawer	25.00
3 drawer	30.00
4 drawer	40.00
5 drawer	45.00
fireproof	75.00
Wood, oak, 4 drawer	250.00

FIREPLACE ACCESSORIES

Fireplace equipment such as andirons, grates, screens, and tools is sold at many "moving" sales. When pricing, consider a piece's condition and decorator value. The better the condition and more ornate, the higher the value. Shine up dull brass andirons for a quicker sale.

Andirons, brass, pair	20.00
Grate, cast iron	5.00
Hearth Rug, fire resistant	2.00

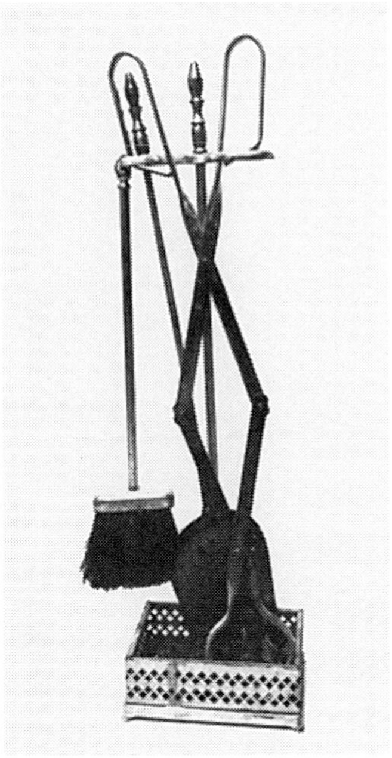

Tool Set, brass, brush, shovel, log lifter, and stand, $15.00.

Leather Gloves	4.00
Log Carrier, wood and rope	2.50
Log Holder, metal hoop	5.00
Screen, brass, traverse rod type	10.00
Tool Set, five pieces, brush, shovel, poker, log lifter, and stand	
brass	15.00
wrought iron	10.00

FISHING EQUIPMENT

Garage sales can be a great source for all the trappings needed for fishing. Nets, vests, and tackle boxes should be priced low for quick sale. Lures, rods and reels that are less than ten years old are bought mainly for reuse and should also be reasonably priced. On the other hand, older lures, decoys, rods, and reels are hot collectibles and should be researched before being priced. Don't throw away those expired fishing licenses – there are collectors for these, too.

Bait Box	.50
Bait Bucket	1.00
Chain Line, metal, 8 hooks	.50
Creel, willow	10.00
Minnow Trap	5.00
License, expired, less than 10 years old	.10
Lure	8.00

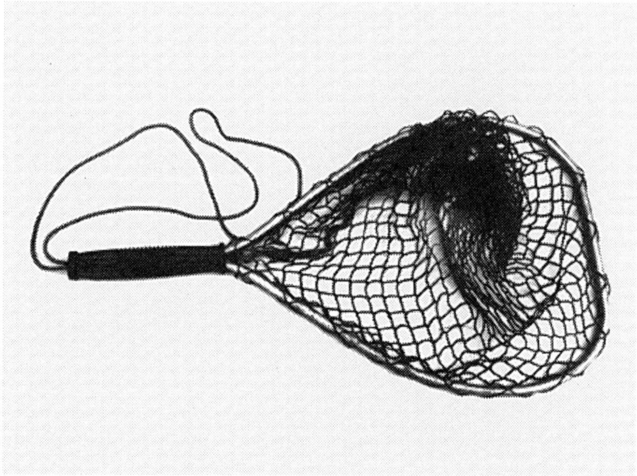

Net, aluminum rim, green plastic handle, 20" l, $5.00.

Net	5.00
Rod and Reel	
child size, plastic	3.00
deep sea, bamboo	25.00
fly rod, split cane	15.00
trout	
plastic	8.00
split cane	10.00
Scaling Knife	2.00
Tackle Box	4.00
Vest	2.00

FLAGS

Flags and banners have become popular household decorations over the last few years. You probably won't find too many of the generic variety, such as holiday or "19th hole" flags for sale yet, but you may find some nice American flags. Size and quality are the deciding factors when pricing 50-star flags. The bigger the flag, the higher the price. Large nylon flags with embroidered rather than printed stars and stripes bring the highest price of all. Be sure to include poles and mounting brackets with the flag.

American Flag, 50 stars	
cotton, printed	
6" long	.50
12" long	1.00
18" long	1.50
24" long	2.00
48" long	5.00
60" long	10.00
72" long	12.00
nylon, embroidered	
48" long	10.00
60" long	15.00
72" long	18.00
72" long, gold fringed border	20.00
Generic Flag (holiday, welcome, etc.)	10.00
Pole	
aluminum, 6' high	2.00
fiberglass, 22' high	50.00
wood, 12' high	10.00
Wind Sock, nylon	2.00

FLASHLIGHTS

Check the batteries and light bulbs on your old flashlights. If they work, price them accordingly. Be wary of buying a used rechargeable flashlight. Chances are it no longer holds a charge.

Left: emergency light, fluorescent tube, flashing warning light, plastic, $5.00; right: lantern, Eveready, red plastic, uses large 6 volt battery, missing hood, $5.00.

Emergency Light, fluorescent bulb, flashing warning lamp	5.00
Household	
lantern, uses large 6 volt battery	5.00
tubular, uses C or D cell batteries	3.00
vest pocket, uses AA batteries	1.00
Penlight	.50
Rechargeable	8.00

FLOWERPOTS & PLANTERS

No matter whether you have a green thumb or a brown one, flowerpots and planters can be great sellers. If your thumb is green, add a plant to the pot and find a new home for some of your unwanted greenery. If your thumb is brown, you probably have a ready supply of used flowerpots to sell.

Some savvy collectors are starting to save early FTD and other florist containers. Many older planters made by potteries like Shawnee and McCoy are not always marked but are still highly collectible. If the planter is marked, either with the company's name or "U.S.A.," take a look in general price guides for identification and price. Figural planters, such as those made in the shape of animals, sell for more than ordinary flowerpots made by the same company.

Flowerpot
- ceramic, unmarked, embossed or painted
  - 3" to 6" diameters 50
  - 8" to 12" diameters 2.00
  - larger than 12" diameter 5.00
- clay, red
  - 3" to 6" diameters 25
  - 8" to 12" diameters 75
  - larger than 12" diameter 2.00

Planter, unmarked, ceramic, figural, two birds and tree stump, orange and yellow, 9½" h, $3.00.

- plastic
  - 3" diameter and smaller 05
  - 4" to 6" diameters 10
  - hanging basket, wire hangers 1.00
- stoneware, glazed, 6" to 8" diameters . 4.00

Jardiniere, bowl and pedestal, modern
- ceramic 5.00
- plastic 3.00
- stoneware 8.00

Planter
- cement
  - swan shaped 3.00
  - urn shaped 5.00
- ceramic, unmarked
  - bowl shaped, florist's 50
  - figural (animal, people, watering can, baby cradle, etc.) 3.00
  - flowerpot or urn shaped 2.00
  - rectangular or square box shaped . . 2.50
- plastic
  - bowl shaped, florist's 10
  - cauldron shaped, 20" diameter 2.00
- pottery, large bowl, hand painted, Mexican design, 24" diameter 4.00
- stoneware, glazed 4.00

Plant Hanger
- macrame 2.00
- wrought iron 1.00

Strawberry Jar, multiple openings
- ceramic 5.00
- stoneware 7.50

FREEZERS

Old chest freezers are very difficult to sell. They weigh a ton and take up far too much space. Older models also need to be defrosted – a major inconvenience when compared to today's frost-free units. Newer, smaller freezers, whether upright or chest style, sell much more easily. Check to see that the freezer works, gaskets seal properly, and whether it is self-defrosting, frost-free, or must be manually defrosted. Some freezer doors lock, be sure to ask the owner for the key.

Chest
- 5.0 cubic feet, manual defrost 35.00
- 12.8 cubic feet, manual defrost 75.00
- 22.7 cubic feet, manual defrost 125.00

Upright
- 5.0 cubic feet, manual defrost 40.00
- 14.6 cubic feet, frostless 75.00
- 19.1 cubic feet, automatic defrost 150.00
- 31.1 cubic feet, manual defrost 175.00

Chest Freezer, Frost Queen, 5.0 cubic feet, manual defrost, $35.00.

FURNITURE

Time to take a trip to the attic and dust off that unwanted furniture. Furniture that is less than 40 years old is bought and sold strictly for reuse. The retail price you paid for furniture has nothing to do with its resale value. A piece of furniture is like a car. The minute it leaves the showroom floor it depreciates rapidly. This is especially true for upholstered furniture. The fact that you paid $500 to reupholster the couch is irrelevant. You will still only get the going rate for a used couch. Upholstered furniture must also be in very good or better condition in order for it to sell at all. Any rips, stains, worn spots, or soiling will greatly reduce your chance of a sale.

If you plan to sell furniture that was manufactured prior to World War II, you should have better luck. Mass-produced oak furniture sells well on today's market. It is sturdy, attractive, and highly desirable. Solid oak pieces should be priced higher than veneered examples.

Standard sizes and styles generally sell better than odd pieces. For example, a king size bed would be much harder to sell than a similar double or queen size. There is simply more demand for the more common sizes. The same holds true for living room furniture. It is much more difficult to find a buyer for a large L-shaped sectional sofa with leopard print upholstery than for a 6 or 7 foot long brown plaid couch.

Finally, remember – you don't want to lug that heavy bureau back up to the attic. Ignore sentimental value and price guide book prices. Be prepared to dicker over prices. The final determination of the value of used furniture is the price the seller and buyer agree upon. If both of you are happy then the price must be right.

Bed, mattress and box spring
- bookcase headboard, metal frame
  - single 10.00
  - double 20.00
  - queen 25.00
- brass
  - single 25.00
  - double 50.00
  - queen 75.00
  - king 50.00
- bunk, pair, with ladder and rail
  - metal 75.00
  - wood 75.00
- canopy, wood, painted white 45.00
- daybed, metal frame 50.00
- Hollywood style headboard, metal frame
  - single 10.00
  - double 20.00
  - queen 25.00
- water
  - double 35.00
  - queen 50.00
- wood headboard, footboard, and side rails
  - youth 10.00
  - single 25.00
  - double 35.00
  - queen 40.00
  - king 40.00

Bedroom Suite
- blonde oak, double bed with metal frame and bookcase headboard, two nightstands, dresser with mirror, and chest of drawers 175.00
- Depression era, wood veneer, includes a double bed, dresser with mirror, chest of drawers, wardrobe, and vanity with mirror and bench 250.00
- French Provincial, painted white, gold trim, single bed, night stand, chest of drawers, and dresser with mirror . . . 150.00
- maple, 2 single beds, chest of drawers, dresser, wall mirror, and end table . 200.00

Bean Bag Chair, black and white striped cotton fabric, $4.00.

other woods, modern, queen size bed with metal frame and wooden headboard, 2 night stands, dresser with mirror and glass top, chest of drawers with glass top 250.00

Bench
- piano, hinged lid 15.00
- vanity 10.00

Blanket Chest 50.00

Bookcase
- flakeboard 10.00
- oak, five shelves, glass doors 200.00
- other woods, open front, modern 50.00
- sectional, oak or mahogany, 4 sections . 300.00

Card Table & 4 Chairs, Samsonite 25.00

Cedar Chest
- Lane 75.00
- other brands 50.00

Chair
- bean bag 4.00
- captain's, wood 15.00
- desk
  - upholstered, swivel 15.00
  - wood
    - non-swivel 10.00
    - swivel 35.00
- dining, wood, upholstered slip seat
  - armchair 10.00
  - side chair 7.50
- kitchen
  - oak, unpainted
    - cane seat 15.00
    - pressed design in back 20.00
  - tubular steel frame, vinyl covered seat and back 2.00
  - wood, painted white 5.00
- living room, upholstered
  - wing back 20.00
  - other styles 10.00
- office
  - molded plastic 2.00
  - upholstered 10.00
- valet 2.00

Chest of Drawers, 5 drawers
- oak, small mirror, unpainted 225.00
- painted wood 35.00
- unpainted wood, modern 50.00

China Closet
- bow front, curved glass, solid oak
  - fancy carving, claw feet 350.00
  - plain example 275.00
- corner cabinet, mahogany 300.00
- Depression era, from dining room suite 45.00

Clothes Tree
- brass 35.00
- wood 25.00

Coffee Table
- brass frame, glass top 50.00
- mahogany, leatherette top 35.00
- wood, modern 20.00
- wood frame, blue glass top 75.00

Computer Desk
- flakeboard 10.00
- metal 10.00
- wood 20.00

Footstool, maple, wool rug covering, $3.00.

Desk
- child's, oak, roll top 75.00
- flakeboard, oak veneer, modern 25.00
- industrial, gray metal 10.00
- mahogany, kneehole 125.00
- oak, old
  - flat top, center drawer 75.00
  - slant front, Larkin style 350.00
- school, hinged lid, metal frame 20.00

Dinette Set, wood, oval table, four chairs . . 100.00

Dining Room Suite
- cherry, 8 pieces, oval table with leaves, 6 chairs, and a 2 piece hutch with lighted interior 400.00
- Depression era, mahogany veneer, 10 pieces, table with two leaves, 2 armchairs, 4 side chairs, server, sideboard, and china cabinet 375.00

Drafting Table, adjustable top 15.00

Dresser, with large mirror
- French Provincial, white, gold trim 25.00
- mahogany or mahogany veneer 35.00
- oak, 4 drawers, ornate, unpainted 350.00
- wood, modern 35.00

End Table
- blonde oak veneer, round legs screw into top, brass caps on legs 5.00
- mahogany, 2 tiers, leatherette tops 30.00
- pine, 1 drawer, base shelf, dark finish . . 20.00

Entertainment Center
- flakeboard, adjustable shelves 25.00
- wood, oak, cherry, or mahogany, adjustable shelves, glass doors 125.00

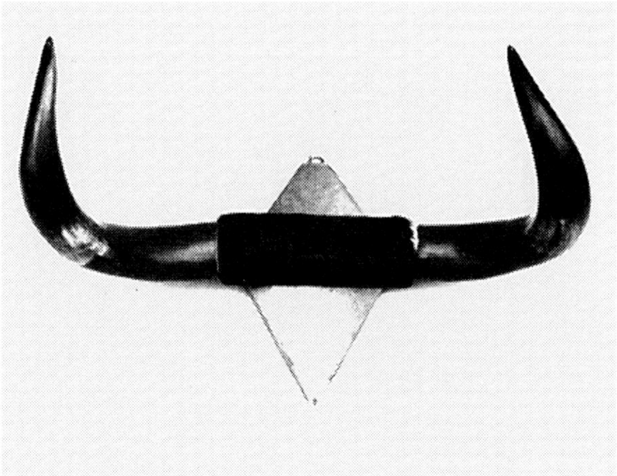

Hat Rack, steer horns, wood plaque, $3.00.

Footstool, small
- needlepoint top 3.00
- wood 5.00

Hassock
- fabric upholstery 2.00
- vinyl covered 1.00

Hutch, wood, 2 pieces
- glass doors on top, lighted interior 150.00
- open shelved top 75.00

Kitchen Base Cabinet, metal, Formica top . . 3.00

Kitchen Cabinet (Hoosier, Sellers, etc.)
- painted 325.00
- refinished 450.00

Kitchen Set, table & 4 chairs
- flakeboard, round oak veneered table with metal pedestal base, 4 vinyl covered upholstered swivel chairs . 50.00
- formica top table with metal legs and 1 leaf, metal frame chairs with vinyl covered seats and backs 35.00
- porcelain top table with wooden frame and silverware drawer, 4 wooden chairs, painted white 100.00

Knick-Knack Shelf 10.00

Living Room Suite
- upholstered
  - sofa and loveseat 100.00
  - sofa, chair, and ottoman 75.00
- wood frame and arms, loose pillow cushions and backs, sofa, chair, rocker, and 2 end tables 100.00

Loveseat
- sleeper, double size mattress 75.00
- standard 50.00

Magazine Rack
- metal 2.00
- wood 7.50

Night Stand, wood, single drawer 15.00

Plant Stand
- brass frame, marble or glass top 10.00
- wood 12.00
- wrought iron 8.00

Recliner, upholstered
- Lazy Boy 75.00
- other brands 40.00

Record Cabinet, wood 40.00

Rocker
- child's, wood frame, paper rush seat . . . 25.00
- oak, pressed back, caned seat 125.00
- porch, splint or slat seat, painted green . 50.00

upholstered, platform base	45.00
walnut, caned back and seat, ornate	200.00
Shelving Unit, wood, four shelves, six threaded supports, 4 ball feet, 4 ball finials	15.00
Sofa	
sectional	
L–shaped	35.00
reclining ends	75.00
sleeper, queen size mattress	75.00
standard	50.00
Toy Chest	
plastic, removable lid	10.00
wood, hinged lid with child safety latch	25.00
TV Stand	
metal	1.00
wood	5.00
Vanity, mirror and bench	45.00
Wardrobe	
metal	
double door	15.00
single door	10.00
wood	
cedar lined	75.00
unlined	
5' high, bank of drawers on left, hanging space on right	40.00
6½' high, oak, break–down, drawer in base	200.00
Washstand, with towel bar	325.00

GAMES

A garage sale can be a gold mine for kids. Outgrown board games end up at garage sales after many years of happy play. Check boxes for instructions and be sure all playing pieces are intact. Be prepared to pay a little extra for more complex or adult games or early versions of common generic titles. Games related to popular television and movie characters are especially appealing to collectors and bring the highest prices. Games manufactured before WW II should be researched before being priced.

Character Related, television or movies	
1950s	20.00
1960s	15.00
1970s	10.00
1980s	7.50
1990s	5.00
Generic Games (Chinese checkers, Parcheesi, Candyland, Ker-Plunk, etc.)	3.00
Monopoly	
metal tokens	4.00
plastic tokens	3.00
Preschool	2.00

GARBAGE CANS

Garbage cans come in all shapes and sizes – made for use indoors and out. Kids' metal cans embossed with cartoon characters and superheroes bring higher prices than plain examples and should be priced accordingly. Outdoors, Rubbermaid's 40 gallon plastic can on wheels is king.

Indoor	
bathroom, small	
metal, embossed design	2.00
plastic, plain	.50
wicker basket	1.00
bedroom	
metal, embossed design	
cartoon character or superhero	4.00
generic	2.00
plastic	
cartoon character or superhero	2.00
plain	.50
kitchen, tall, plastic, lidded	2.00
office	
metal	2.00
plastic	.50
wood	3.00
Outdoor	
metal	
cinder can	2.50
full size	4.00
plastic, full size	
no wheels	3.00
wheels	5.00
Trash Can Cart, holds 2 cans, wheeled	7.50

GARDEN HOSES & REELS

Need more hose to reach your garden or driveway? Garden hoses and reels found at garage sales should be checked for rusted connectors, dry rot, and holes. Nozzles should be free of mineral deposits. Worn washers are not a problem, they can be easily replaced. Make sure reels run smoothly.

Garden Hose
- rubber
  - 25' long 3.00
  - 50' long 5.00
  - 50' long, soaker hose 3.00
  - 75' long 7.50
  - 100' long 10.00
- vinyl
  - 50' long 2.00
  - 75' long 4.00

Hose Hanger, metal, wall mounted 1.00

Reel
- metal
  - wall mounted 3.00
  - wheels 5.00
- plastic
  - wall mounted 4.00
  - wheels 6.50

GARMENT BAGS

Now that you've decided to sell that old prom gown and unused clothing, you may as well add the garment bag to the garage sale. Dust if off, check the zipper, and add a few hangers to help it sell.

Hanging
- coat bag, 62" long 1.00
- dress bag, 54" long
  - double wide 1.50
  - single wide 1.00
- handbag file, 8 pockets ..... .50
- shoe bag, holds 10 pairs 2.00
- sweater bag, 10 shelves 1.50
- suit bag, 42" long 1.00

Storage Chest, sweaters 2.00

Under-The-Bed, 6" high, 42" long 1.50

GAS CANS

If your used gas cans have been used for anything other than gas, be sure to label them accordingly. Never sell kerosene cans if you've used them to store gas. Unsuspecting buyers could be seriously hurt. Properly dispose of the contents of cans before you sell – nobody wants to drive from sale to sale constantly exposed to the smell of gasoline fumes.

Gas Can, 5 gallon, metal, red, pouring spout, $5.00.

Gasoline
- 2 gallon
  - metal
    - pouring spout 3.00
    - no spout 2.00
  - plastic
    - pouring spout 1.50
    - no spout 1.00
- 5 gallon, metal, pouring spout 5.00

Kerosene, 5 gallon, metal
- pouring spout 3.00
- no spout 5.00

GERIATRIC SUPPLIES

Getting old can be quite expensive. The elderly often require specialized equipment. Many items exist to make their life a little easier and safer. Canes, walkers, and other health care products usually outlive their usefulness and end up being discarded. Why not offer them for sale? Care givers often search garage sales for walkers or commodes when medical insurance won't pick up the tab. If it's a cane you're after, be sure to buy a sturdy one.

Retail prices for health care products are exorbitant. If you're left with unsold items at the end of your sale, try calling local community service agencies. Many groups will collect used health care equipment for distribution to those in need.

Bathtub Bench	3.00
Bathtub Brace, adjustable	2.00
Cane	
metal, 3 prong base	2.50
wood	2.00
Commode	5.00
Hospital Bed	
electric	50.00
manual	15.00
Walker	
adjustable height, folding	10.00
fixed position	5.00
wheeled	7.50
Wheelchair, nonelectric	5.00

GLASSWARE

Box lots of mismatched glasses are common garage sale finds. To get the most money for your unwanted glassware, wash each piece and display it attractively. Put a tablecloth (preferably a solid dark color) on your card table for optimum effect. Search your attic for forgotten wedding and shower gifts – if you haven't used that decanter during the first ten to twenty years of your marriage, chances are you never will.

All glassware should be examined for scratches, chips and flakes. Make a note of flaws by writing "as is" on the price sticker. Damaged glassware should be tagged at a fraction of the price of undamaged items. Assign highest prices to complete sets or *new* items with original labels and/or packaging.

Sort out any old pink, green, or yellow glassware. Take the time to consult a price guide specializing in Depression era glass for these pieces. Knowing the pattern name will make the job easier. Don't expect to get book value. Instead, set your prices lower to ensure a quick sale. Remember, the idea is to sell, not to carry it back into storage.

Accessory Pieces	
basket	4.00
cake server	
pedestal base	5.00
plate	3.00
candle holder	.50
candlesticks, pair	1.00
candy dish, covered	3.00
cigarette box, covered	4.00
compote	5.00
creamer	2.00
decanter	7.50
pin dish, covered	2.50
pitcher	8.00
relish dish	3.00
salt and pepper shakers, pair	3.00
sandwich tray, 2 handles	3.00
sugar bowl	2.00
toothpick holder	1.00
Stemware	
brandy snifter	.25
champagne	.50
martini glass	.25
sherbet	.50
water goblet	.50
wine goblet	.50

Candy Dish, etched design, divided interior, $3.00.

Creamer, etched design, $2.00.

Water Set, Depression era, pitcher and 10 tumblers, $20.00.

Water Glass
- highball glass .... .25
- iced tea size .... .25
- jelly glass type
  - 1/2 pint .... .25
  - pint .... .50
- juice size
  - decorated .... .25
  - plain .... .15
- water glass ....
  - individual .... .50
  - matching set of 8 .... 5.00

Water Set, pitcher and tumblers
- 1940s, Depression era, striped, pitcher and 10 tumblers 20.00
- 1950s era, enameled decoration 15.00
- 1960s era, solid color 10.00
- 1970s era, reproduction Depression glass type 5.00

HAIR CUTTERS & CLIPPERS

Buzz hairstyles are back in fashion. With the ever rising costs of haircuts, now is the time to buy a set of hair clippers. Inspect the cord for worn spots. Plug it in to see that it works. Make sure the various attachments are included.

Electric Clippers 4.00
Thinning Shears 2.00
Trimming Shears 2.00
Vacuum Cleaner Kit 5.00

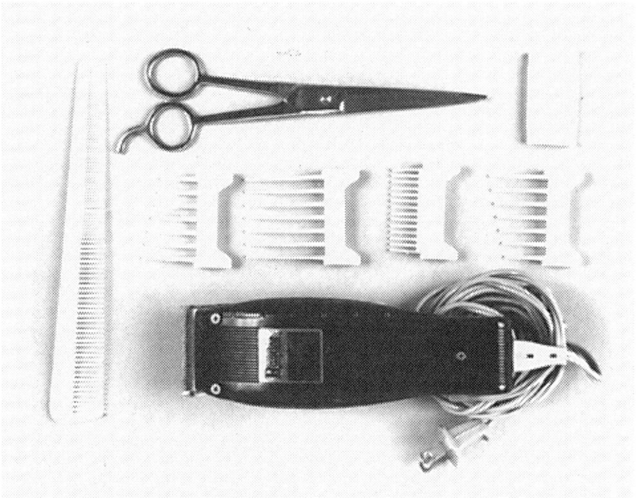

Clippers, Raycine, clippers, scissors, styling comb, and 5 attachments, $4.00.

HAIR DRYERS

Not all hair dryers are created equal. Some models have multiple heat and power levels, including a cold setting ideal for inflating air mattresses. Ask the seller if the hair dryer works. Check the cord. If you're buying an older bonnet type, inspect the hood for age cracks and cleanliness.

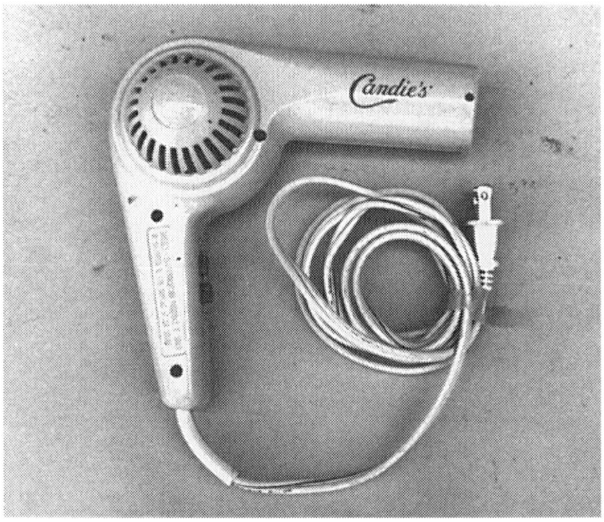

Hair Dryer, hand held, Candie's, 2 speed, $3.00.

Bonnet Type
- hard bonnet, hairdresser's model 5.00
- soft bonnet, fitted carrying case 1.50

Hand Held
- full size
  - multiple settings 3.00

single setting	2.00
professional stylist's type, multiple heat settings, diffuser attachment	2.50
travel size, single setting	2.00

HAMMOCKS

Hammocks come in two styles, self-supported by a metal frame, and the type you string up between two trees. Both have their advantages. The former can be set up and used anywhere, anytime. But for the true hammock personality, the latter doesn't need to be moved at grass cutting time.

Metal Frame	
canvas hammock	15.00
rope hammock	12.00
Tree Suspended	
canvas hammock	10.00
rope hammock	7.50

HANGERS

Why is it every home has either too many or never enough hangers? There never seems to be a happy compromise. Untangle wire hangers and bundle them together. Discard any that are either too misshapen or show signs of rust.

Padded	.10
Pants, metal, holds five pairs	.75
Plastic	
heavy duty	.05
lightweight, store giveaways	.02
Skirt or Trouser, spring clips	.25
Wire	.01
Wooden	
coat hanger	.05
suit hanger, with pants holder	.10

HARDWARE

Did you ever have to make a special trip to the hardware store just to buy a bolt to finish that repair job? That's why so many people have an assortment of miscellaneous hardware on hand. Use old jars and cans to group like objects together. Sell small items in quantity – a whole can of screws for $2 should ensure a quick sale.

Cabinet Knob	
glass	.50
metal	.25
porcelain	.50
wood	.25
Coat Hook, large	
brass	.50
iron	.50
Curtain Hooks, metal, 12 pieces	1.00
Curtain Tiebacks, pair	
brass or plated	1.00
glass, Depression era	3.00
wrought iron	2.50
Doorknob	
modern, brass plated	5.00
old, glass, metal, or wood	10.00
Drawer Pull	
brass, bail handle	.50
wood knob	.25
Hardware Organizer, plastic	
12 drawers	4.00
24 drawers	8.00
Hinges, pair	
indoor, furniture or cabinet doors	1.00
outdoor, large, gate or barn door type	2.00
Key	
clock	1.00
skeleton, door or furniture	.75
Miscellaneous Hardware (wire nuts, hooks and eyes, tacks, etc.) can full	2.00
Nails, Nuts and Bolts, or Screws, can full	2.00
Springs, can full	2.00
Washers, metal or rubber, assortment	1.00

HEATERS

Ever rising energy costs and recent harsh winters have resulted in an increased demand for portable heating devices. Prices are season–oriented. Heaters command higher prices when sold in late autumn or early winter than during the heat of summer.

If you're shopping for an electric heater, inspect the cord carefully – look for bare spots or melted insulation. This is often the result of the unsafe practice of using extension cords with heaters. Also, space heaters should be equipped with an automatic shutoff switch to prevent a fire should the heater be accidently tipped over.

Baseboard, electric	5.00

Space Heater, Presto, $5.00.

Kerosene	
large, household	35.00
small, camp style	10.00
Oil Filled Electric Radiator	10.00
Quartz	5.00
Space Heater	
large	10.00
small	5.00
Torpedo	40.00

HEATING PADS

Heating pads are available in electric and microwaveable varieties. As usual, examine electrical cords carefully for damage. Microwaveable heating pads provide moist heat and temperature is determined by the length of heating time. This type is generally problem free, providing the covering is clean and free of holes.

Electric, dry heat	
flat	
single heat setting	1.00
three heat settings	2.00
wrap around type	4.00
Microwaveable, moist heat	4.00

HELMETS

Many states now require both bicycle and motorcycle riders to wear helmets. Before you purchase a helmet, try it on for size and be sure it meets your state and local safety codes.

Bicycle Helmet, Cruzer, $3.00.

Bicycle	
adult	5.00
child	3.00
In-Line Skates	
adult	5.00
child	3.00
Motorcycle	12.00

HOLIDAY DECORATIONS

Christmas is just around the corner! While you're cleaning that attic or closet to find garage sale merchandise, don't overlook holiday decorations. Some older items are highly collectible and quite valuable. Christmas items manufactured before 1950 are particularly pricey. For example, a German feather tree (early artificial tree) sells for an average of $100 per foot and Santa Claus figures made in Japan following WW II can exceed $40. Once again, it pays to do a little research before you sell.

Halloween costumes dating from the 1960s and 1970s with TV or cartoon themes are also highly prized. A Herman Munster costume made by Ben Cooper books at over $200 and an Underdog suit from Collegeville at $70. Check price guides for a ball park figure but remember, these are book values. Don't expect to get these prices at a garage sale.

Homemade costumes, while not as collectible, are usually sturdy, well made, and more elaborate and detailed. When considering the time spent and cost of materials to make them, homemade costumes are really the best buys.

Christmas Tree Stand, metal, heavy duty, $5.00.

Jack-O'-Lantern, candy carrier, plastic, orange and black, ©1980 Carolina Enterprises, Inc., $1.00.

Christmas
- artificial tree
  - aluminum, silver, 4' high 1.00
  - plastic, green, 6' high 2.00
- color wheel with spotlight 2.50
- creche, 10 plaster or papier mâché figures and manger 12.00
- garland, tinsel, single strand .... .25
- knick-knack, ceramic
  - Christmas tree, 25 watt light bulb illuminates plastic mini bulbs on branches, 18" high 4.00
  - figurine (angel, elf, etc.) .... .50
- lawn statue, electric 8.00
- lights, string with bulbs
  - Christmas tree.............. 2.00
  - outdoor 5.00
- ornaments, tree
  - glass balls, box of 12 .... 2.00
  - satin balls, box of 12............ 1.00
  - wood figures, set of 12 .... 2.50
- tree skirt, fabric.................. 2.00
- tree stand, metal
  - heavy duty, holds real tree 5.00
  - lightweight, holds artificial tree 1.50

Easter
- basket
  - plastic...................... .50
  - woven splint or wicker 3.00
- egg
  - ceramic, price per dozen 1.50
  - glass, white, price each.......... .75
  - plastic, egg tree type, price per dozen .50
  - polished stone, price each .... .50
  - Pysanki...................... 2.00
- knick-knacks (bunny, chick, etc.) ..... .50

Halloween
- costume
  - homemade
    - adult sizes 4.00
    - children's sizes 3.00
  - store bought, generic 2.00
- jack-o'-lantern
  - ceramic, electric, window decoration 3.00
  - plastic, candy carrier............ 1.00
- knick-knacks (witch, ghost, pumpkin, etc.) .50
- lawn statue 8.00
- window cutout, cardboard .... .10

Independence Day
- bunting, red, white, and blue 5.00
- carbide cannon, uses bangsite 7.50
- flag, 50 stars, nylon, embroidered stars, 60" long 15.00

New Year's Eve
- hat, cardboard or plastic 1.00
- lei, plastic...................... .25
- noisemaker
  - cardboard, horn .... .50
  - metal (bells, ratchets, etc.)........ 1.50

Thanksgiving
- dinnerware serving pieces, figural turkey
  - gravy or sauce tureen 3.00

salt and pepper shakers, pair 2.00
knick-knacks (pilgrim, turkey, cornucopia) .50
planter, figural turkey 5.00
turkey platter 10.00

HUMIDIFIERS

Give your humidifier a good cleaning to remove lime scale before you attempt to sell. If you are selling the large rotating drum type, remove the old crusty filter and if possible, replace it with a new one. Smaller, table top humidifiers need less space and are easier to clean and maintain. One with a 2 gallon tank should run for 24 to 48 hours before needing to be refilled. Newer humidifiers with built-in medication cups can also be used as vaporizers.

Floor Model, plastic cabinet
9 gallon capacity, 3 speed 25.00
11 gallon, drum type 12.00
Table Top Model
½ gallon capacity 5.00
2 gallon capacity 7.50
5 gallon capacity 15.00
Vaporizer, cool mist 3.00

ICE SKATES

Ever notice how fast kid's grow, especially their feet? They only wear ice skates a few times before they're too small. Most used skates look practically brand new. Polish them up and label them with the size and price.

Boy's, Canadian Royal, black, size 3, $3.00.

Adult
figure 5.00
hockey 8.00
speed 3.00
Child
figure 3.00
hockey 2.00
training, double blades 2.00

IRONS & IRONING BOARDS

Despite the invention of permanent press fabrics, there is still a need in most homes for the old-fashioned iron and ironing board. Newer lightweight models with Teflon plates may be easier to lift, but the older, heavier irons worked just as well and seemed to do most of the work for you. Blocked vent holes are a steam iron's biggest problem. Examine the plate for telltale green and white lime stains. If they're present, chances are a previous owner used tap water rather than distilled water in the tank. Plug it in and check it out.

Iron, General Electric, steam/spray, $2.00.

Clothes Hanger
metal, over-the-door 50
vinyl coated wire, hooks on end of board to hold ironed clothing 50
Iron, electric
dry 1.00
steam/spray 2.00
traveling, carrying pouch 1.00

Ironing Board
full size
metal, adjustable height 7.50
wooden, folding 4.00
sleeve board, 2 sleeve sizes 1.00
traveling, table top model, 28" long . . . 1.00
Pressing Cloth 50
Rack, over-the-door, vinyl coated wired, holds
iron and ironing board 1.00
Sprinkler Bottle, glass or plastic 1.50

JEWELRY

Costume jewelry is garage sale gold. Gaudy beaded necklaces, old rhinestone earrings, and overwound wristwatches sell equally well.

As you sort through your jewelry, look for gold or silver items. Genuine gold or sterling silver will be marked. If it isn't marked *sterling* or *14 K,* then assume it's not. Prices for gold jewelry are dependent upon the weight of the items and the current gold market. Have gold jewelry appraised. Gold plated or gold filled jewelry will also be marked. The actual gold or silver content in these pieces is minimal.

Use old egg cartons to display small pieces of jewelry. Pair up your earrings, cuff links, and any other jewelry sets. Indicate the manufacturer's name on the price tag. Jewelry marked *Carnegie, Coro, Eisenberg, Miriam Haskell, Joseff of Hollywood, Monet, Schiaparelli, Schreiner, Trifari, Weiss, or Whiting Davis* is popular with collectors and should be priced slightly higher than unmarked pieces.

This is one area where you shouldn't throw anything away. What looks like junk to you may be a diamond in the rough to someone else.

Bracelet
bangle
bakelite, carved 25.00
copper 4.00
plastic 1.00
plated metal 2.00
sterling silver, narrow 5.00
chain 2.00
charm, sterling silver, 8 charms 15.00
identification 2.00
Charm
plated 50
sterling silver 1.50

Beaded Necklaces, $.50 each.

Cuff Links, pair 5.00
Earrings, pair
clip–on 1.00
pierced 2.00
Lapel Pin 3.00
Necklace
beads 50
chain
gold plated, 18" long 5.00
silver 2.50
locket 7.50
pendant 1.00
Pin, figural (animal, flower, etc.)
metal, enameled or set with stones 2.00
plain metal, plastic, or wood 1.00
Ring, cocktail, adjustable 5.00
Stickpin 2.50
Sweater Guard 75
Tie Bar 3.00
Tie Tack 2.00

JEWELRY BOXES

Don't sell a jewelry box with the contents intact. Empty the box, sort through the jewelry, and price pieces either individually, in small groups, or in sets. Price the jewelry box separately. You will realize higher prices by itemizing.

Cardboard, imitation leather covering, velvet lining, fitted interior, cantilever shelves, mirror inside, locking
- 1 shelf
  - musical, dancing ballerina 2.00
  - non-musical 1.00
- 3 upper compartments with shelves, 2 fitted drawers in bottom 7.50

Cedar, souvenir, 10" long.............. 5.00
Leather Case, locking, travel size, 8" long.. 5.00
Wood, chest of drawers, 15" high........ 5.00

KITCHEN GADGETS & UTENSILS

Old kitchen gadgets are highly collectible. The two most important factors in determining value are age and uniqueness. Early models of apple peelers and egg beaters were produced in more variations than can be imagined. If they are still in good shape and working order, they should sell quickly.

Utensils from the 1940s and earlier with painted handles also sell well. The most common colors are red or green, with or without white stripes. If you buy any of these utensils, keep in mind you'll have to wash them by hand. One cycle through the dishwasher is sufficient to strip the paint.

Cast iron bottle openers made during the 1950s and early 1960s can be found in a myriad of shapes. Condition is the primary consideration. Broken pieces and the presence of rust greatly reduces value. If the paint is either badly chipped, completely worn, or has been touched-up, value is also lower. Check general price guides for further guidance in pricing old gadgets and utensils.

Apple Peeler, crank handle
- modern, peels, slices, and cores 5.00
- old, cast iron, peels only............ 35.00

Apple Peeler/Corer
- modern plastic or wooden handle .... .50
- painted wooden handle 1.00

Bag Clip, reseals food bags, plastic .... .50
Baked Potato Baker, aluminum, four skewers .25
Basting Brush .... .25
Bottle Brush .... .10
Bottle Opener/Can Opener Combination
- aluminum, beer advertisement .... .75
- metal, plastic handles .... .50

Butter Churn, glass jar, crank handle, wooden paddles 10.00

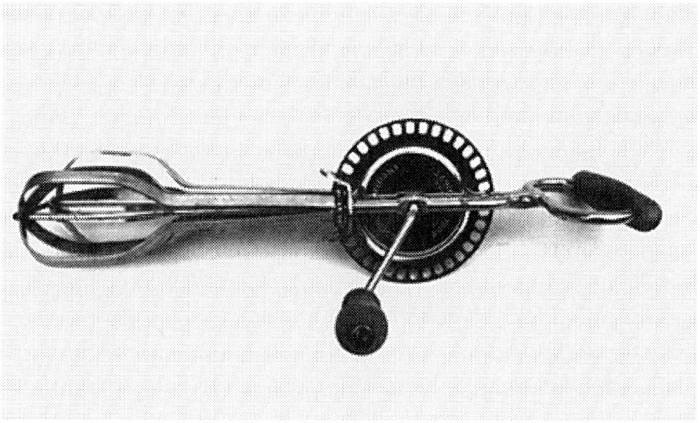

Egg Beater, Edlund Co., Burlington, VT, stainless steel blades, red wooden handles, $4.00.

Cake Tester .... .25
Can Opener, crank handle
- hand held....................... 1.00
- mounts on wall 3.00

Cheese Grater, crank handle, plastic, fits on jar 1.00
Cheese Slicer .... .50
Cherry Pitter....................... 25.00
Chocolate Mold, tin 18.00
Chopper, curved metal blade, wooden handle 4.00
Citrus Peeler, plastic................. .25
Coffee Grinder, crank handle, wood box .. 25.00
Coffee Scoop, metal or plastic .... .10
Colander 2.00
Corkscrew, modern 1.00
Corn Huller, metal, leather strap handle ... 1.00
Corn Skewers, set of 4 .... .50
Crab Mallet 1.00
Egg Beater 4.00
Egg Poacher, single egg, aluminum 1.00
Egg Separator .... .50
Egg Slicer, hard boiled eggs .... .75
Fizz Saver .... .25
Flour Scoop, red wooden handle 1.00
Flour Sifter 5.00
Fondue Skewers, metal, set of 4 .... 1.00
Food Mill, conical, aluminum sieve and stand, wooden masher 2.50
French Fry Cutter
- 1 piece, circular blade, red wooden handles 2.00
- 2 interchangeable blades, red wooden handle, 10" long............... 5.00

Fruit Baller .... .50
Funnel, glass, metal, or plastic .... .50

- Garlic Press — 3.00
- Grapefruit Knife — 1.00
- Grater, stainless steel, 4 cutting patterns — 2.50
- Gravy Shaker, aluminum or copper — 1.00
- Hamburger Press, plastic — 1.00
- Honey Dipper, wooden — .75
- Ice Cream Scoop
  - one piece, no moving parts, aluminum — .50
  - thumb release, green wooden handle — 5.00
- Ice Pick, advertising on wooden handle — 1.00
- Ice Tongs — 1.00
- Jar Wrench — 1.50
- Kabob Skewers, set of 8 , bamboo — .50
- Knife Sharpener, 2 wheels — 1.00
- Ladle
  - graniteware — 5.00
  - modern plastic or wooden handle — .50
  - painted wooden handle — 1.00
- Lemon Squeezer, aluminum — 5.00
- Measuring Cup
  - dry, plastic or metal, set of 4 — 1.00
  - liquid
    - glass
      - 1 cup — 1.00
      - 2 cup — 1.50
      - 4 cup — 2.50
    - plastic, any size — .50
- Measuring Spoons, set of 4, plastic or metal — .50
- Meat Fork
  - modern plastic or wooden handle — .50
  - painted wooden handle — 1.00
- Meat Grinder, with attachments — 12.00
- Meat Tenderizer, wooden hammer — .50
- Meat Thermometer — 1.00
- Noodle Cutter — 1.50
- Nut Set, 2 nut crackers, 4 picks — 2.00
- Nutmeg Grater, painted wooden knob — 5.00
- Onion Chopper, spring action, glass jar, plastic lid, wooden disc in bottom — 1.50
- Pastry Blender, 4 blades, painted wooden handle — 2.50
- Pea Sheller — .75
- Pie Crimper, painted wooden handle — 1.50
- Pie Server — 1.00
- Pineapple Snip — .75
- Pizza Cutter — .50
- Pot Scrubber, wire rings — 1.00
- Potato Masher
  - modern plastic or wooden handle — 1.00
  - painted wooden handle — 2.00
- Potato Ricer — 2.50
- Poultry Shears — 3.00

Flour Sifter, Bromwell's Bee, Pat. No. 1753.995, tin, wooden crank handle, $5.00.

- Powdered Sugar Shaker, plastic — 1.00
- Raisin Seeder — 12.00
- Reamer, glass, clear, unmarked — 5.00
- Salad Server, plastic, large scissor action fork and spoon — 1.00
- Serving Spoon, solid or slotted
  - modern plastic or wooden handle — .50
  - painted wooden handle — 1.00
- Shrimp De-veiner, plastic — .50
- Soda Bottle Cap — .10
- Spaghetti Lifter, plastic — .50
- Spaghetti Measurer — .50
- Spatula
  - bowl scraper, rubber blade — .50
  - cake icer, metal blade — .50
  - pancake flipper
    - modern plastic or wooden handle — .50
    - painted wooden handle — 1.00
- Strainer
  - plastic, fits over pot for draining liquids — .25
  - wire mesh, fits over bowl — .75
- Strawberry Huller — .75
- Sugar Cube Tongs — 1.00
- Tea Ball, aluminum, acorn shaped — .50
- Tongs, hot dog or corn on the cob size — 1.00
- Turkey Baster — .50
- Vegetable Brush — .50
- Vegetable Peeler — .50
- Veg-O-Matic — 2.00
- Wire Whisk — .50
- Wooden Spoon — 1.00

KNICK-KNACKS

It's amazing how dirt and dust builds up on knick-knacks. Before you attach that price sticker, wash each piece in soapy water. You'll be surprised at the difference it makes. Check the base of figurines for the maker's mark. If there is a specific name (rather than *made in Japan* or just a mold number) you may want to do a little research before pricing.

Whoever said "one man's junk is another man's treasure" must have been talking about the brick-a-brack that accumulates in the average household over a number of years. If you like to buy knick-knacks but dread the extra housework, don't despair. A hair dryer set on low will speed up your dusting chores.

Statue, pot metal, United Nations Building, $1.00.

Bank
- ceramic, circus elephant sitting on stool, 8" high 1.50
- glass, pig, 4" long 1.00

Bud Vase, pottery, cornucopia shaped, floral decal, $5\frac{1}{2}$" high 1.00

Figurine (animal, person, etc.)
- ceramic
  - birthday angel 1.00
  - cottage, hand painted, $4\frac{1}{4}$" long . . . 1.50
  - poodles, mother and 3 puppies, attached together by chain leash, mother is 7" high 1.00
  - zebra, plaster, 10" long 2.00
- glass
  - swan, clear, filled with colored water .50
  - unicorn, blown glass, $2\frac{1}{2}$" high 50

LADDERS

How high does it go? Ladders are generally sold by the foot. The higher the ladder, the higher the price. When comparing ladders of equal size, aluminum and fiberglass ladders are preferred over wooden models because of their lighter weight and subsequent easier manageability. Price them higher than their wooden counterparts. Inspect ladders before you buy. Make sure they are safe to use – no broken rungs or missing ropes or shoes.

Stepladder, wooden, 6' high, Type 1 Industrial, $5.00.

Escape, 3 story, steel chains and rungs 7.50

Extension
- 16'
  - aluminum 15.00
  - fiberglass 20.00
- 24'
  - aluminum 20.00
  - fiberglass 25.00
- 32'
  - aluminum 35.00
  - fiberglass 45.00
- 40'
  - aluminum 50.00
  - fiberglass 65.00

Step
- 4'
  - aluminum 7.50
  - fiberglass 10.00
  - wooden 4.00

6'
aluminum 10.00
fiberglass 15.00
wooden 5.00
8'
aluminum 15.00
fiberglass 20.00
wooden 7.50
12'
aluminum 20.00
fiberglass 25.00
wooden 10.00
Three Level, adjusts to 18 different positions, aluminum
12' straight/6' step/3' scaffolding...... 20.00
14' straight/7' step/4' scaffolding...... 22.50
16' straight/8' step/4' scaffolding...... 25.00
Upright, wooden
16' 5.00
24' 7.50

LAMPS

The styles and varieties of lamps available at garage sales is infinite. They are designed for use from floor to ceiling, and to grace every piece of furniture in between. Examine electrical cords for bare spots and frays. If the lamp is old and has a fabric covered cord, be prepared to replace it. If you find a lamp that you really like, but it doesn't work, don't be discouraged from buying it, especially if it has only one socket. Lamps are very easy to repair – most consist of just a socket and cord, both of which are easily replaced.

Bed Lamp, metal or plastic, attaches to headboard, dimmer switch.............. 3.00
Bedroom
candlestick, clear glass 10.00
child's
ceramic, figural cartoon character . . 20.00
plastic, ABC blocks............. 7.50
hurricane lamp, milk glass, floral design 2.00
Desk, gooseneck, high intensity light bulb . 2.00
Floor Standing
1 socket, metal 10.00
4 sockets, 3 regular bulbs, center mogul light, 2 switches, metal 20.00
Heat Lamp 5.00
Lava, bottle shaped 30.00

Bedroom Lamp, clear glass chimney, white milk glass shade, bronze colored metal base, $2.00.

Motion, revolving plastic cylinder 35.00
Nursery, ceramic, figural (clown, nursery rhyme character, etc.)............... 4.00
Pole, 3 lights, spring tension pole 5.00
Swag, hanging chain
leaded glass 15.00
wicker 2.00
Table
ceramic (urn, ginger jar, etc.) 3.00
Tiffany type, pot metal frame, slag glass panels in dome shade........... 200.00
Television
ceramic, figural (panther, ship, etc.) . . . 20.00
seashell 8.00
Workshop, 2 fluorescent tubes, 3' long.... 7.50

LAWN & GARDEN TOOLS

Leaf blowers, edgers, and weedwackers all are meant to make lawn care easier. Unless you have ample storage for these tools, the time saved using them can be eaten up just trying to get at them. If you are fortunate enough to own a large garage, the muscle power and exertion they eliminate can certainly make them well worth the price paid at a garage sale.

Check all tools to ensure that they work. Manual tools are easy. Electric models must be plugged in. Ask the seller to start up gas powered engines. Be sure hardware and accessories are included when appropriate.

When choosing between electric and gas powered models, base your decision not only on cost, but also on the size of your yard and how many feet of extension cord would be needed to reach the far corners. Keep in mind that some tools can serve double duty – lawn rollers can also be used to flatten newly laid linoleum flooring; leaf blowers are great for cleaning out your home's gutters.

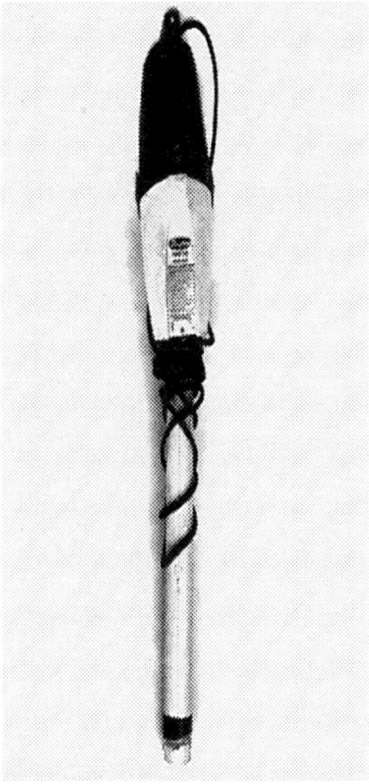

Leaf Blower, Dayton Hand Vac, Dayton Electric Mfg Co., Chicago, IL, 5.8 amps, $15.00.

Apple Picker	2.00
Blower	
electric	12.00
gas powered, 25 cc engine, 2 cycle	25.00
Blower/Vacuum	
electric	15.00
gas powered	30.00
Brushwacker, gas powered	
25 cc engine, 17" wide cut	35.00
40 cc engine, 18" wide cut	75.00
Chain Saw	
electric, 2.75 hp, 12 amps	15.00
gas powered	
2.0 cubic inch	20.00
2.5 cubic inch	35.00
3.3 cubic inch	50.00
Chipper/Shredder	
electric, 12 amp	50.00
gas powered	
5 hp	75.00
8 hp	125.00

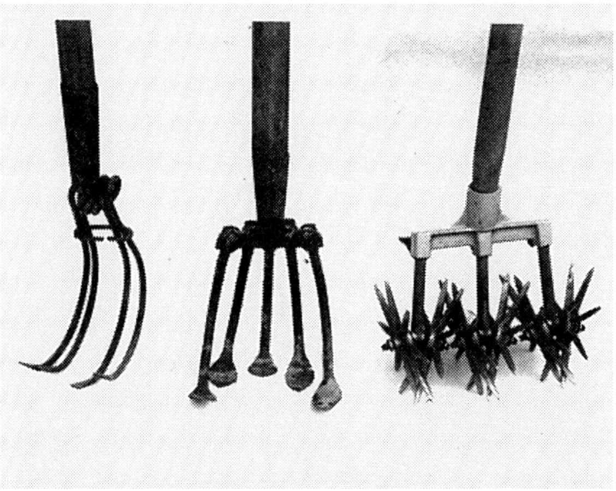

Cultivators, left and center: fixed tines, $5.00 each; right: Garden Weasel type, $10.00.

Compost Bin	7.50
Cultivator	
electric	20.00
gas powered, 2 cycle engine	35.00
manual	
fixed tines	5.00
Garden Weasel type, four wheels	10.00
Dandelion Puller	2.00
Edger	
electric	15.00
gas powered	
21 cc engine, 2 cycle	25.00
3 hp, 4 cycle	75.00
manual	2.00

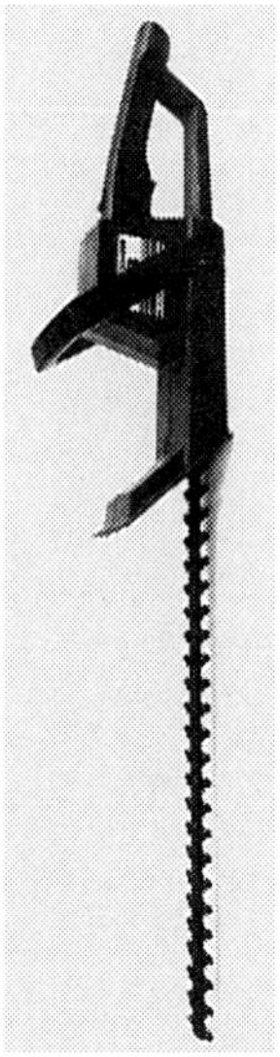

Hedge Trimmer, electric, Sears Craftsman 18 Bushwacker, $15.00.

Rakes, leaf and lawn, bamboo and metal, $2.50 each.

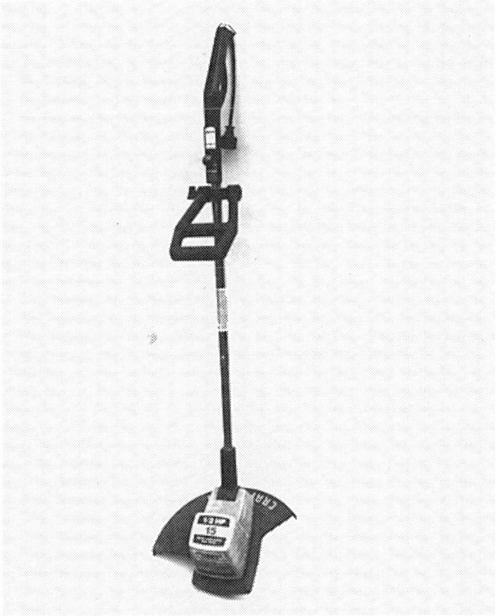

Weed Trimmer, Sears Craftsman Weedwacker, electric, 1/2 hp, 15" wide path, $15.00.

Garden Tool Set, trowel and claw	4.00
Grass Shears	1.00
Hedge Trimmer	
electric	15.00
gas powered	30.00
manual	2.00
Hoe	2.50
Lawn Cart, steel, 5 1/2 cubic foot capacity	20.00
Lawn Vacuum, 5 hp, self-propelled, 30" nozzle, hose attachments	125.00
Log Cart, wooden, steel frame, removable front panel, 300 lb capacity	15.00
Pitchfork	4.00
Post Hole Digger	
gas powered, 3 1/2 hp, 2 cycle	
1-man	65.00
2-man	100.00
manual	5.00
Pruner, hand held	2.00
Rake	
garden	2.50
leaf and lawn, bamboo, metal, or plastic	2.50
thatch	3.00
Rototiller, gas powered, 5 hp	
front tine	50.00
rear tine	125.00
Sieve, dirt sifter, wooden frame, fits over wheelbarrow	5.00
Spade	2.50
Sprayer, plastic, 2 gallon capacity	2.00
Spreader, drop or broadcast, 55 lb capacity	5.00
Sprinkler	4.00
Tree Pruner	
buck saw	
metal frame	5.00
wooden frame	5.00
high limb cutter, 48" chain blade, reaches up to 25' high, add rope for additional height	7.50
manual, wooden handles, cuts small branches	2.00
pole pruner, fiberglass, telescopes from 6' to 12' high	10.00

Wheelbarrow, steel, 6 cubic foot capacity, pneumatic tire, $12.00.

Watering Can
- galvanized 5.00
- plastic 2.50

Weed Trimmer
- electric
  - 3.1 amp, converts to edger 20.00
  - 3.3 amp 10.00
  - 6 amp 15.00
  - 12 volt, cordless, rechargeable 25.00
- gas powered
  - 21 cc, 15" wide cut 25.00
  - 32 cc, 18" wide cut 45.00

Wheelbarrow, 6 cubic foot capacity, steel, pneumatic tire, wooden handles 12.00

LAWN & PORCH FURNITURE

Before the introduction of plastic lawn and patio furniture, home owners invested in sets of redwood or Adironack style wooden chairs, settees, and tables. These pieces were built to last. Even today, they usually only require a good cleaning, fresh coat of paint, or at worst, a new woven seat. More and more home owners are making a decorating statement with the furniture they use on their porches and decks. Old rockers and park benches or even brightly colored molded plastic furniture is certainly more appealing than an old over–stuffed chair!

Chair
- aluminum frame, plastic webbing
  - child's size 1.00
  - full size 2.00
- molded plastic
  - child's size 1.50
  - full size 2.50
- redwood, upholstered cushion 5.00
- twig 15.00
- wooden frame, canvas back and seat . . 5.00

Chaise Lounge, adjustable back
- aluminum frame, plastic webbing
  - child's size 3.00
  - full size 4.00
- molded plastic, white 5.00
- redwood, upholstered cushion 12.00
- wood and wicker, magazine pockets on both sides, painted dark green 45.00

Glider
- aluminum frame, plastic webbing 10.00
- metal frame, upholstered cushions 15.00

Chair, wooden frame, canvas back and seat, $5.00.

Park Bench
- cement ends, wooden boards 7.50
- wrought iron ends, wooden slats 20.00

Porch Swing, wooden, chains for suspending from ceiling 30.00

Rocker
- aluminum frame, plastic webbing 2.50
- metal, 1 piece, painted yellow 5.00
- wood, woven splint back and seat, painted dark green 50.00
- twig 25.00

Sand Chair, aluminum frame, plastic webbing or canvas seat and back 2.00

Swing, wood A–frame, 2 facing bench seats suspended by chains 25.00

Table
- metal, folding, 24" diameter top 1.00
- molded plastic, white 1.00
- plastic, stacking, set of 3 . . . . . 2.00
- redwood, 24" square top 2.50

LAWN GAMES

Outdoor games such as volleyball and bean bags will always be popular summertime activities. Make sure you have the complete game assembled and packaged together. If you're buying, inspect all the pieces carefully. These games were usually played hard – bent racquets, torn beanbags, and punctured volleyballs are commonplace.

Lawn Darts, price for complete set, $5.00.

Badminton, complete set includes net, posts, stakes, ropes, 4 racquets, 2 birdies	7.50
Beanbags, set includes 2 wooden targets and 8 bags	5.00
Bocce Ball, set includes eight 4" balls and $1^1/_2$" jack ball	5.00
Croquet, set includes 2 stakes, 6 different colored balls and mallets, 9 wire wickets, and wheeled cart	10.00
Frisbee	.50
Hoops, complete set includes 2 posts and 4 bicycle tires	5.00
Horse Shoes, set includes 2 stakes and 4 horseshoes	
iron set, adult's	7.50
plastic set, child's	2.00
Lawn Darts, set includes 2 rings and 4 darts	5.00
Quoits, complete set	
2 slate boards, four rubber quoits	45.00
2 iron pins, four iron quoits	7.50
Tetherball, complete set includes pole, tethered ball, and two paddles	10.00
Volleyball, complete set includes net, posts, ropes, stakes, volleyball	15.00

LAWN MOWERS & TRACTORS

Those old rotary type mowers are becoming popular again. Postage stamp yards don't need gasoline powered self-propelled mowers, the old rotary type is sufficient. Electric mowers are also good for smaller yards, but make sure you have enough cord to get you where you need to go.

If you're shopping for a power mower and don't know your way around a gasoline engine, ask the seller to start the mower to ensure that it works. While this is no guarantee that it will last for any length of time, it certainly is a start. If you're handy and don't mind making minor repairs, garage sales can be a ready source for inexpensive used mowers. Many people prefer older, simpler mowers over the newer, more complex models with electric starters, safety shut-off levers, and self-propulsion.

Lawn tractors can be equipped with attachments to handle every conceivable garden chore. If you're in the market for attachments, have your tractor's specifications on hand to ensure compatibility.

Accessories	
gas can, 5 gallon, metal, pouring spout	5.00
lawn mower cover, vinyl	
push mower	2.00
riding mower	7.50
Attachments	
push mower	
bagger, side or rear	5.00
side discharge chute, push mower	3.50
riding mower and tractor	
aerator, steel, $2^1/_2$" spikes	15.00
broadcast spreader, 100 lb capacity	20.00
dethatcher, steel, rear tow, 40" wide	15.00
disc harrow, 2 gangs, 40" wide	40.00
grader blade, reversible steel blade	35.00

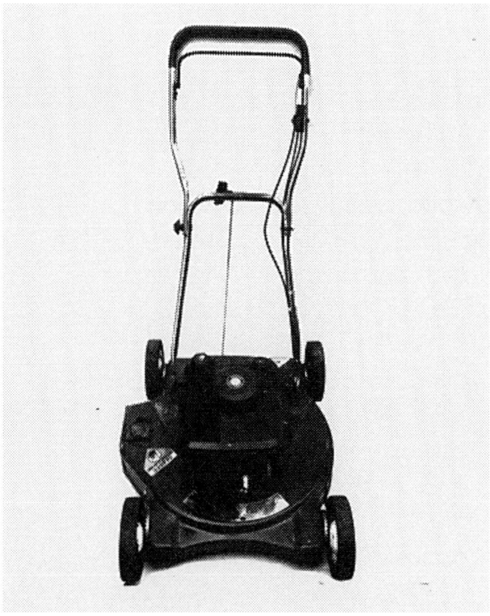

Push Mower, gas powered, safety shut-off lever, 22" cutting deck, $30.00.

lawn cart, steel
- 4 cubic foot capacity 10.00
- 10 cubic foot capacity 25.00
- 20 cubic foot capacity 40.00

lawn roller, steel drum, 180 lbs . . . 10.00
lawn sweeper, 10 cubic foot capacity 10.00
lawn vacuum, two 32 gallon bins, 12 bushel capacity 150.00
plow, 3 position yoke 45.00
sleeve cultivator, steel frame, 5 adjustable sweeps, 43" wide 65.00
snow blade, 42" wide 50.00
snow thrower, 40" path 175.00
sprayer, 14 gallon, tractor mounted 25.00
trailer sprayer, 25 gallon 40.00

Power Mower
- electric, push mower 25.00
- gas powered
  - mulching
    - 3-in-1, converts to rear bagger or side discharge, self-propelled, safety shut-off lever, 21" cutting deck 50.00
    - converts to side discharge only, push mower 40.00
  - rear bagger, converts to side discharge, self-propelled, rechargeable battery, electric start 45.00
  - side bagger, push mower, 22" cutting deck 35.00
  - side discharge only, push mower, 20" cutting deck 30.00

Riding Mower
- 5 hp, 25" cutting deck, 3 speed, manual start, side bagger, cloth bag 200.00
- 10 hp, 3-in-1 mulching, side discharge, or rear bagger, 5 speed, electric start, 30" cutting deck, 7 bushel polyethylene grass catcher 500.00

Rotary 2.00

Tractor
- 12.5 hp, 3-in-1 mulching, side discharge, or rear bagger, 5 speed, electric start, 38" cutting deck, full bag indicator, double bin bagging system 750.00
- 14 hp, 3-in-1 mulching, side discharge, or rear bagger, automatic transmission, electric start, 42" cutting deck, infinite height adjustments, double bin bagging system 1,000.00
- 18 hp, side discharge, 6 speed, 2 reverse speeds, electronic ignition, electric clutch, 44" cutting deck, adjustable seat 1,250.00

LAZY SUSANS

Lazy Susans have more uses than just as turntables for condiments on the dinner table. While these are probably the most decorative examples, inexpensive plastic models can also be found organizing spices in the kitchen and medicines in the bathroom. Before you buy, give it a quick spin to see that it turns smoothly.

Plastic
- double tier 1.50
- single tier 75

Wooden, inlaid decoration, matching salt and pepper shakers 5.00

LINENS

Separating and labeling your freshly laundered linen will make it easier for potential buyers to find what they're looking for. Keep sets, such as sheets, towels, or dresser sets together. Pin labels on sheet sets listing bed size. If there are any defects such as stains or small holes, make a note of these, too.

Old handmade quilts can range in price from under $100 to well over $1,000. Various factors can affect value, including age, condition, quality, size, and maker. Sellers would be wise to have old quilts appraised before trying to determine their value.

Bathroom Set, 5 pieces, tank set, toilet lid cover, U-shaped rug, bath rug 5.00
Bath Rug 2.00
Bedspread 5.00

Blanket
- thermal
  - twin size 2.00
  - double size 4.00
  - queen size 6.00
  - king size 8.00
- wool
  - twin size 2.50
  - double size 5.00
  - queen size 7.50
  - king size 10.00

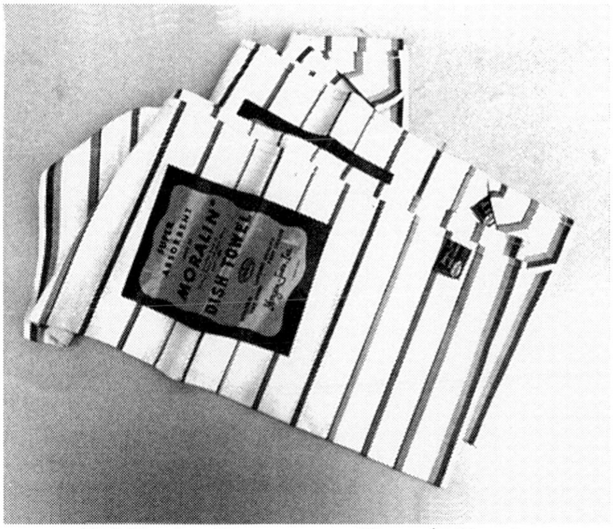

Dish Towels, cotton, rayon, and linen, $1.00 each.

Hot Pad, woven basketry, $.50.

- Comforter
  - down filled
    - twin size . . . 7.50
    - double size . . . 10.00
    - queen size . . . 12.50
    - king size . . . 15.00
  - poly fill
    - twin size . . . 5.00
    - double size . . . 7.50
    - queen size . . . 10.00
    - king size . . . 12.50
  - quilt squares, machine stitched, hand tied
    - twin size . . . 10.00
    - double size . . . 15.00
- Dish Towel . . . 1.00
- Dish Cloth 50

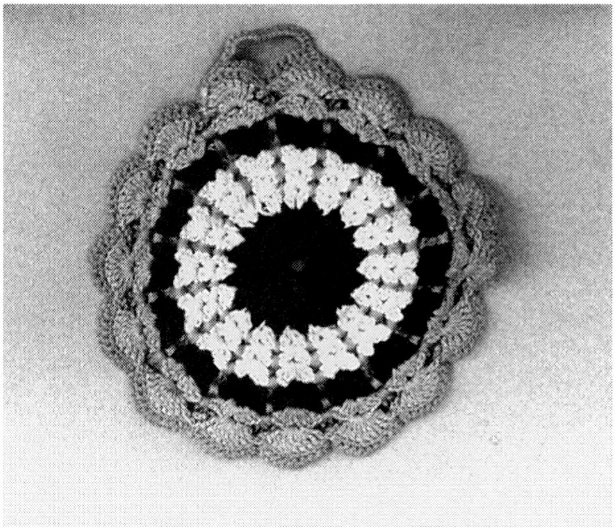
Doily, hand crocheted, 7" diameter, $2.00.

- Doily
  - crocheted . . . 2.00
  - machine woven 50
- Dresser Scarf
  - hand embroidered, crocheted edging . . 4.00
  - machine made . . . 1.00
- Electric Blanket
  - twin size . . . 5.00
  - double size . . . 7.50
  - queen size . . . 10.00
  - king size . . . 12.50
- Hot Pad 50
- Mattress Pad
  - twin size . . . 2.00
  - double size . . . 4.00
  - queen size . . . 6.00
  - king size . . . 8.00
  - sofa bed
    - double size . . . 5.00
    - queen size . . . 7.00
- Oven Mitt 50
- Pillow
  - backrest, corduroy . . . 5.00
  - bed pillow
    - down filled . . . 5.00
    - polyester foam . . . 2.00
  - throw pillow . . . 2.00
- Placemat
  - fabric . . . 1.00
  - plastic 50
- Quilt
  - craft kit, embroidered, hand quilted . . . 200.00
  - machine made
    - twin size . . . 5.00

double size	7.50
queen size	10.00
king size	12.50
Sheet Set, fitted sheet, flat sheet, 2 pillowcases	
twin size	2.50
double size	5.00
queen size	7.50
king size	10.00
sofa bed	
double size	6.00
queen size	8.50
Shower Curtain	3.00
Shower Curtain Liner	1.00
Tablecloth	3.00
Towels	
bath mat	1.00
bath sheet	3.00
bath towel	1.50
beach towel	3.00
hand towel	.50
wash cloth	.25

LOCKS

Padlocks, combination locks, and bicycle locks – they all sell well at garage sales, providing the keys or combinations are available. Retail prices for locks are inexpensive – garage sale locks must be priced even lower.

Assorted Padlocks, all made in USA, $1.00 each.

Bicycle, chain	2.50
Combination	1.00
Padlock	1.00

LOG SPLITTERS

If your home has a fireplace or wood burning stove, and you've ever chopped a cord of wood by hand, you can appreciate the value of a log splitter. If you're looking to buy, expect to pay a reasonable price – log splitters are a luxury, not a necessity, and there aren't many to be found at garage sales.

Log Splitter	100.00

LUGGAGE

Luggage design has changed drastically over the last thirty years. Old cardboard suitcases would never hold up to the abuse meted out at the baggage turnstile. Today's luggage is better constructed and can last decades with minimal care.

Examine luggage for damaged stitching, broken zippers, and torn or missing interior straps. Don't forget to ask the seller for the keys or combination for locking suitcases.

Beach Bag, waterproof	1.00
Duffle Bag, canvas	5.00
Foot Locker	5.00
Gym Bag	2.50
Knapsack, fabric or vinyl	2.00
Matching Set, large wheeled suitcase, overnight bag, vanity case	25.00

Overnight Bag, American Tourister, blue vinyl, $5.00.

Overnight Bag	5.00
Suitcase, large	
hard sided	7.50

soft sided
- leather 15.00
- vinyl or fabric 10.00

wheeled, hard sided 12.00

Suit Bag 3.00

Vanity Case, makeup mirror and tray 5.00

Vintage, cardboard 1.00

LUNCH BOXES

The most popular lunch boxes are embossed metal boxes decorated with popular children's television and cartoon characters. In order to achieve premium prices, lunch boxes must have their original thermoses intact. Leading manufacturers of children's lunch boxes include Aladdin Company, Ohio Art, and Thermos/King–Seely. If you still have your lunch kit dating from the 1960s or 1970s, and it's in very good condition with no rust or scratches, take a look in collectibles price guides for more specific pricing.

Lunch Box
- embossed metal, child's
  - character (TV, superhero, etc.) 25.00
  - generic (plaid, US map, etc.) 10.00
- hard plastic
  - adult's, plain, dome top 1.00
  - child's
    - character (GI Joe, Cinderella, etc.) 5.00
    - generic (space, animals, etc.) . . 1.00
- metal, adult's, plain, dome top 2.00
- vinyl, soft sided
  - child's, zipper closure
    - character (fairy tale, cartoon, etc.) 3.00
    - generic (plaid, sports, etc.) 1.00
  - plain, lunch bag style, Velcro closure 1.00
- vinyl covered cardboard, child's
  - character (Sesame Street, Disney, etc.) 5.00
  - generic (ABCs, animals, etc.) 2.00

Lunch Kit, matching box and thermos, child's
- embossed metal box, metal thermos
  - character (TV, Disney, etc.) 50.00
  - generic (basketweave, rocket, etc.) . 20.00
- embossed metal box, plastic thermos
  - character (TV, superhero, etc.) 40.00
  - generic (plaid, cowboys, etc.) 15.00
- hard plastic box, plastic thermos
  - character (James Bond, ET, etc.) . . . 10.00
  - generic design (flowers, animals, etc.) 5.00

Thermoses, Aladdin, plastic, left: GI Joe, © 1986 Hasbro; right: Minnie 'n Me, Disney Company; $2.00 each.

- vinyl soft sided box, plastic thermos
  - character (cartoon, superhero, etc.) . 5.00
  - generic design (stripes, stars, etc.) . . 2.00
- vinyl covered cardboard box, plastic thermos
  - character (TV, sports, etc.) 15.00
  - generic design (plaid, cowboys, etc.) 7.50

Thermos
- metal, glass insert
  - character, child's (TV, Barbie, etc.) . 15.00
  - generic design, adult's or child's (plaid, stripes, etc.) 1.00
- plastic
  - character, child's (TV, Barbie, etc.) . 2.00
  - generic design, adult's or child's (plaid, stripes, etc.) 1.00
- stainless steel, adult's
  - 1 pint 2.00
  - 1 quart 5.00

MAGAZINES

Most people with magazine subscriptions tend to save their old magazines – they are too good to just throw away. The sorry news is, most of them are practically worthless. In order for an individual magazine to have any real value, it must be in excellent condition and possess one or more of the following characteristics: the cover was designed and signed by a famous illustrator; the cover story is of historic significance; the magazine contains many popular full page advertisements; or the magazine is scarce due to its limited circulation.

The price tag on a box of magazines should be set lower than the price you would get if you totaled the cost of each individual issue. People will pay a higher unit price for a particular magazine that is of interest to them than they will for a whole stack which may contain only one or two *good* copies. Another rule of thumb is: the more popular the magazine, the greater the supply. As always, supply and demand are key factors in determining price.

National Geographic, January, February, and July 1974 issues, $.25 each.

Bulk Prices (multiply price times the number of magazines in the lot)
- art (*Art and Beauty, Modern Art*) 25
- automotive (*Automobile Quarterly, Automotive Magazine*) 1.00
- children's (*Boys Home Weekly, Teen, Youth Companion*) 25
- economic (*Fortune, Money*) 10
- educational (*National Geographic, Nature Magazine*) 25
- farm life (*Farm and Fireside, Successful Farming, The Farmer's Wife*) 50
- fashion (*Cosmopolitan, Domestic Monthly, Glamour*) 25
- girlie (*Esquire, Penthouse, Playboy*) . . . 1.00
- hobbies (*Popular Photography, Needlecraft*) 10
- literary (*Literary Digest, Readers Digest*) .10
- movie (*Glamour of Hollywood, Motion Pic ture, Screen Stories*) 1.00
- music (*Billboard, The Beatles are Back*) .50
- news (*Newsweek, Time, World's Events Magazine*, etc.) . . . . *.25*
- outdoor (*Hunting & Fishing, Outdoor Life, Rocky Mountain Sportsman & Western Wild Life*) .50
- pictorial and general interest (*Collier's, Life, Look, Saturday Evening Post*) . 1.00
- political (*Democratic Digest, The Independent, Success*) 25
- religion (*Catholic Digest, Extension – National Catholic Monthly*) 10
- romance (*True Confessions, True Romance*) . . . . *.25*
- sports (*American Golfer, Sports Review, Sports Illustrated*) 50
- television (*TV Guide*) 50
- travel (*Arizona Highways, Travel*) 10
- women's (*Ladies Home Journal, McCall's, House & Garden, Woman's Home Companion*) 50

MAIL BOXES

A used mailbox needs to be in good condition in order to find a buyer. If the door doesn't close properly or the red flag is missing, give it to the garbage man. Figural decorator boxes can afford to have slight damage, but again, it must be functional in order for it to be of any use.

Business Size
- metal
  - decorated 12.00
  - plain 10.00
- plastic
  - decorated 10.00
  - plain 7.50

Decorative, figural (house, goose, etc.) . . . 15.00

Standard Size
- metal
  - decorated 10.00
  - plain 5.00
- plastic
  - decorated 7.50
  - plain 5.00

Wall Mounted
- metal 4.00
- plastic 2.00
- wood 6.00

MEDICINE CABINETS

If you plan on remodeling the bathroom, don't throw out the old medicine cabinet, you may be able to find it a new home. Some people buy old wooden cabinets to use as knick-knack shelves. Others may be restoring an old home and looking for a medicine chest to match the claw foot tub and pedestal sink.

Modern
- metal
  - mirrored doors 10.00
  - mirrored doors and overhead lighting 15.00
- wood
  - mirrored doors 15.00
  - mirrored doors and overhead lighting 20.00

Old, wood, mirror on door 35.00

METAL SHELVING

Everyone needs more storage space and metal shelving is great for the garage, basement, attic or shed. Look for clean, rust free units without dents or bowed shelves. While you should expect to pay a little extra for industrial strength shelving, it is well worth the investment if you plan to store heavy items. Remember to measure your wall space before you leave home and take a tape measure along to measure prospective units.

Industrial Shelving, heavy duty
- 4 shelf unit 8.00
- 6 shelf unit 12.00
- 8 shelf unit 15.00

Lightweight Shelving
- 4 shelf unit 2.50
- 6 shelf unit 5.00
- 8 shelf unit 10.00

MIRRORS

Polish your mirrors before you sell. If the mirror is dirty, it could be mistaken for needing re-silvering, a major undertaking and often more costly than the mirror itself. Make sure the mirror fits securely in its frame or backing. Measure large mirrors and include this information on the price tag. If you no longer need it, include with the mirror any hardware needed for mounting.

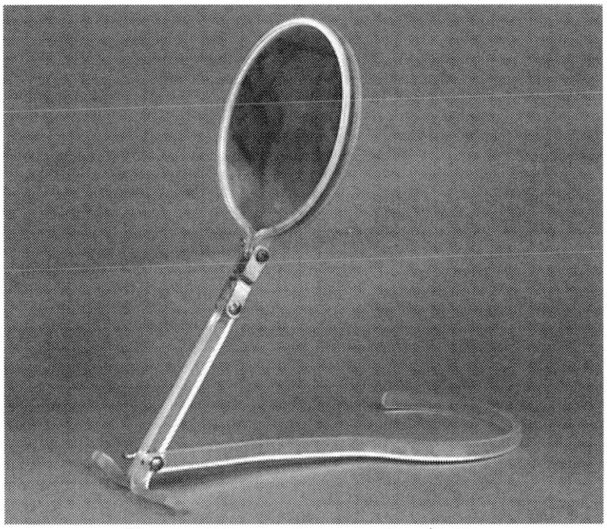

Shaving Mirror, clear acrylic, $2.00.

Mirror
- cheval, wood frame and legs, swivel mirror, 60" high 20.00
- convex, 15" diameter 5.00
- dresser tray, gold colored metal gallery . 3.00
- full length, wall mounted, 18" x 60" . . . 7.50
- hand held
  - celluloid frame 5.00
  - metal frame 3.00
  - plastic frame 1.00
- makeup, lighted, double sided, regular and magnified views 2.50
- mirror tile, 12" square. 50
- pocket size
  - advertising on back 5.00
  - plain back 1.00
- shaving
  - plastic, wall mounted, adjustable swivel arm. 2.00
  - wood frame, swivel mirror, 2 small drawers 20.00
- wall
  - self-framed, etched border design
    - 10" x 14", bathroom 3.00
    - 18" diameter, foyer 5.00
    - 36" x 24", dining room 10.00
    - 36" square, bedroom 12.00
  - wood frame
    - 10" x 14" 10.00
    - 18" diameter. 15.00
    - 36" x 24" 20.00

Mirror Clips, plastic, for mounting wall mirrors, set of 4 with screws 1.00

MIXING BOWLS

Modern mixing bowls are meant strictly for utilitarian use and are usually made of either glass or stainless steel. Porcelainized metal bowls with dainty floral decals and plastic lid seals, while attractive, are better suited for serving than for serious mixing. If your mixing bowls have plastic lid seals, add 50¢ to the price listed below for each bowl.

Be careful when pricing older stoneware, pottery, and yellow ware bowls. They are very popular with country collectors and value can range anywhere from $5 for a small bowl to hundreds of dollars for a nesting set.

Dinnerware companies from the 1940s and 1950s produced kitchenware items, including mixing bowl sets, to coordinate with their more popular lines. Look on the bottoms of bowls for makers' marks. Names to look for include Bauer, Hall, Homer Laughlin (Fiesta), and Watt. Dealers and buyers searching for pieces to complete their pattern will pay higher prices for these bowls than the average shopper.

China	
dinnerware pattern	
small	10.00
medium	12.00
large	15.00
extra large	25.00
nesting set of 4	75.00
plain, unmarked	
small	5.00
medium	7.50
large	10.00
extra large	15.00
nesting set of 4	45.00
Glass	
opaque	
solid color or decorated	
small, 1½ pint	2.00
medium, 1½ quart	4.00
large, 2½ quart	6.00
extra large, 4 quart	8.00
nesting set of 4	25.00
transparent	
blue	
small	5.00
medium	8.00
large	10.00
nesting set of 3	25.00
clear	
small, ½ quart	1.00
medium, 1 quart	2.00
large, 1½ quart	4.00
extra large, 2½ quart	6.00
nesting set of 4	15.00
Mixer Bowls, base fits electric mixer stand	
glass	
clear	
small	2.00
large	4.00
opaque green	
small	8.00
large	12.00
opaque white	
small	2.00
large	4.00
stainless steel	
small	1.00
large	3.00
Plastic	
small	.25
medium	.50
large	.75
extra large	1.00
nesting set of 4	2.50
Porcelainized Metal	
small, 1½ pint	1.00
medium, 1½ quart	2.00
large, 2½ quart	4.00
extra large, 4 quart	6.00
nesting set of 4	15.00

Mixing Bowls, glass, Pyrex, solid colors, yellow, green, red, and blue, nesting set of 4, $25.00.

Stainless Steel
- small, 1½ pint . . . 1.00
- medium, 1½ quart . . . 2.00
- large, 2½ quart . . . 3.00
- extra large, 4 quart . . . 5.00
- nesting set of 4 . . . 12.00

Stoneware, unmarked, blue trim
- small, 1 quart . . . 5.00
- medium, 1½ quart . . . 10.00

Yellow Ware, unmarked
- green sponged decoration, modern
  - small, 1½ pint . . . 2.00
  - medium, 1½ quart . . . 4.00
  - large, 2½ quart . . . 6.00
- pink and blue stripes, old
  - small, 1 quart . . . 15.00
  - medium, 2 quart . . . 35.00
  - large, 4 quart . . . 75.00

MUSIC STANDS

Musicians of all ages and abilities need a place to hold their music during those long hours of practice. You might also find the type band members tuck under their arms or attach to their instruments to hold their music while marching in parades.

Floor Stand
- portable, metal, folding, leather case . . . 5.00
- institutional, metal, black . . . 2.00

Marching Band
- clip-on . . . 2.00
- other . . . 4.00

MUSICAL INSTRUMENTS

Musical instruments of all kinds end up in garage sales as their usefulness in one household comes to an end. How many kids do you know that started playing an instrument in elementary school, only to lose interest after one or two years? If it's your child's turn, you may want to shop at garage sales for a good secondhand instrument. Examine the instrument carefully for signs of wear and tear. Ask the owner if it has been used lately and if it is still in tune.

If you're selling a used instrument, expect to recoup less than 50% of its original purchase price. Don't forget to include the carrying case and other accessories.

Harmonica, Hohner Pocket Pal, $5.00.

Instrument
- banjo . . . 65.00
- bugle, soprano . . . 75.00
- clarinet . . . 75.00
- drum
  - bass . . . 35.00
  - snare . . . 30.00
- drum set, includes bass drum with pedal, two mounted toms, floor tom, snare drum on stand, hi-hat and cymbal stand, and two drumsticks . . . 175.00
- flute . . . 80.00
- guitar
  - acoustic . . . 75.00
  - acoustic/electric . . . 100.00
  - electric . . . 100.00
- harmonica . . . 5.00
- keyboard, electric
  - 49 midsize keys . . . 30.00
  - 61 full-size keys . . . 50.00
- organ . . . 20.00
- piano
  - electronic, 61 full-size keys . . . 175.00
  - upright . . . 25.00
- piccolo . . . 75.00
- saxophone
  - alto . . . 200.00
  - soprano . . . 175.00
- trombone
  - slide . . . 125.00
  - valve . . . 175.00
- trumpet . . . 85.00

ukulele	40.00
violin	75.00
Accessories	
amplifier, 10 watt	20.00
keyboard bag, nylon	15.00
keyboard stand, steel, adjustable height	5.00
guitar case, hardshell	10.00

OFFICE SUPPLIES

While you're getting ready for your garage sale, sort through the desk drawers. Gather up old rulers, compasses, pens, and miscellaneous stationery. Bundle interesting objects together and price them to move quickly. If you have child-related supplies such as markers, ruler, stencils, etc., why not box them together as a *Back to School Kit?* If your supplies are more suited to the 18 to 21 year old range, try assembling a *Going Away to College* package with envelopes, stapler, pens, pencils, and a ruler. Take a little extra time to creatively market and package your odds and ends, it could pay off!

Clipboard	
vinyl, folding	1.50
wood, metal clip	1.00
Desk Organizers	
drawer organizer, plastic	.50
pencil cup, plastic	.25
Drawing Compass	1.00
File Drawer, metal, holds index cards	
1 drawer	2.00
2 drawer	4.00
Hole Punch, single or triple	1.50

Stapler, heavy duty, $1.00.

In-Out Basket, plastic	1.00
Markers, set of 10	1.00
Paper Clip Dispenser, magnetic	.50
Paper Clips, box of 100	.50
Pencil Sharpener	
battery operated	2.00
electric	3.00
manual	
hand held, plastic	.25
wall mounted, metal	1.00
Pencils, bundle of 10	.50
Pens, Bic type, bundle of 10	.75
Rolodex	2.00
Rubber Bands, box of 100	.50
Ruler	.50
Scissors	.50
Stacking Tray, plastic, holds files, price each	.50
Stamp Dispenser	.25
Stapler	
electric	4.00
manual	1.00
Staples, box	.50
Stationery, envelopes and paper, box of 20	3.00
Tape Dispenser	
Scotch tape	1.00
strapping tape	2.00

PAINT SPRAYERS

Examine sprayers for clogged nozzles and cracked hoses. Be sure that all attachments are included. Original instructions are also helpful.

Automotive, air compressor type	10.00
Household	
power roller	15.00
sprayer	
indoor	15.00
outdoor, cordless	35.00

PATIO LIGHTS

Although patios lights are not as popular for everyday use as they once were, they are still in demand for dressing up the camper and as a festive touch to summer evening picnics. Search garage sales for just the right shapes and color to accent your decor. Check the wiring and plug to be sure they are in working order.

The tiki torch also lost favor when it was replaced by the electric bug zapper. If you prefer the romance of an open flame and the aroma of kerosene over harsh black light and sizzling sounds, pick up a set of torches. They're often found at garage sales for bargain prices.

- Patio Lights, plastic, multicolored, string of 12
  - beer cans 4.00
  - Japanese lanterns 2.00
  - owls 3.00
  - seashells 3.00
- Tiki Torches, pair 5.00
- Umbrella Lights, string attaches to ribs of patio umbrella 5.00

PET SUPPLIES

Buying a pet can be a costly undertaking. Used pet supplies are common garage sale bargains, priced at a fraction of their original cost. Look over every item before you buy, but be especially careful when shopping for aquariums. If you plan to raise fish, it *must* be watertight!

- Bird
  - cage
    - floor standing 25.00
    - hanging 10.00
  - toys (mirror, ladder, perch, etc.) 25
- Cat
  - bed, hooded basket 3.00
  - carrier, plastic 5.00
  - collar 50
  - comb or brush 50
  - feeding dish, plastic 50
  - kitty condo 5.00
  - leash 1.00
  - litter box with hood 3.00
  - litter tray 1.50
  - scratching post 2.00
  - sunning shelf, attaches to windowsill . . 2.00
  - toy 25
- Dog
  - bed, basket with cushion 5.00
  - carrier
    - small 5.00
    - large 10.00
  - collar 50
  - comb or brush 50
  - feeding dish, plastic 1.00
  - hair clippers 4.00
  - harness 2.00
  - house, homemade, wood 7.50
  - invisible fence, complete 50.00
  - kennel, wire
    - small 10.00
    - large 15.00
  - leash
    - 6' long 1.00
    - 16' long, retractable 3.00
  - muzzle 2.00
  - nail clippers 1.00
  - portable gate 4.00
  - sweater 1.00
  - tether spike, metal, spiral 1.00
- Fish
  - aquarium
    - hexagonal, 15 gallon 20.00
    - rectangular
      - 10 gallon 5.00
      - 20 gallon 10.00
  - aquarium accessories
    - aerator 2.00
    - algae sponge 50
    - decorations (plant, house, etc.) 50
    - gravel 1.00
    - guppy nursery 50
    - fish net 50
    - heater 2.00
    - light 4.00
    - mural 50
    - pump/filter 4.00
  - aquarium stand, wrought iron 10.00
  - goldfish bowl 2.50

Hamster Setup, 10 gallon aquarium, feeding dish, exercise wheel, and water bottle, $8.00.

Hamster, Gerbil or Mouse
- cage
  - aquarium, 10 gallon 5.00
  - Habitrail, plastic 5.00
  - wire 2.00
- exercise ball, clear plastic, for use on floor 1.50
- exercise wheel 1.00
- feeding dish 50
- screen lid, for use on aquariums 1.00
- toys (plastic house, tube, etc.) 50
- water bottle 50

Hermit Crab, cage, plastic 1.50

Rabbit
- feeding dish 50
- hutch, wooden, two room 5.00
- water bottle 1.00

PHONOGRAPHS

While phonograph records have been phased out in favor of CDs, there is still a market for phonographs. Everyone who owns old 45s and albums needs a phonograph on which to play them. Be reasonable in determining value. Remember these two major drawbacks when pricing old phonographs: their sound quality is miserable by today's standards and there are still plenty of them out there – the supply far exceeds the demand.

Adolescent's, plastic, plays 45 and 33⅓ rpms, two speed, automatic record changer, detachable speakers 5.00

Child's, plastic, plays 45 rpms, electric, single speed 5.00

PHOTO ALBUMS

Looking for something to store all your photographs in? Photo albums can be readily found in a variety of sizes, colors, and styles.

Album
- Grandma's Brag Book, 1 picture per page 1.00
- magnetic pages, 6 photos per page, 11" x 14" 1.50
- plastic pocket pages, 6 photos per page 2.50

Photo Index, covered cardboard box and dividers, shoe box size 1.00

Photo Album, magnetic pages, decorated cover, $1.50.

PICNIC BASKETS

Not all picnic baskets are baskets. Lithographed tin "baskets" from the 1950s and 1960s also qualify, as do plastic examples manufactured today. Many are equipped with all the trappings needed for a picnic, including plastic plates, utensils, cups, and a tablecloth. Add $2 to the basket prices listed below if the contents are still intact.

Lithographed Tin, basketweave design, hinged lid, 2 swivel handles 5.00

Oak Splint, hinged lid, swivel handles, removable shelf, $10.00.

Oak Splint, elastic utensil holder on inside of hinged lid, swivel handles, removable inside shelf 10.00
Plastic, removable lid, handles 2.00
Wicker, 2 flap lids hinged at center, 2 swivel handles 5.00

PICNIC SETS

The traditional redwood picnic set has given way to a myriad of styles made from combinations of metal, plastic, and glass. No longer limited to a simple rectangular table with two benches, newer tables may be round, oval, square, or hexagonal, with comfortable cushioned seats. Prices vary according to comfort, construction, and ease of care.

Aluminum, white
- 40" round table with plastic table top, 4 chairs with full cushions 50.00
- 48" round table with glass table top, 4 chairs with full cushions 75.00
- 60" rectangular table with glass table top, 4 chairs with full cushions 100.00

Plastic
- 48" round table, 4 folding chairs 35.00
- 55" rectangular table, 4 molded chairs . 25.00
- 60" hexagonal table, 6 molded chairs . . 45.00

Steel Frame
- 42" round table with glass table top, 4 chairs with full cushions 50.00
- 42" round table, 4 chairs 25.00
- 45" square table with glass table top, 4 chairs with full cushions 75.00

Redwood
- 36" rectangular table with 2 attached benches, child's 10.00
- 42" round table, 4 benches 25.00
- 60" rectangular table, 2 benches 25.00

Wrought Iron
- 36" round table with glass top, 4 chairs with seat cushions 50.00
- 48" round table with mesh top, 4 barrel chairs with full cushions 65.00
- 66" oval table with mesh top, 4 chairs with full cushions 100.00

Umbrella, tilt and crank, 7 1/2' diameter 10.00

Umbrella Base
- plastic, sand filled 2.00
- wrought iron 7.50

PICTURE FRAMES

Every size, shape, and color of picture frames can be found at a garage sale. Know what sizes you need and bring a tape measure along. Replacing glass is easy and inexpensive, but figure it into the final price of any frame you buy.

Picture Frame, silver colored metal, silver and black cardboard mat, easel back, 7 x 9", $1.00.

Modern Frames
- ceramic, floral decals, easel back
  - 2 1/2" x 3 1/2" 50
  - 3" x 4 1/2" 75
  - 5" x 7" 1.00
  - 8" x 10" 2.00
- metal, rectangular or oval, easel back
  - 2 1/2" x 3 1/2" 25
  - 3" x 4 1/2" 50
  - 5" x 7" 75
  - 8" x 10" 1.00
  - 11" x 14" 1.50
- plastic, rectangular or oval, easel back or hanging
  - 2 1/2" x 3 1/2" 10
  - 3" x 4 1/2" 25
  - 5" x 7" 50
  - 8" x 10" 75
  - 11" x 14" 1.00
- wood, hanging
  - oval
    - 5" x 7" 2.50

8" x 10" 5.00
11" x 14" 7.50
rectangular
5" x 7" 1.50
8" x 10" 2.50
11" x 14" 4.00

Old
gesso over wood, oval, acorn design, gold leaf liner, 8" x 10" opening 40.00
gilt, rectangular, gold colored wood, applied moldings, 11 x 14" opening . . 10.00
mahogany, rectangular, deep well, ornate molding, 8" x 10" opening 35.00
oak, rectangular, intricately carved and/or pressed design on 3½" wide boards, 24" x 32" opening 20.00

PING PONG SETS

Ping pong tables are available in two styles: freestanding models and table tops made to fit on pool tables. They are also made for both indoor and outdoor use, depending on the construction. Indoor tables are made with particleboard tops, while outdoor models have aluminum compound tops for weatherproof durability. When buying a complete set, be sure all accessories including net, two net posts with tension adjustments, four paddles, balls, and hardware are included.

Balls, package of 4 50
Net, with net posts and hardware 2.00
Paddles, set of 4 . . . . 4.00
Ping Pong Set, indoor, complete 25.00
Ping Pong Table, 108" x 60" x 30"
indoor, particleboard top
freestanding 20.00
pool table cover, converts pool table to ping pong table 15.00
outdoor, aluminum compound top 50.00

PLAYING CARDS

Count the deck before you buy. Poker decks should have 52 playing cards and two jokers. Pinochle decks should contain 48 playing cards, nines through aces, two of each card. Decks with advertising bring higher prices than decks without. Big faced decks have oversized letters and numbers for sight-impaired players. Don't bother selling decks with creased or missing cards – buyers will count cards.

Playing Cards, advertising, pinochle deck, $3.00.

Advertising, single deck, poker or pinochle 3.00
Child's Deck (old maid, fish, etc.) 50
Double Deck, boxed set
canasta 3.00
poker or pinochle 4.00
Playing Card Kit, imitation leather folder with snap closure holds 2 poker decks, pencil, and note pad 5.00
Single Deck, poker or pinochle
big faced 1.00
standard size 1.00

POGO STICKS

Pogo Sticks are practically indestructible. If the pole is still straight and the spring's not broken, it should be a safe buy.

Pogo Stick 5.00

POOL EQUIPMENT

If there's a pool in the backyard at a garage sale don't be surprised to find pool related toys, tools, and cleaning supplies. If there's a new pool filter hooked up, be suspicious as to why the old one is being sold. Ask questions. The only safe way to purchase rafts and other inflatable toys is if they're still in their original packaging, or if you see them inflated.

Pool
baby pool
inflatable 2.00
molded plastic, turtle shape 4.00

child's pool, 12' diameter, 3' deep	30.00
Pool Accessories	
boogie board	5.00
chemical test kit	1.50
chlorine dispenser, floating	2.00
cover, fits 21' round pool	15.00
face mask	1.00
filter	
diatomaceous earth	
1 hp, molded plastic tank	125.00
$1\frac{1}{2}$ hp, 24 hour programmable timer, molded plastic tank	175.00
poly–perm, molded plastic tank	
$\frac{3}{4}$ hp	75.00
$\frac{1}{25}$ hp	20.00
sand	
$\frac{1}{3}$ hp, galvanized steel tank	50.00
$\frac{3}{4}$ hp, stainless steel tank	100.00
$1\frac{1}{2}$ hp, 24 hour programmable timer, molded plastic tank	150.00
games (volleyball, basketball, etc.)	3.00
goggles	.50
ladder	
inside pool	15.00
over-the-wall	25.00
life vest	2.00
lounge chair, floating	5.00
raft	
canvas	2.00
vinyl	1.00
skimmer net, telescoping pole	3.00
snorkel, plastic	1.00
solar cover, fits 21' round pool	12.00
solar cover reel	40.00
toys (diving rings, diving sticks, etc.)	1.00
vacuum kit	15.00

POOL TABLE ACCESSORIES

Garage sales can be great sources for finding used cue sticks, racks, and even balls. A quick tip to see if a cue stick is straight: roll it on a flat surface (preferably a pool table) and watch for any uneven spots or warping. If it rolls smoothly, buy it!

Balls	
Belgian phenolic with molded-in colors, 6 oz	15.00
plastic, 4 oz	10.00
Bridge Stick	3.50

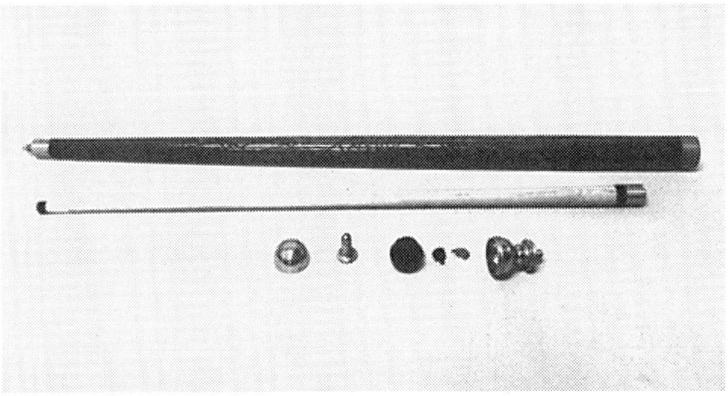

Cue Stick, 2 piece, $5.00.

Chalk, box of 6	.50
Cue Stick	
1 piece	3.00
2 piece, carrying case	5.00
Kelly Peas and Bottle	1.00
Table, portable, particleboard, folding legs with levelers, 39" x 79" playing area	75.00
Table Brush	1.00
Table Cover, vinyl	3.00
Triangle	
plastic	2.00
wood	4.00
Wall Rack, holds 8 cue sticks	5.00

POSTERS

Most posters found at garage sales will not be in pristine enough condition to attract the attention of true poster collectors. Thumbtack holes and fading mean that your buyer will probably be under the age of 16. Price posters within their reach.

Children's Theme (animals, cartoons, rock stars, sports, etc.)	
12" x 18"	.50
24" x 36"	1.00

POTPOURRI BURNERS

There are two kinds of potpourri burners: those that are heated electrically, and those that use small candles called tea lights. Electric models are often burned out due to being left on too long after the liquid has evaporated. Plug in electric models to see that they still heat properly. Tea light burners consist of a base to hold the candle, a bowl for the potpourri, and a perforated lid. Examine tea light burners for cracked bowls and bases.

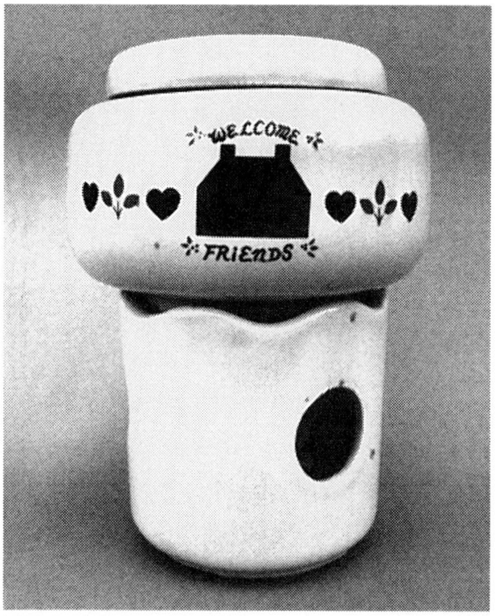

Potpourri Burner, tea light variety, ceramic, $1.00.

Burner	
electric	2.50
tea light	
ceramic	1.00
copper	1.50
Potpourri	
dry, full package	.50
liquid, full bottle	1.00
Tea Lights, box of 12	1.00

POTS & PANS

Scour your pots and pans thoroughly before adding them to your sale. If nonstick surfaces are scratched or pitted, reduce the price accordingly. Rather than tossing everything in a large box, arrange pots and pans attractively on a table with sets together and matching lids in place.

Cast iron frying pans are sought by collectors but not all brands are equal. Two names to look for are Griswold and Wagner, with Griswold usually priced slightly higher. Unmarked ironware is not highly collectible and should be considered solely utilitarian. Cast iron prices listed below are for unmarked examples.

The most commonly found enameled cookware was produced during the 1950s and 1960s in white with red or black trim. It is attractive and nostalgic, but not very durable. For this reason, it is used more on camping trips than in modern kitchens, where chips and scratches would be unacceptable. Coffeepots and tea kettles are often purchased for their decorative appeal, although it may be difficult to find pieces in good condition.

If you're lucky enough to own a set of Farber or Revere Ware, price it slightly higher than other stainless steel sets. Buyers are familiar with the names and quality and will pay a premium for these brands.

Although it may be expensive to buy a set of stainless steel cookware at retail prices, individual used pots and pans never bring high prices. Mark them low if you want them to sell. If you're selling a complete set, mark it at roughly twice the price of the sum of the individual pieces.

Coffeepot, percolator	
aluminum	.50
enamelware	2.00
glass	1.50
Double Boiler	
aluminum	1.50
glass	1.50
stainless steel	3.00
Dutch Oven, covered, 5 quart	
aluminum	3.00
enamelware	2.00
glass	2.00
Silverstone interior	3.00
stainless steel	4.00
Teflon interior	2.00
Egg Poacher	
aluminum, small pan, single egg poacher, and lid	.25
stainless steel, 12" diameter skillet, 12" diameter rack to hold 5 removable egg cups, and lid	4.00
Pressure Cooker, 6 quart	
aluminum	3.00
stainless steel	5.00
Pressure Cooker/Canner Combination, aluminum, holds seven 1 quart jars	3.00
Roasting Rack, aluminum, round	.50
Saucepan, covered	
1 quart	
aluminum	1.50
enamelware	1.00

Pots & Pans, Teflon coated, various prices.

glass 1.00
Silverstone interior 2.00
stainless steel 2.50
Teflon interior. 1.50

2 quart
aluminum. 2.00
enamelware 1.50
glass 1.50
Silverstone interior 2.50
stainless steel 3.00
Teflon interior. 2.00

3 quart
aluminum. 2.50
enamelware 2.00
glass 2.00
Silverstone interior 3.00
stainless steel interior 3.50
Teflon interior. 2.50

Set, 8 pieces, 8" and 10" skillets, 1 and 2 quart saucepans, 5 quart Dutch oven, and 3 interchangeable lids
aluminum. 20.00
enamelware 15.00
glass 15.00
Silverstone interior 25.00
stainless steel 30.00
Teflon interior 20.00

Skillet
8" diameter
aluminum. 1.50
cast iron 2.00
enamelware 1.00
glass 1.00
Silverstone interior 2.50
stainless steel 2.50
Teflon interior. 1.50

10" diameter
aluminum. 2.00
cast iron 2.50
enamelware 1.50
glass 1.50
Silverstone interior 3.00
stainless steel 3.00
Teflon interior. 2.00

12" diameter
aluminum. 2.50
cast iron 3.00
enamelware 2.00
glass 2.00
Silverstone interior 3.50
stainless steel 3.50
Teflon interior. 2.50

Steamer, 2 quart, fits in 2 quart sauce pan
aluminum. 1.00
stainless steel 1.50

Stock Pot, covered, 8 quart
aluminum. 3.00
enamelware 3.00
Silverstone interior 5.00
stainless steel 6.00
Teflon interior 2.00

Tea Kettle
aluminum. 1.50
enamelware 2.00
glass 2.00
stainless steel 3.00

Wok, aluminum, $2.00.

Wok
- aluminum 2.00
- cast iron 3.00
- nonstick surface 00

PUNCH BOWLS

A punch bowl is the ultimate bridal shower gift. How many brides do you know that haven't received one? Although punch bowls spend the majority of their lives in storage, when the need for one arises, it's great to have it on hand. If you come across a punch bowl at a garage sale, it will probably be in it's original box with all cardboard dividers and packaging intact. With the exception of an occasional broken cup, sets are usually found complete.

Bowl, 12 cups, plastic ladle
- acrylic 2.00
- glass 5.00

Bowl and Pedestal Base, glass, 12 cups, glass ladle 8.00

Ladle
- glass 2.50
- plastic 1.00

PURSES

There was a time when women owned a closet full of purses in various colors and styles. Proper dressing required matching shoes and handbags. This is no longer the case. Most women today own several purses, but they are more likely meant to accompany various styles of dress such as evening dress, work, or sportswear, rather than to perfectly match a particular outfit. A garage sale held by a mature homeowner is a bonanza for clothing accessories. Keep an eye out for alligator purses from the 1960s and earlier. While they're no longer produced, they are currently back in style and hot, hot, hot!

Fabric, large or small 1.00

Imitation Leather, large or small 1.00

Leather
- Etienné Aigner 3.00
- other brands
  - large 3.00
  - small 2.00

Metallic Mesh, evening bag, small 5.00

Plastic or Vinyl, child's, small 50

Purse, suede, satin lining, metal chain strap and closure, $1.00.

QUILTING FRAMES

If your grandmother was a quilter, chances are you have a quilting frame stashed somewhere in your home. If you're a novice quilter and looking for a frame, garage sales and estate auctions are the places to shop.

Look for four straight wooden slats, two longer and two shorter, each with a folded strip of canvas or ticking tacked the length of one side. A set of four sawhorses, each with a notch cut in the top the width of a slat, completes the frame. Four C-clamps are needed to hold the slats in position, but if the original clamps are missing, a new set can be purchased at any hardware store.

C-clamps, set of 4 . . . . . . 2.00

Frame, wood, four slats and horses
- large, will hold from crib size to queen size quilts 15.00
- small, crib size only 10.00

Quilting Hoop, 36" diameter 8.00

RADIOS

When selling a radio at a garage sale, plug it in and tune in to a good, clear station. What better way to demonstrate to your customers that it works? Don't forget to put a conspicuous sign on it so people will know it's for sale.

CB 5.00

CB Radio, Midland Model 13-883B, $5.00.

Headphone Radio	2.00
Multiband Scanner	5.00
Portable	3.00
Stereo Component	10.00
Table Top, clock	3.00
Transistor	3.00
Walkman Type, radio and headphones	5.00

AM/FM Radio, Sony, $3.00.

RANGES, KITCHEN

If a remodeling project has left you with a saleable range, you might find a buyer at your garage sale. Electric stoves tend to sell more quickly, though for a lesser price, than gas models. While most cooks prefer gas over electric, most modern kitchens are equipped with electric ranges and therefore the demand for electric models is higher. Clean your range inside and out, find the instruction book, and price it to sell. If it's not priced reasonably and it doesn't sell, you may end up having to pay someone to haul it away.

Electric	40.00
Gas	50.00

RAZORS

Plug in razors to see that they run. Examine the razor's head for cracked screens or damaged blades. If you buy a used electric razor, clean it thoroughly before you attempt to use it.

Electric Razor, Norelco, three rotary heads, $1.00.

Razor	
cordless, rechargeable	3.00
rotating blades or microscreen	1.00
hair removal system, Lady Remington	1.00
Trimmer, beard and mustache	1.00
Voltage Converter, 5 adapters, converts voltage to 110/120, fabric travel case	2.00

RECORDS

The invention of the compact disc brought an end to the production of phonograph records. Records can be garage sale gold. Sort through old 45 and 78 rpm records. Look for either early works by unknown artists who later became stars or records by popular artists who are now deceased. Not all Elvis records are worth a fortune, but many sell in the $10+ range. Records that are missing their original covers and sleeves should be discounted to half the price of those which are complete. Many people buy the album as much for the cover's artwork as the music.

Display records in the shade! Baking in the hot sun will quickly warp your merchandise.

$33\frac{1}{3}$ LP, original sleeve	1.00
45 rpm, original cover	3.00
78 rpm, original sleeve	3.00

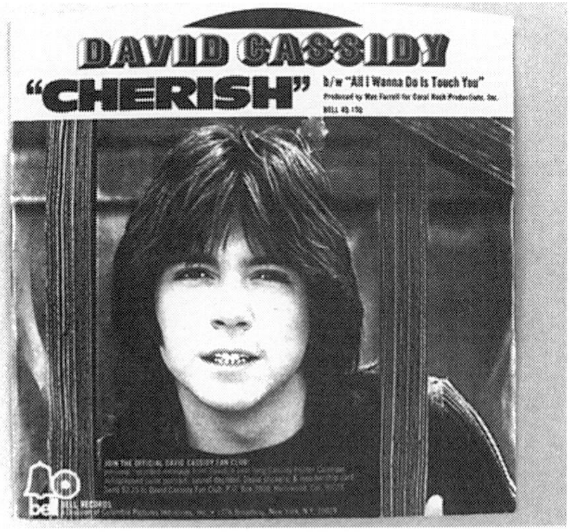

45 rpm, David Cassidy, "Cherish/All I Wanna Do Is Touch You," Bell Records, $3.00.

REFRIGERATORS

To get the best possible price for your refrigerator, empty it, clean it, and have it running the day of the sale so prospective buyers can see for themselves that it works. Obviously, larger sizes sell for more than apartment size models. Self-defrosting and frost-free models are better than those with manual defrost. The presence of a working ice maker is an added bonus. Old timers are often bought to be refitted for beer kegs. A hole is drilled through the door for the installation of a tap.

Buyers, if you're shopping for a second fridge and come across one that isn't plugged in, ask questions. Does it work? How old is it? Examine gaskets. Evidence of mold around doors means poor sealing. Open the refrigerator door and take a whiff. Does it smell bad? Refrigerators that are allowed to remain unplugged with closed doors will acquire a foul odor that is difficult to erase. Ask the owner to plug it in. If the lights go on, the motor starts running, and it doesn't make strange noises, great. However, it's impossible to tell in a short period of time whether it will refrigerate properly. An older model that has been sitting idle for a long period of time may take hours or even a day to reach its correct temperature.

One last thing to keep in mind if you buy – transport the refrigerator in an upright position if you want it to work when you get it home.

Compact, manual defrost	
1.7 cubic feet	20.00
3.6 cubic feet	30.00
6.0 cubic feet	50.00
Draft Beer Dispenser, holds $\frac{1}{4}$ or $\frac{1}{2}$ keg	85.00
Old, one-door, type refitted for beer keg	10.00
Side-by-Side	
exterior ice/water dispenser	
22 cubic feet	200.00
25.1 cubic feet	275.00
no ice/water dispenser	
19.8 cubic feet	150.00
21.6 cubic feet	175.00
Top Freezer	
10 cubic feet	100.00
15.6 cubic feet	125.00
20.6 cubic feet	175.00
25.1 cubic feet	250.00

ROASTING PANS

Roasting pans come in several shapes and sizes and are most commonly made from graniteware or aluminum. Expect to pay a little more for a pan with a matching lift-out roasting rack. Carefully examine graniteware pans for signs of misuse such as dents, chips, and dull scratched interiors from scouring with harsh abrasives.

Cast Aluminum, covered, oval, turkey size	5.00
Clay Cooker, covered	
oval	
chicken	5.00
fish	7.00
turkey	10.00
round, baked potato	3.00
Graniteware	
oval, covered	
chicken	3.00
turkey	8.00
rectangular, open, 9" x 13"	2.00
round, covered, 12" diameter	2.50

Roasting Pan, graniteware, 12 7/8" long, $3.00.

Stainless Steel, rectangular, open, 9" x 13", with wire rack 3.00
Stamped Aluminum, covered, oval, steam vent, turkey size 2.00

ROLLAWAY BEDS & COTS

Rollaway beds and cots are great to have on hand when unexpected guests spend the night. Make sure the mattress is clean and the springs are sturdy and free of rust. Don't be embarrassed to ask the seller to show you how to set it up and fold it back together. Convertible chairs and love seats are modern versions of rollaway beds. Before you buy, open them up and check for tears and stains.

A final alternative is the inflatable air mattress. Made of vinyl, it is available in several sizes. Most commonly used on camping trips, they can serve double duty as emergency sleeping space at home. Some mattresses have flocked tops to help hold sheets in place. Display your air mattress inflated. Shoppers will be more inclined to buy if they can see the mattress holds air.

Air Mattress, vinyl
flocked top
twin 7.50
double 10.00
queen 12.50
king 15.00
no flocking
twin 5.00
double 7.50
queen 10.00
king 12.50
Army Cot, wood frame, canvas cover 6.00
Convertible Bed
chair, twin 10.00
love seat, double 15.00
sofa, queen 25.00
Folding Cot, metal frame, canvas cover
52" long, child size 3.00
72" long 5.00
84" long 7.50
Futon, wood frame, folding foam mattress
twin 15.00
full 20.00
queen 25.00
Inflater
auto, 12 volt 5.00
electric 5.00
foot pump 2.50
Rollaway Bed, metal frame on wheels, foam mattress
30" wide 7.50
38" wide 10.00
47" wide 15.00

ROLLER BLADES & SKATES

Roller skates have evolved over the last ten years. Metal skates that clamp onto shoes and are tightened with a key are practically unheard of today, although a plastic strapping version for toddlers is available. Old-fashioned shoe skates, with two front and two back wheels are also losing ground to the current rage – roller blades or in-line skates.

In-line skates have molded plastic boots with removable liners and four wheels positioned in a straight line. These are by far today's best selling skates.

In-Line Skates
adult 15.00
child 10.00
Protective Gear
helmet
adult 5.00
child 3.00
pads, set of 6, 2 each elbows, wrists, and knees
adult 5.00
child 3.00

In–Line Skates, Streets, child's size, $10.00.

Roller Skates	
clamp-on	
metal, with key	2.00
plastic	1.00
shoe skate	4.00

RUGS

Rugs of all sizes, from hall runners to room-size, are bought and sold at garage sales. The ideal way to display your rug, weather–permitting, is to spread it out on your lawn. This way buyers can examine the whole rug for signs of wear and fading. Tag each rug with its dimensions. You might also include washing instructions, if applicable.

If you are the proud owner of a genuine Oriental rug, don't attempt to sell it at your garage sale unless you are sure of its value. If you don't know what it's worth, have it appraised. Alternative markets include advertising in your local paper and selling it privately for a firm price, or consigning it to auction, where it will receive proper advertising and exposure.

Area, bound edges	
3' x 5'	
design (floral, border, etc.)	7.50
plain, 2 fringed edges	5.00
4' x 6'	
design (floral, border, etc.)	15.00
plain, 2 fringed edges	10.00
5' x 7'	
design (floral, border, etc.)	25.00
plain, 2 fringed edges	20.00
5' 10" x 8' 10"	
design (floral, border, etc.)	35.00
plain, 2 fringed edges	30.00
9' x 12'	
design (floral, border, etc.)	60.00
plain, 2 fringed edges	50.00
27' x 8', runner	
design (floral, border, etc.)	20.00
plain, 2 fringed edges	15.00
Carpet, bound, solid color	
6' x 9'	10.00
9' x 12'	20.00
12' x 12'	25.00
12' x 15'	35.00
12' x 18'	40.00
Bathroom, nonslip backing	2.00
Braided	
2' x 3', oval	3.50
3' x 5', oval	5.00
5' x 8', oval	10.00
7' x 9', oval	30.00
8' x 11', oval	45.00
8' round	25.00
9' x 2', runner	10.00
Loom, woven, rag type	
22" x 40"	2.00
22" x 66"	3.50
22" x 108"	5.00
30 x 48"	3.50
42" x 66"	7.50
57" x 89"	15.00
Hearth, fire resistant	2.00
Novelty, kid's design, 2' x 3'	2.50
Oriental Style, wool	
2' x 4½'	7.50
4' x 6'	15.00
5½' x 8½'	30.00
8' x 11'	60.00
9' x 2½', runner	15.00

SAFES, COMBINATION

Not everyone feels the need to own a safe. But if you keep valuables at home such as old coins, expensive jewelry, large sums of money, or even important documents, it could be a good investment.

Ask the seller for the combination, and whether it can be changed. Don't spend your money on a cheap, lightweight safe unless you plan to bolt it to the floor. If a burglar can pick it up and carry it off, what purpose does it serve? Buy a sturdy, heavy safe. Be prepared to have plenty of help to bring it home. Very large safes (like the type once used in railroad offices) may even require the use of a chain hoist or electric lift. Decide in advance where you're going to put it. Once you get it home and in place you don't want to have to move it again.

16" x 13" x 8³/₄", 1.1 cubic feet, 85 lbs. . . .	20.00
17" x 13¹/₂" x 19", 2.5 cubic feet, 200 lbs. .	30.00
30" x 30" x 24", 4.5 cubic feet, 350 lbs . . .	50.00

SCALES

From kitchen to nursery to bathroom to office, many things need to be weighed around the house. Scales can be expensive when new. Smart shoppers look for secondhand scales at garage sales.

Kitchen Scale, Columbia Family Scale, Landers, Frary & Clark, metal, $2.50.

Balance Beam, doctor's office type	
full size	25.00
waist high	15.00
Bathroom	
electronic	7.00
mechanical	3.00
Kitchen	2.50
Postage	2.00

SCREENHOUSE ENCLOSURES

Screenhouses are available in two basic varieties, those with steel accordion-like frame panels and separate vinyl roof, and one-piece tent style units with support posts and stakes. When buying a screen house, be sure all necessary hardware and assembly instructions are included.

10' 4" x 10' 4", steel frame panels	50.00
12' x 12', tent style	15.00

SECURITY SYSTEMS

There is a wide range of home security systems available on the market today. Modern systems are wireless, easy to install, and contain battery backup power. Give the new owner all the necessary installation and operation instructions. If they're no longer available, provide a set of handwritten instructions.

Buyers need to check local regulations to determine whether a permit or license is required for installation. Then check you yellow pages for a monitoring company in your community. Finally, call your insurance company to see if you qualify for a break on your homeowners insurance.

Automotive	
alarm, remote controlled	15.00
club, steering wheel locking system . . .	5.00
Home	
alarm and lock bar, for use on sliding glass doors or windows	2.50
alarm/disarm transmitter	1.00
child locator smoke detector, smoke triggers alarm and flashing light	3.00
complete system, control console, power alarm, 2 arm/disarm transmitters, and 6 door/window transmitters	20.00
door/window transmitter	2.00
entry alarm, magnetic contact switch, identification number keypad	3.00
flasher/dialer interface, dials preprogrammed number after 40 second delay, battery backup system	3.50
glass break detector	3.50
infrared sensor alarm and light	5.00
light activated socket	3.00
light activated timer	3.00
motion detector, pet alley lens	7.50

personal alarm, squeeze to activate	1.50
portable door knob alarm	2.00
power alarm, battery backup system	
exterior	5.00
interior	3.50
power failure light	2.50
remote light controller, 100' radius	2.50
sensor switch	1.00

SEWING BOXES

Spools of thread, bobbins, thimbles, needles, and pincushions are just a few of the objects commonly found in sewing boxes. Generally, the box itself is of less value than its contents. Unless your sewing box contains an old sewing bird, or some other valuable collectible, sell it with its contents intact. The more items and variety, the greater the value. Add up the prices on the items below to get a rough idea of the total value of your sewing box.

Box	
plastic, hinged lid, compartment trays	2.00
wood, round, 10" diameter	5.00
Contents	
bobbin	.05
button hook	2.00
crochet hook	.50
darner	
gourd	1.00
wood	1.50
embroidery floss, full skein	.25
embroidery hoop, plastic	1.00
grommet tool	2.50
hemming gauge, metal	.25
knitting counter	.50
knitting needles, pair	.50
latch hook	.75
miscellaneous (elastic, lace, rickrack, seam tape, zippers, snaps, buttons, etc.) price per package	.25
needle packet, 12 needles	.50
needle threader	.10
pattern (Simplicity, Butterick, etc.)	.25
pincushion, fabric, tomato shape	.75
pins, box	
safety	.75
straight	.50
quilter's beeswax	.25
scissors	
embroidery	.50
pinking shears	2.00
shears	1.00
seam ripper	.50
sewing kit, plastic sleeve	.10
six inch ruler, metal	.25
tailor's chalk	.25
tape measure	
folding, yellow	.25
retractable	1.00
thimble	
leather, thumb, quilter's	.50
metal	.50
plastic	.10
sterling silver	2.50
thread, full spool	.10
tracing wheel and paper	1.00

SEWING MACHINES

Used sewing machines are like many other small appliances and machines – they sell for big bucks when new and not much at all when on the secondary market. Include all the instruction books, extra belts, bobbins, needles, and attachments with the sewing machine. Cabinet models sell for more than portable machines. Treadle sewing machines have little utilitarian value. Models with fancier cabinets and carved or applied molding are sometimes bought and sold for use as decorator pieces. The more ornate the cabinet, the higher the price.

Cabinet	
no storage space in cabinet	
plain model, straight stitch only	20.00
zigzag	30.00
zigzag and embroidery stitches	50.00
storage space and drawers in cabinet	
plain model, straight stitch only	30.00
zigzag	40.00
zigzag and embroidery stitches	60.00
Portable	
overlock	75.00
plain model, straight stitch only	20.00
zigzag	30.00
zigzag and embroidery stitches	40.00
Treadle	
ornate cabinet	50.00
plain cabinet	35.00

SHOE POLISHERS

Shoe polishers for the traditionalist consist of a good brush, a tin of polish, and plenty of elbow grease. Modern shoe polishers can be either electric or battery operated and come with interchangeable heads. If you have a son or daughter in the military, or you are an executive that requires highly shined shoes, these modern versions can save time and energy. Be sure the various buffing and brush attachments are present and the polisher is operational.

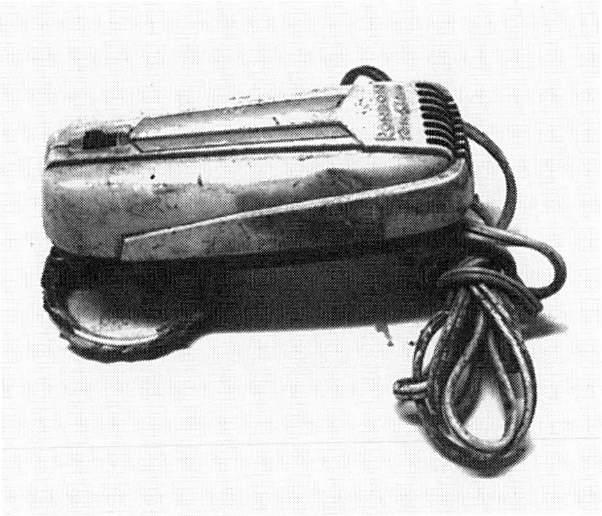

Shoe Polisher, electric, Ronson Roto-Shine, various attachments, $2.00.

Battery Operated, traveling kit	1.00
Electric	2.00

SHOE RACKS

Shoe racks help to keep your shoes paired up and scuff–free. Some racks are made to hang on the back of a bedroom door, others fit under the bed or on the closet floor. Wire racks are great for drying wet shoes and snow boots.

Metal, 2 tiers, expands to 4' wide	3.00
Vinyl, quilted, garment bag type	
closet hanger, holds 4 pairs	1.00
over-the-door, holds 10 pairs	2.00
shoe chest, holds 12 pairs	2.50
Wire	
floor model, holds 12 pairs	2.00
over-the-door, holds 21 pairs	4.00

SILVERWARE

Every bride starts housekeeping with at least one set of silverware. Many start with multiple sets. Unfortunately, through the years pieces are damaged or lost and the set becomes smaller and smaller. Because of the vast number of patterns on the market, it would be extremely difficult to match a particular silverware pattern at a garage sale. However, similar patterns or complementary pieces are readily found.

If your set of flatware is complete, keep it that way. You'll get a better price for a set than for odd pieces. Flimsy imported sets obviously sell for less than better quality, heavier duty services.

Thinking of disposing of great grandmother's sterling silver flatware? Have it appraised first, or sell it to a replacement service or at auction. Another alternative, when the market is favorable and sentimentality is not an issue, is to sell it for its meltdown value. A final note on the family silverware – monogrammed sets tend to bring lower prices than those not monogrammed due to the more limited pool of prospective buyers. Meltdown rates are unaffected, but if you plan to sell a monogrammed set at your garage sale, reduce its price by about 25%.

Flatware	
mismatched flatware, approximately 50 pieces, tray lot	
silverplated	2.00
stainless steel	4.00
service for 8, complete, 46 pieces including 8 dinner forks, salad forks, teaspoons, soup spoons, and dinner knives, 2 serving spoons, and a hostess set including butter knife, sugar spoon, serving fork, and pastry server	
plastic handles	10.00
silver plated	
good condition	10.00
poor condition, plating worn off in some places	5.00
stainless steel	
good quality, heavy duty (Oneida, Wm. A. Rogers, etc.)	
gold wash	7.50
silver	15.00
lesser quality, imported, bends easily	10.00
Flatware Chest, wood, lined	5.00

SINKS, TUBS & TOILETS

Yes, you can even sell the kitchen sink at your garage sale. Home remodelers can recoup some expenses by selling used plumbing fixtures. Home renovators often search garage sales for period pedestal sinks and cast iron claw footed bathtubs. Before you scrap those unwanted fixtures, try selling them first.

Shower Stall, molded fiberglass, 1 piece . . . 25.00
Sink
- bathroom
  - pedestal 30.00
  - standard, porcelain 10.00
  - vanity cabinet 20.00
- kitchen
  - porcelain 10.00
  - stainless steel
    - double 30.00
    - single 20.00
- laundry room, utility, plastic 5.00
- wet bar, stainless steel 15.00

Toilet 25.00
Tub
- cast iron, claw feet 35.00
- fiberglass, molded walls, 1 piece 30.00
- porcelain 20.00

SKATEBOARDS

Price old skateboards reasonably – chances are the buyer will be spending a few weeks' allowance in order to purchase his new set of wheels.

Skateboard, Powell Peralta, $5.00.

Protective Gear
- helmet
  - adult 5.00
  - child 3.00
- pads, set of 6, 2 each elbows, wrists, and knees
  - adult 5.00
  - child 3.00

Skateboard 5.00

SLEDS & TOBOGGANS

Today's sleds differ greatly from their predecessors both in materials and durability. It's still possible to find old wooden sleds in very good condition, while the newer, plastic models tend to last only one season. Although the demand for modern sleds may be higher because they can be used on a wider range of snow depths, older, better–built sleds still command higher prices.

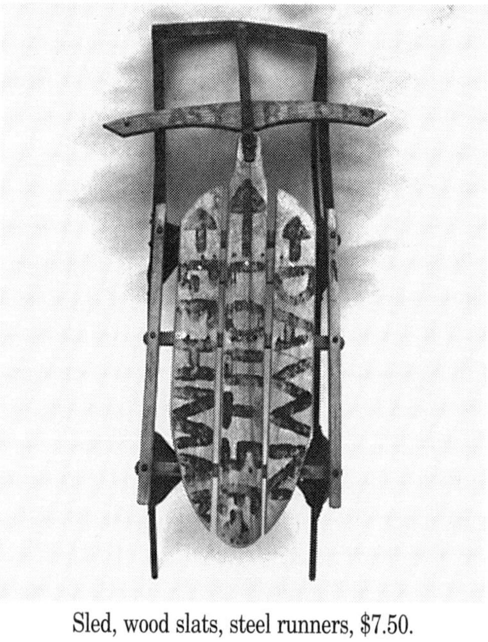

Sled, wood slats, steel runners, $7.50.

Inner Tube, truck tire, black 2.00
Saucer
- metal 4.00
- plastic 2.00

Sled
- molded plastic
  - single seater
    - with steering device 2.00
    - without steering device 1.50
  - two seater 2.50

wood slats, metal runners
- single seater 7.50
- two seater 10.00

Snow Board 15.00
Snow Runner, rolled-up sheet of plastic 50
Snow Tube, inflatable 2.50
Toboggan
- molded plastic 5.00
- wood 15.00

SMOKE DETECTORS

Every home should be equipped with working smoke detectors. If you're selling your excess detectors, install fresh batteries so prospective buyers can see they work. Also, be sure to include all necessary mounting hardware and instructions.

Smoke Detector, Family Gard Smoke Detector and First Alert Smoke Alarm, $2.00 each.

Fire Extinguisher, multi-purpose 2.00
Smoke Alarm or Detector 2.00

SNOW THROWERS & SHOVELS

Snow removal tools sell best at an autumn garage sale. Like lawn mowers and air conditioners, they're season oriented. People tend to postpone making major purchases until it is absolutely necessary. If you must sell your snow blower in the middle of a heat wave, expect to get a lower price. Be prepared to start up electric and gas powered equipment to demonstrate that it works.

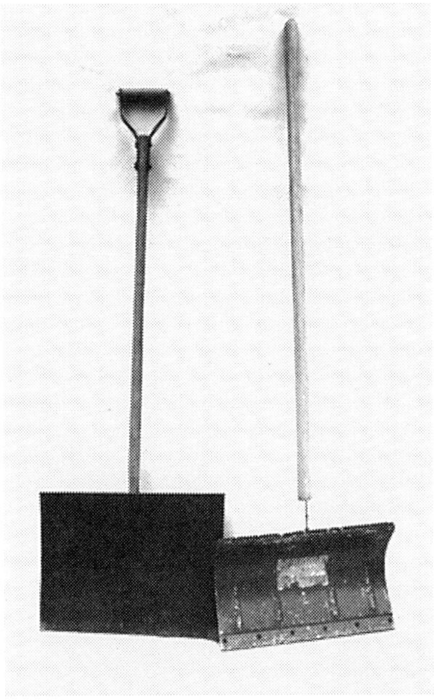

Snow Shovels, right: black steel blade, $2.00; left: Ames, blue nonstick surface, scooped blade, $3.00.

Ice Chopper 2.00
Ice Scraper, auto .50
Snow Shovel
- electric, 1 hp, 4.5 amp 25.00
- manual
  - non-stick 3.00
  - steel 2.00

Snow Thrower
- electric, 3 hp, 12 amp 40.00
- gasoline
  - 3 hp, wheels, 20" path
    - electric start 75.00
    - manual start 65.00
  - 5 hp, manual start, wheels, two-stage discharge, 22" path 125.00
  - 10 hp, electric start, track system, two-stage discharge, 32" path 200.00

SPORTING GOODS

Children's sporting equipment is outgrown as rapidly as clothing and toys. Many items, such as baseball mitts, hockey skates, and skis, need to grow with the athlete. Children's sporting goods should be priced lower than adult's full–size equipment. Regardless of whether it's a child's or adult's, expect to pay a little more for a left hander's baseball mitt than for a right hander's. Lefty mitts are harder to come by and therefore will command a higher price. Inflate your basketball, football, etc., so buyers can see it really does hold air. Bowling balls are hard to sell because the holes need to be drilled to fit the individual's hand. Unless it's an extremely high quality ball, most people don't want a plugged and re-drilled bowling ball.

Archery
- arrows, set of 3
  - adult's, anodized aluminum 4.00
  - child's, wood or plastic 2.00
- bow
  - child's 2.00
  - compound, fiberglass
    - 45 – 60 lb draw weight 30.00
    - 65 – 80 lb draw weight 45.00
- bow case, holds compound bow 5.00
- quiver, child's 1.00
- rack, wood, holds 2 compound bow and 18 arrows 7.50
- target and stand, reversible, self–healing, 36" diameter 10.00

Baseball
- ball
  - hardball 2.00
  - softball 1.00
  - T–ball 1.00
  - whiffle .... .25
- bases, set of 4 plus pitcher's plate 2.00
- bat
  - aluminum 4.00
  - whiffle .... .50
  - wood 2.00
- batting glove
  - adult 1.00
  - child .... .50
- batting helmet 3.00
- batting tee 3.00
- catcher's chest protector 5.00
- catcher's mask 3.00
- catcher's shin guards, pair 5.00
- mitt, leather
  - catcher's
    - adult
      - left handed 7.50
      - right handed 5.00
    - child
      - left handed 5.00
      - right handed 4.00

Baseball Mitt, child's, Regent Eagle Tan, cowhide, $4.00.

  - fielder's, hardball or softball
    - adult, full size
      - left handed 10.00
      - right handed 7.50
    - child, small size
      - left handed 4.00
      - right handed 3.00
    - youth, medium size
      - left handed 7.50
      - right handed 5.00
- pitch–back 3.00
- shoes
  - metal cleats, adult 5.00
  - plastic or rubber cleats
    - adult 4.00
    - child 2.00

Basketball, MacGregor X1000, full size, $4.00; football, Rawlings R5, full size, $4.00.

Bowling Ball and Bag, ball: Bonanza, plastic, marbleized red, $1.00; bag: vinyl, maroon, $2.50.

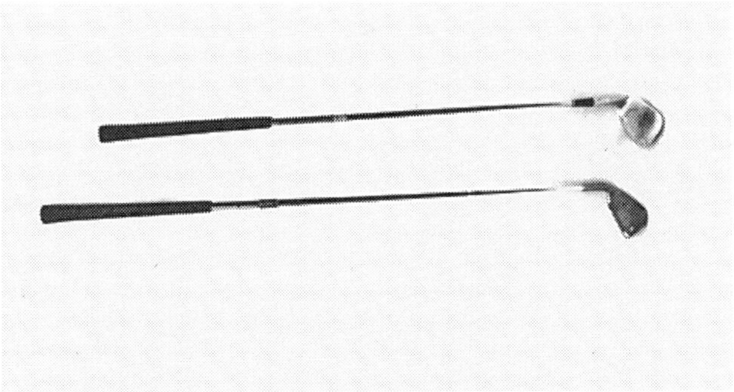

Golf Clubs, left: True-Temper Unique Gold, 5 iron; right: Tru-Flite X-Ploder; $5.00 each.

Basketball
- backboard
  - freestanding
    - child size, molded plastic 5.00
    - full size, graphite board, adjustable height 35.00
  - wall mount, fiberglass 10.00
- ball, full size 4.00
- net 1.00

Bowling
- bag 2.50
- ball, any weight 1.00
- shoes, any size 1.00
- wristband ..... .50

Field Hockey
- ball 1.00
- goal 5.00
- shin guards, pair 5.00
- stick, wood, any size 5.00

Football
- ball
  - full size, leather 4.00
  - youth size
    - leather 2.50
    - plastic or rubber 1.00
- kicking tee 1.00
- shoes, rubber cleats
  - adult 4.00
  - child 2.00

Golf
- bag 10.00
- balls, dozen 3.00
- cart, metal frame, holds bag 10.00
- clubs, set, 1, 3, and 5 woods, 3 through 9 irons, and pitching wedge
  - full size 65.00
  - junior size 20.00
- headcovers, knit, set of 3 ..... .50
- practice mat 2.00
- practice net 7.50
- putter 5.00
- shoes, metal cleats, any size 4.00
- tees, dozen 1.00
- umbrella, wood or fiberglass shaft 5.00

Ice Hockey
- glove 1.00
- goal 5.00
- goalie blocker pad 5.00
- goalie catch mitt 5.00
- goalie face mask 3.00
- goalie shin pads, pair 7.50
- helmet
  - adult 5.00
  - child 3.00
- knee/shin guards, pair 5.00
- puck 1.00
- skates, any size 8.00
- stick
  - plastic 3.00
  - wood shaft, plastic blade, any size 5.00

Racquetball
- balls, can of 3 ..... 1.00
- racquet
  - aluminum 7.50
  - wood 3.00
  - racquet bag 2.00

Skiing
- boots, any size . . . 8.00
- clothing
  - bibbed pants . . . 10.00
  - gloves . . . 1.00
  - hat 50
- jacket . . . 10.00
- goggles . . . 2.00
- poles . . . 5.00
- skis
  - cross country . . . 20.00
  - downhill . . . 25.00
  - water . . . 20.00

Soccer
- ball
  - hand sewn . . . 4.00
  - laminated . . . 2.00
- goal . . . 5.00
- practice kicker, ball attached to elastic cord . . . 5.00
- shin guards, pair . . . 5.00
- shoes, plastic or rubber cleats
  - adult . . . 4.00
  - child . . . 2.00

Street Hockey
- glove . . . 1.00
- goal . . . 5.00
- goalie blocker pad . . . 5.00
- goalie catch mitt . . . 5.00
- goalie face mask . . . 3.00
- goalie shin pads, pair . . . 7.50
- helmet
  - adult . . . 5.00
  - child . . . 3.00

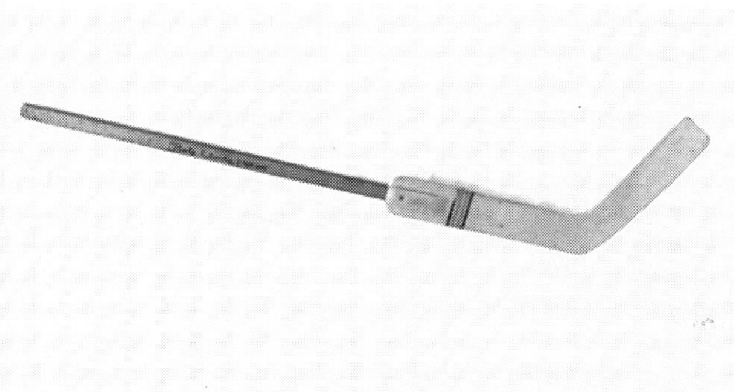

Street Hockey Stick, Official Bobby Clarke Street Hockey, wood stick, plastic blade, 48" l, $5.00.

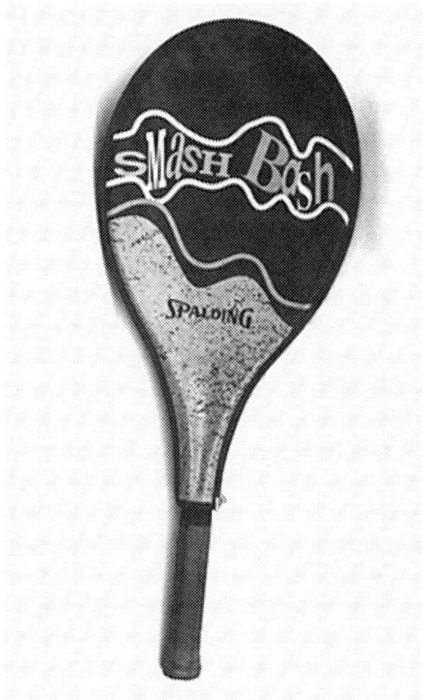

Tennis Racket, Spalding Smash Bash, aluminum, zippered vinyl case, $10.00.

- in–line skates
  - adult . . . 15.00
  - child . . . 10.00
- knee/shin guards, pair . . . 5.00
- puck . . . 1.00
- stick
  - plastic . . . 3.00
  - wood shaft, plastic blade, any size . 5.00

Tennis
- ball pickup/dispenser, holds 60 balls . . 2.50
- balls, can of 3 . . . 1.00
- racquet
  - aluminum . . . 7.50
  - wood . . . 3.00
- racquet case, vinyl, zippered . . . 2.00
- tennis trainer, rebounding device . . . 2.00

Volleyball
- ball
  - hand sewn . . . 4.00
  - laminated . . . 2.00
- net and poles . . . 15.00

STEP STOOLS

Every old–fashioned kitchen, with its high ceiling and counter top–to–ceiling cabinets, needed a step stool to get to those hard–to–reach shelves. They also served double duty as extra seating at the kitchen table when there weren't enough chairs.

Today's best sellers are sturdy and untippable. They fold up to require minimal storage space when not in use.

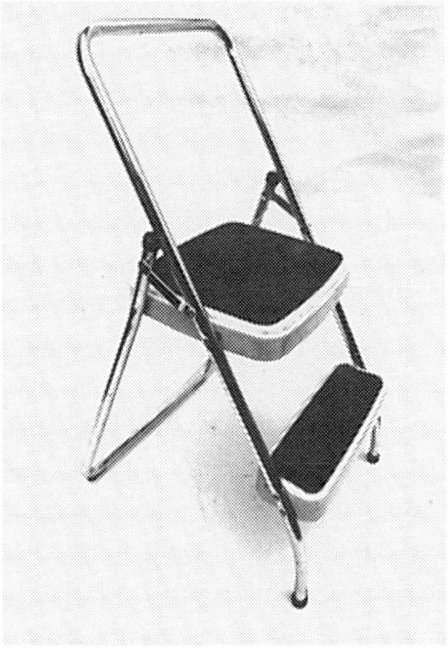

Step Stool, Cosco, metal, two-step, black rubber treads, $5.00.

Step Stool 5.00

STEREO COMPONENTS & EQUIPMENT

Now that CDs are commonplace, stereo systems with turntables and tape decks will soon be obsolete. Many brands of stereo equipment are interchangeable. You could sell a single component, such as the turntable or receiver, or sell your sound system as a unit. Either way, dust it off and remove any fingerprints and smudges. If you plan on demonstrating the tonal quality, be sure to replace the dull phonograph needle or run head cleaner through the tape deck.

Remember the console stereos from the 1960s with their beautiful wood cabinets and great sound? Today they're worthless. If you plan on selling yours, be content if someone will give you a few dollars. You may even have to give it away in order to avoid paying the garbage man an extra fee. Most people don't have the room for such an unwieldy piece of furniture, and phonograph records are joining 8–track tapes in extinction.

CD Player
- multi disc, remote 75.00
- single disc 50.00

Console 1.00
Headphones 3.00
Radio, AM/FM, programmable 10.00
Receiver
- 60 watt 35.00
- 100 watt 50.00

Speaker
- 60 watt 10.00
- 150 watt 25.00

Tape Deck, dual cassette 35.00
Turntable 10.00

STUFFED TOYS

Kids love stuffed toys. The more colorful and exotic the animal, the better. The vast majority of stuffed toys found at garage sales are generic in nature and were acquired as prizes from carnival games and coin operated machines or were bought at toy stores as gifts. Modern stuffed animals that are looking a little shabby can be run through the dryer on fluff cycle (no heat) to remove dust and stale or musty odors. Display these toys at young shoppers' eye level in order to enhance sales. Prices generally increase with size, the bigger the toy, the higher its value. Rarer specimens such as a buffalo or walrus, popular characters like Tweety Bird or the Genie from Aladdin, or stuffed toys with a gimmick like Puppy Surprise will also bring higher prices.

Not all stuffed animal collectors are under the age of ten. Mature buyers may be merely young at heart. Sophisticated collectors will be looking either for early examples of specific characters like Mickey Mouse, or manufacturers such as Steiff, Gund, or Knickerbocker. Steiff animals are easily identified by their distinctive ear button.

Teddy bears predating World War II are also highly collectible and can be worth several hundred dollars. Check a price guide for further help in pricing these toys and display them at a higher level, out of reach of small hands.

Character (Goofy, Stimpy, Lion King, etc.)
- smaller than 6" 50
- 6" to 12" 75
- 12" to 24" 1.50
- 24" to 36" 3.00
- larger than 36" 00

Generic
- common (bear, rabbit, dog, etc.)
  - smaller than 6" 25
  - 6" to 12" 50

Rabbit, purple and white, Prettique label, c1990, $2.00.

12" to 24"	1.00
24" to 36"	2.00
larger than 36"	3.00
uncommon (whale, giraffe, parrot, etc.)	
smaller than 6"	.50
6" to 12"	.75
12" to 24"	1.50
24" to 36"	3.00
larger than 36"	5.00
Gimmick (talking, secret compartment, etc.)	
character	
smaller than 6"	.75
6" to 24"	1.50
generic	
smaller than 6"	.50
6" to 24"	1.00

Rajah from the Disney movie *Aladdin*, Mattel, Inc., $1.50.

SWING SETS

Modern gym sets made from pressure treated wood are more popular than old–fashioned metal swing sets. They command higher prices because they're more durable, complex, and attractive. Metal swing sets, especially older or cheaper sets, may be too rusted to sell at all. If the set is too far gone have it hauled away for scrap. For sets in good condition, the higher the number and complexity of the activities, the higher the price.

Before you buy a gym set, see that it can be disassembled for transportation. Then bring plenty of help and a pickup truck. Don't leave behind any swings, bars, chains, or other accessories.

Metal, 2 swings, glider, hanging rings, sliding board, and 2-seater swing	20.00
Wood, 2 swings, hanging rings, rope ladder, sliding board, climbing rope, elevated fort, and vertical and overhead ladders	60.00

TAPE PLAYERS, TAPE RECORDERS & TAPES

Portable cassette players have been replaced in many homes by CD players. However, you might be able to find a buyer for your old tape player if it is priced reasonably. As with a radio or television, have it playing during the garage sale to attract attention and demonstrate its quality. Eight–track tape players, whether for home or auto, are obsolete. There is practically no market for either the players or the tapes.

Miniature tape recorders, on the other hand, are still in demand for educational and vocational purposes. Install fresh batteries and be prepared to show that it works.

Tape	
cassette	2.00
eight–track	.25
Tape Player	
cassette	
automotive	10.00
personal, headphones	2.50
portable (boombox)	
dual cassette	15.00
single cassette	5.00
stereo component	
dual cassette	35.00

single cassette 15.00
eight–track
automotive .25
portable 25
stereo component 25
Tape Recorder, hand held
microcassette 5.00
standard size cassette 7.50

TEAPOTS

Ceramic teapots of all shapes and sizes are common garage sale finds. Few people buy teapots for utilitarian purposes. Today they are more often purchased for use as decorative accents than for serving afternoon tea. Collectors are most interested in figural and unusually shaped teapots and those made by specific dinnerware companies such as Hall, Homer Laughlin (Fiesta), or Shawnee. Hall produced a vast array of teapots with prices now ranging from $30 to hundreds of dollars, depending on shape, rarity, and color. Take the time to research the mark found on your teapot. The least desirable teapots are unmarked or ceramic's class varieties.

Common Shape, unmarked 5.00
Figural, unmarked (cat, car, football, etc.) . . 20.00
Unusual Shape, unmarked 15.00

TELEPHONES & ACCESSORIES

Make sure the telephone equipment you sell is in working order. If the original instructions are no longer present, include a set of handwritten directions for the new owner. This is especially important for programmable telephones and answering machines. If your answering machine can be accessed by remote, be sure to provide the new owner with the security code number. Finally, erase personal numbers from programmable telephone memories.

Answering Machine
dual standard cassettes 15.00
microcassette 10.00
Caller ID
single function 7.50
3 functions, includes call blocking and
last number redial 10.00
Pager 12.50

Telephone, desktop model, push button, touchtone, beige, $2.00.

Telephone
cordless, 10 channel selectable, 2–way
page/intercom, 9 number memory,
last number redial 12.50
multiple features, pulse/tone switchable,
push button, 13 number memory,
last number redial 5.00
push button, touchtone 2.00
rotary, pulse 1.00
Telephone/Answering Machine
cordless, microchip and microcassette, 10
number memory, digital call counter,
2–way page/intercom 25.00
standard telephone, last number redial,
12 number memory, remote access,
battery backup system
microcassette 15.00
microchip 15.00
standard cassette 20.00

TELESCOPES

Telescopes come equipped with either altazimuth or equatorial mounts. Altazimuth mounts adjust both horizontally and vertically and are easier to use. Equatorial mounts are recommended for longer periods of sky watching when tracking is needed.

All telescopes should include a tripod as part of the package. Features include variable powers and accessories such as additional eyepieces and lenses, sun projection screens, and moon filters.

Altazimuth Refractor, 700 mm, 2 eyepieces,
3 lenses 25.00
Equatorial Reflector, 900 mm, 4½" diameter mirror, 2 eyepieces, 2 lenses, finder–scope, moon filter 35.00
Equatorial Refractor, 900 mm, 3 eyepieces, 2 lenses, sun projection screen, moon filter 25.00

TELEVISIONS & ACCESSORIES

Black and white or color, television sets are so expensive when new, many people will take a chance and buy a used model at a garage sale. The same is true for VCRs. If possible, have them hooked up and running to show buyers their condition. Be prepared to answer questions concerning age, number of channels received, and stereo capabilities.

If you were unfortunate enough to have purchased a Beta VCR don't expect to sell it. Both the popularity and production span of Beta were short–lived and there is little demand for them.

Many older televisions and VCRs receive a limited number of channels – sometimes as few as thirty-six. Newer models can receive as many as 181 channels and possess additional features such as a universal remote to operate both the TV and VCR, onscreen clock, and sleep and alarm timers. Adjust your prices according to the features available on your set. Don't forget to include the remote control unit.

Amplified Coupler, cable signal booster . . . 2.50
Antenna Amplifier, 300–ohm 5.00
Antenna Booster 5.00
Antenna Rotator 5.00
Cable Converter, converts rotary dial TV to remote control, expands channel capability from 13 to 36 or more channels . . 5.00
Surge Protector 1.00
Television
- big screen, color, 32" screen 250.00
- console, 27" screen
  - black and white 5.00
  - color
    - with remote 40.00
    - without remote 30.00
- miniature
  - under-the-cabinet, kitchen model, color, remote, 10" screen 20.00

Portable Television, Toshiba, color, remote control, 20" screen, $30.00.

- Watchman, Sony, black and white, battery operated, earphone jack, 2.7" screen 10.00
- portable
  - black and white
    - 13" screen 5.00
    - 20" screen 5.00
  - color
    - with remote
      - 13" screen 25.00
      - 20" screen 30.00
      - 27" screen 40.00
    - without remote
      - 13" screen 15.00
      - 20" screen 20.00
      - 27" screen 30.00

VCR, VHS, Sharp, 40 cable-capable channels, $50.00.

Television Stand
metal 1.00
plastic 1.00
wood 5.00
Television Turntable
plastic 1.00
wood 2.50
Television/VCR Combination 100.00
Universal Remote Control 3.00
VCR
Beta 1.00
VHS
40 cable-capable channels 50.00
181 cable-capable channels 75.00
VCR Cover, plastic 1.00
Videotape, VHS
blank
Beta .... .25
VHS 1.50
prerecorded
Beta .... .50
VHS 3.00
Videotape Case, plastic .... .25
Videotape Player, 2 head 40.00
Videotape Rack, plastic, rotating......... 2.50
Videotape Rewinder.................. 2.50

TIE RACKS

Tie racks can be plain or fancy, stationary or battery operated. They can hold anywhere from eight to twenty-four or more ties. Pick one you like, all should be reasonably priced.

Battery Operated, holds 24 ties.......... 2.00
Decorative, holds 10 ties 2.00
Plain, holds 12 ties 1.00

TIMERS

Today's timers serve many purposes. They can be a deterrent to burglars by turning on lights, televisions, and radios. Kitchen timers remind cooks to check the oven. Some timers even automate the use of outdoor sprinklers or pool filters. Include the original instructions with the timer. If they're no longer available, be prepared to explain the timer's use to the new owner.

Egg, hourglass, 3 minutes .... .25

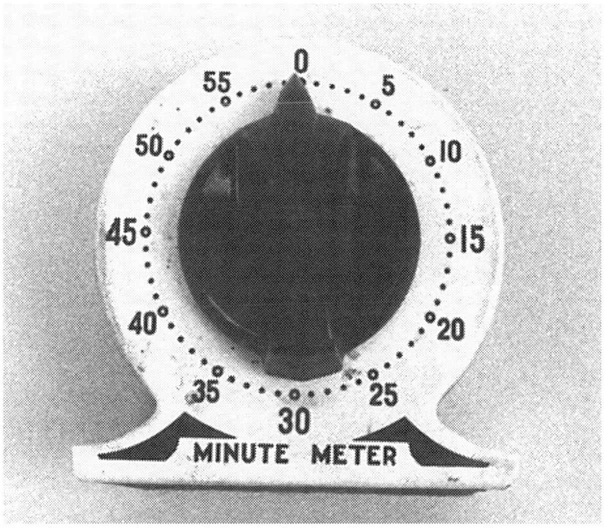

Kitchen Timer, Minute Meter, Robertshaw Controls Co., metal, enameled, $1.00.

Kitchen, 60 minutes 1.00
Lamp, electric, 24 hour programmable 2.00
Security, electric, turns lights on at dusk, off according to program setting 3.00
Water, 24 hour programmable 3.00

TOMATO CAGES

Tomato cages are cheap to buy when new – mark them even cheaper if you hope to sell them used. Cages can also be used for other vegetables, flowers, and shrubs. Before you sell, clean them off and straighten their legs.

Tomato Cage, wire
large.......................... .50
small .... .25
Tomato Stake, wood................. .10

TOOL BENCHES

Tool benches can either be homemade or store–bought and can offer a varying amount of work and storage space. Measure your workshop area before you buy. Tool benches can weigh a ton – be sure to have a pickup truck and plenty of muscle to help with the transportation.

Commercial, steel base, reversible wood top, storage drawers and cabinet 30.00
Homemade, base shelf 5.00
Workmate Type 35.00

TOOL CHESTS

Tool chests can be small enough to fit under the car seat, or large enough to hold all the tools necessary to rebuild your car's engine. Sizes vary according to use. If your tool box is small, you may have a better chance of a sale if you include a variety of tools with it. Larger roll–away chests like those used by mechanics need no accessories to encourage a sale, providing they are relatively clean and free of major dents and rust.

Plastic, 22" long, plastic tote tray 3.00
Steel
- 10" long, locking 2.00
- 15" long, plastic tote tray 3.00
- 20" long, 12" high, cantilever tray in top, two locking drawers 10.00
- 26" long, 17" high, metal steel tote tray, five divided drawers 20.00
- 26" long, 32" high, five divided drawers, roll–away 25.00
- 30" long, steel tote tray 5.00

TOOLS

An easy way to increase the value of your hand tools is by cleaning. All tools should be free of grease and oil. If a buyer is hesitant to touch the tools, he will be even more reluctant to buy them. Cleanliness also indicates that the tools have been well cared for – an added selling point.

Plug in power tools to ensure that they work. Test rechargeable tools like screwdrivers to see that they still have sufficient power to get the job done.

Old Stanley planes may be valuable. Check out your plane's number in a tool price guide for more specific information.

Craftsman hand tools, with their quality reputation and full unlimited warranty, bring premium prices. If your hand tools are Craftsman, add an extra 25% to the prices listed below.

Hand Tools
- anvil, 35 lb 5.00
- awl 1.00
- axe 2.50
- bolt cutter, 24" long 4.00
- caulking gun 1.00
- center punch 50

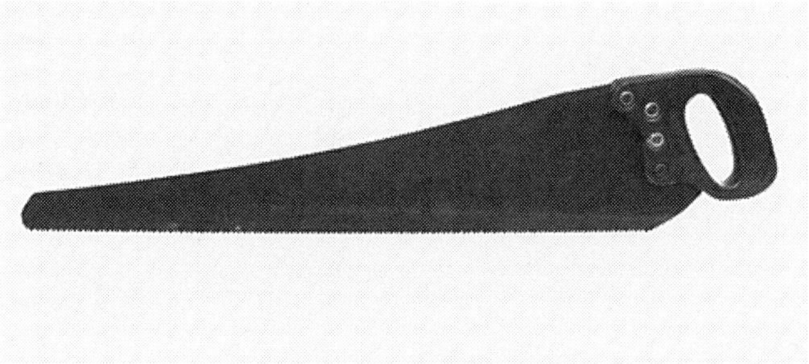

Hand Saw, 26" long, $2.50.

- chisel
  - cold chisel 50
  - wood chisel 1.00
- clamp
  - C–clamp 50
  - pipe 1.50
  - spring 50
- combination square, 16" blade, angle finding rotating vial 2.50
- drain snake 1.00
- drive set, 1/4" drive, 4 1/2" slide bar, flex extension, speed bar, and 1 1/2" extension bar 2.50
- drive socket set, 9 sockets, 2 extension bars, and spinner handle 4.00
- file 1.00
- flaring tool, 45° flares 5.00
- hammer
  - ball peen, 16 oz 1.00
  - claw, 20 oz 2.50
  - deadblow, 1 1/2 lbs 4.00
- hatchet 1.50
- level
  - aluminum
    - 24" long 3.00
    - 48" long 5.00
    - 72" long 10.00
  - mahogany, brass edges
    - 24" long 5.00
    - 48" long 7.50
- mitre box and saw 5.00
- nipper, end–cutting 1.00
- nut driver set, 7 drivers 3.00

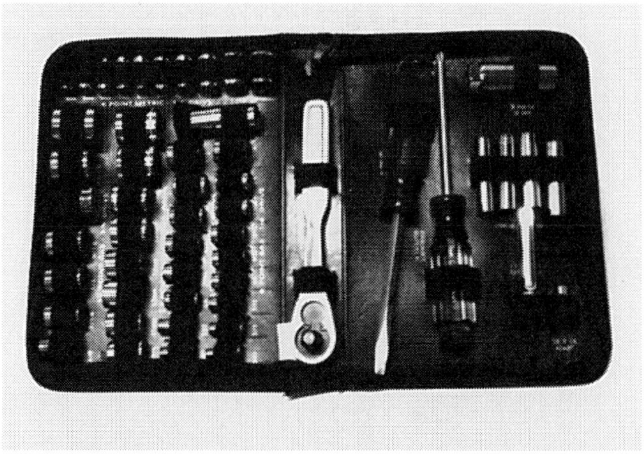

Socket Set, 1/4" and 3/8" drive, 10 metric sockets, 32 standard sockets, 5 deep sockets, spark plug socket, extension, adapter, Phillips screwdriver, and slotted screwdriver, zippered case, $20.00.

pickaxe 4.00
pipe cutter 5.00
plane
  bench, #4, 10" long 5.00
  block, 7" long 2.50
  jack, #5, 14" long 7.50
  rabbet, bull nose 2.50
pliers
  arc joint 1.50
  diagonal cutter 1.00
  needle nose 1.00
  slip joint 1.00
propane torch set 5.00
rubber mallet 1.00
sanding block .50
saw
  coping 1.00
  dovetail 2.00
  hacksaw 2.00
  hand saw, 26" long 2.50
screwdriver
  offset 75
  Phillips or slotted
    1 1/2" stubby 25
    4" long 50
    8" long 75
sledge hammer 4.00
snips
  compound leverage, serrated edge . 1.50
  duckbill 1.00
  offset aviation 1.50
  tin, heavy duty, 16" long 3.00
socket set, 11 sockets, spark plug socket, ratchet, extension bar, and case
  1/2" drive 5.00
  3/4" drive 20.00
squeezedriver, high speed reversible screwdriver, nut driver, and drill combination 5.00
staple gun 2.00
tap and die set, 10 tap and die sizes, die stock, T–handle tap wrench, tap driver, plastic case 3.50
tape measure
  12' long 50
  25' long, locking 1.50
T–square, steel 1.00
tubing cutter 5.00
utility knife 50
vise
  bench
    3 1/2" jaws 5.00
    5 1/2" jaws 10.00
  pipe, anchors to workbench, with pipe bending accessories 15.00
  woodworker's, 12" capacity 17.50
vise grips 2.00
wire stripper 1.00
wrench
  adjustable
    6" 1.00
    10" 1.50
  box end, open end, or combination .25

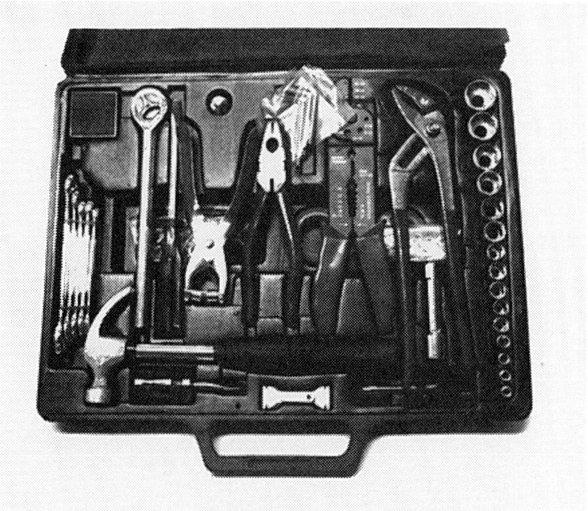

All-Purpose Tool Set, 40 tools, $25.00.

- hex key set, 20 pieces 2.50
- pipe
  - 1 1/2" capacity 2.00
  - 3" capacity 5.00
- ratchet tap, T–handle 1.00
- Stillson 3.00
- tap/reamer, 1/4" to 3/4" tap capacity . 2.00
- torque
  - beam type, 1/2" drive 2.50
  - micrometer style, 1/2" drive 7.50

X–acto knife set, #1 knife with #11 blade, #2 knife with #2 blade, #6 knife with #24 blade, woodcarving knife with #104 blade, 17 other blades, fitted wooden box 5.00

Power Tools

- buffer/polisher, orbital, 2 bonnets 7.50
- dado, adjustable
  - 16 tooth 5.00
  - 48 tooth 10.00
- drill
  - cordless, 5 cell, 3/8" capacity 7.50
  - electric, 1/2 hp, 3/8" drive, reversible, variable speed 10.00
- drill bits
  - high speed, 14 bits, 1/16" through 1/2" sizes 4.00
  - wood boring, 12 bits, 1/4" through 1 1/2" sizes 3.00
- grinder, bench top, 2 wheels 10.00
- hammer drill, 3/8" hp, 3/8" capacity, variable speed, reversible 17.50
- hole saw set, 7 saws, 7/8" to 1 1/2" sizes, 1/4" round arbor, arbor adapter, plastic case 5.00
- impact wrench, reversible, 1/3 hp, 1/2" drive 17.50
- lathe, wood, 1/2 hp, 12" 35.00
- router, 1 1/2 hp, single speed 10.00
- router bit, carbide tip, 1/4" shank 1.00
- sander
  - band, bench top, 1/3 hp, 10" 25.00
  - belt, 1/2 hp, 3" belt 7.50
  - belt/disc, bench top, 1/2 hp, 6" disc, 1" x 42" belt 25.00
  - pad, 1/4 hp 12.50
- sander/grinder, disc, 1 3/4 hp, 7" disc ... 15.00
- saw
  - band, bench top, 1/3 hp, 10" 20.00
  - circular, 2 1/2 hp, 12 amp 15.00
  - compound mitre, 10" 25.00
  - radial, 3/4 hp motor 75.00
  - reciprocating, 3/4 hp 2.00
  - sabre, 1/4 hp, scrolling mechanism . . 7.50
  - scroll, bench top, 16" 15.00
  - table, 1 1/2 hp, 10" 30.00
- screwdriver, cordless 5.00
- shaper bit 2.00
- spindle shaper, 7/8 hp 30.00
- wood shaper, 1 hp, 3 cutters 60.00

Electric Drill, Rockwell, 1/3 hp, 1/4" drive, $5.00.

TOYS

Many toys manufactured before 1970 can be extremely valuable. Early tin windup toys, cast iron cars and trucks, and old dolls or electric train sets are prime examples of toys that should be well researched before being priced. Even early Fisher Price toys have become highly collectible. If you own a sizeable collection of toys identified in toy price guides and they're still in good condition, consider consigning the lot to an auction. Specialty auctions are well advertised – drawing toy buyers and collectors prepared to pay premium prices. Piecemealing your collection at a garage sale could mean selling off the best toys at bargain prices and winding up with no market for the less desirable items.

Most toys sold at garage sales are less than ten years old, often incomplete, and have seen plenty of hard play. Pick through the toy box carefully to find all parts and accessories. If a toy has numerous pieces, assemble, package, and price them as a single unit. This applies to dolls and action figures as well as Legos and Micro Machines. If they're still on hand, include the directions and assembly instructions for more complex toys such as race tracks or Erector Sets.

Pull Toy, Playskool Dairy Wagon, wood, $3.00.

Infant Toys, ages 6 months to 2 years
- activity center . . . 1.00
- blocks, set
  - plastic 50
  - wood . . . 1.00
- cash register, drawer opens, plastic 50
- chime ball 25
- cobbler's bench 50
- corn popper 50
- jack–in–the–box 75
- piano 75
- rail rocker, musical, windup . . . 1.00
- See 'N Say, pull string . . . 1.00
- snap–lock beads 50
- soft sculpture, stuffed figure 25
- stacking rings 50
- telephone 50
- television, windup . . . 1.00

Toddler Toys, ages 2 to 5
- bop bag, inflatable . . . 1.50
- building blocks
  - plastic, 18 blocks, storage wagon . . 1.00
  - snap together, large size blocks, storage bucket (Legos, Tyco, etc.) . . 2.00
  - wood, 110 blocks, different colors, sizes, and shapes . . . 2.00
- doll
  - 2" to 4" high, miniature, with accessories (Quints, doll house, etc.) . .50
  - 10" to 12" high
    - plain 50
    - special features (wets, cries, talks, walks, etc.) . . . 1.00
  - 12" high and over
    - plain 75
    - special features (wets, cries, talks, walks, etc.) . . . 1.50
- doll accessories
  - carriage . . . 2.50
  - clothing, outfit 50
  - crib
    - plastic . . . 2.00
    - wood . . . 4.00
  - highchair
    - plastic . . . 2.00
    - wood . . . 4.00
  - infant seat . . . 1.00
  - playpen . . . 1.50
  - stroller . . . 2.50
  - swing, windup . . . 1.50
- doll house
  - plastic . . . 2.00
  - metal . . . 4.00
  - wood . . . 8.00
- doll house furniture (couch, refrigerator, bed, bureau, etc.)
  - plastic 25
  - metal or wood 75
- Etch–A–Sketch 75
- figure (My Little Pony, Battle Troll, etc.) .50
- golf set, plastic, clubs, balls, and 18 holes 2.00
- housekeeping toys
  - dinner service, plastic, 4 plates, cups, saucers, cereal bowls, knives, forks, and spoons . . . 3.00
  - food, price each set 50
  - iron and ironing board . . . 1.00
  - kitchen, 1 piece, refrigerator, range, oven, and sink combination . . . 10.00
  - pots & pans, price each 50
  - sewing machine . . . 1.50
  - tea set, plastic, teapot, creamer, sugar, tray, 2 cups, saucers, and spoons . . . 2.00
  - vacuum . . . 1.50
- jigsaw puzzle, frame tray
  - cardboard 50
  - plastic or wood 75
- Lite–Brite, complete . . . 2.00
- magnetic desk top, alphabet letters . . . 1.50
- Mr. Potato Head, complete . . . 1.00
- musical instrument, plastic, (horn, guitar, drum, etc.) 75
- play set (Fisher Price Play Family Farm, Weebles, etc.) . . . 3.00

Hess Truck, plastic, 14" l, $3.00.

Action Figure, Mantech Robot Warrior, Remco, $1.00.

pull toy, musical	.75
push toy (lawn mower, musical wagon, grocery cart, etc.)	1.00
radio/microphone, battery operated	2.50
record player, windup	1.50
ride–on toys (car, giant shoe, etc.)	1.00
rocking horse	
plastic	1.50
wood	5.00
spring horse	7.50
tool bench	1.00
vehicles	
airplane, plastic, spinning props	1.50
car	
Hot Wheels	.50
Matchbox	.75
others	
miniature	.25
large	.50
truck	
Hess	3.00
Hot Wheels	.50
Matchbox	.75
Tonka	5.00
others, large	
metal	3.00
plastic	1.00
weapons	
cap gun	1.00
laser tag set, gun and target	2.50
rifle	
plastic	1.00
wood	4.00
six-shooters, pair, metal, holster	3.00

Children's Toys, ages 6 and up

action figure (GI Joe, Teenage Mutant Ninja Turtles, etc.)	1.00
action figure accessories	
dress-up toy (sword, armor, etc.)	.75
play set	
large (Technodrome type)	3.00
miniature (Mighty Max type)	1.00
vehicle	1.50
arcade games	
hand held	1.00
table top, 8" high	2.00
building toys	
K'nex, storage bucket	2.00
Legos, storage bucket	4.00
Lincoln Logs, set	3.00
Tinkertoys, storage bucket	2.00
camera, takes real pictures	1.50
cassette player, battery operated	2.50
computer toys (Alphie, Simon Says, etc.)	2.50
Creepy Crawler Oven	4.00
doll	
Barbie, less than 10 years old	1.50
other fashion dolls	.75
doll accessories	
clothing outfit	.25
play set	2.00
vehicle	1.00
Erector Set	2.50
football game, electric, vibrating board	2.50
frisbee	.25
hockey game, control rods	2.50
jigsaw puzzle, cardboard	.50
jump rope	.25

Draw Poker, battery operated, $1.00.

Magic Oven	2.50
marbles, dozen	.50
Nerf	
sports equipment (football, basketball, baseball, etc.)	1.00
weapon (bow & arrow, crossbow, dart rifle, etc.)	2.50
poker machine	1.00
race track	
electric	5.00
manual (Domino Rally, Hot Wheels Speed Shifter, etc.)	3.00
Rubik's Cube	.50
Skip–It, plastic, lap counter	.75
Spirograph	2.00
squirt gun	
pistol	.50
rifle, Super Soaker type	2.00
tape player, battery operated	2.00
train set, HO scale, less than 10 years old	4.00
vehicles	
car	
battery operated	2.00
remote control	10.00
truck	
battery operated	2.00
remote control	10.00
View Master	
reel	1.00
viewer	.10
walkie–talkies, pair	2.00
Waterfuls	1.00
yo–yo, plastic or wood	.50

Turtles Sewer Ball, Milton Bradley Waterfuls, $1.00.

TRASH COMPACTORS

When selling a trash compactor at a garage sale, clean it thoroughly and be prepared to sell it fairly cheap. A compactor is a luxury kitchen appliance that never evolved into a "necessity." Be sure to have the operating instructions handy.

Compactor	35.00

TRIVETS

Ceramic tile, wood, and various metals are all materials used to make the trivets found at today's garage sales. A decorative trivet meant to be used as a wall plaque is usually cast from pot metal, while functional, heavy duty trivets are more often cast from brass, pewter, or iron. The larger, heavier examples should be priced slightly higher.

Decorative	
cast metal, Pennsylvania Dutch theme	2.00
ceramic, souvenir	1.50
Functional	
basketry	.50
ceramic tile, 6" square	1.50
metal, cast	
brass	3.00
iron	3.00
pewter	2.00
pot metal	2.00
wood, inlaid design	1.00

Trivets, cast pot metal, black, 9" l, $2.00 each.

TROPHIES

When was the last time you looked through that box of trophies stored in the attic that documents your accomplishments at bowling, baseball, and track? If you've decided it's time to find them a new home, be resigned to letting them go cheaply. Few people are interested in used trophies unless they are very old and either made of sterling silver or inscribed with the name of a famous sports figure.

The trophies you are likely to find today will consist of plastic statues mounted atop imitation marble bases. Slightly older trophies may have metal statues on a metal or wood base. The subject matter, materials and size of the trophy are three key factors in determining price.

Trophies, left: Little League Baseball, 1994, $.25; center: Boy Scouts' Pinewood Derby, 1994, $.50; right: gymnastics, 1995, $.50; all with plastic statues on imitation marble bases.

6" high	
metal and/or wood	.50
plastic	.25
12" high	
metal and/or wood	.75
plastic	.50
18" high	
metal and/or wood	1.00
plastic	.75

TUPPERWARE

The name Tupperware has become so common and well known it is often used generically to refer to any plastic food storage container. Genuine Tupperware generally outsells its imitators, most likely due to Tupperware's higher quality and its generous lifetime replacement policy. Tupperware is also the pioneer in marketing new shapes and sizes. There is a special container designed for almost every imaginable need. All Tupperware containers have lids. Be sure to include the proper lids and any other accessory pieces.

Tupperware	
bacon keeper	.50
bowl	
2 cups	.25
$4^1/_2$ cups	.25
$8^1/_2$ cups	.50
15 cups	.50
26 cups	1.00
32 cups	1.00
cake saver	1.50

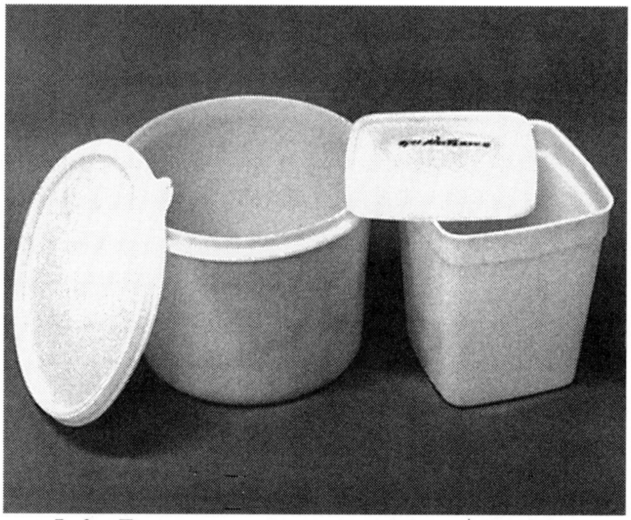

Left: Tupperware, 2 quart container, $.25; right: imitation brand, $1^1/_2$ quart container, $.10.

cereal bowl	.25
chip and dip server, seven sections	2.00
colander	.50
creamer and sugar	.75
deviled egg carrier	1.50
divided plate	1.00
food mold	.50
frozen juice molds, tray with 6 cups, lids, and handles	1.50
ice bucket	.50
ice cream cube, holds 1/2 gallon	.75
ice cube tray	.25
lettuce crisper	.75
lid organizer	1.50
measuring cup, liquid, 4 cups	.50
mug	.25
pickle jar, lift-up strainer	2.00
pie saver	1.50
pitcher	
1 quart	.50
2 quart	.75
1 gallon	1.00
plate	.25
salad set, 6 quart bowl, 6 individual bowls, and 2 servers	2.00
salt and pepper shakers, pair	
large	.75
small	.25
shaker cup, 2 cups	.75
sip cup	.25
toy (blocks, stencils, etc.)	1.00
tumbler	.25
Other Brands	
bowl	
2 cups	.10
4 1/2 cups	.10
8 1/2 cups	.25
15 cups	.25
26 cups	.50
32 cups	.50
divided plate	.25
frozen juice molds, tray with 6 cups, lids, and handles	.50
ice cream cube, holds 1/2 gallon	.25
ice cube tray	.10
lettuce crisper	.50
measuring cup, liquid, 4 cups	.25
pitcher	
1 quart	.25
2 quart	.50
1 gallon	.75

TV TRAY TABLES

Now that instant dinners are available in meal-sized microwaveable containers, will TV tray tables make a comeback? Probably, and with today's hectic schedules, those handy snack tables should do well at a garage sale. Look for metal tables with no dents or rust. Tray table sets should have four folding tables and a storage cart. Expect to pay more for nested wooden sets.

Bed trays are also useful for sickroom duty or serving Mother's Day breakfast in bed. Folding wooden or wicker tables should be priced higher than the more common metal or plastic varieties.

Bed Tray	
metal	2.00
plastic	1.00
wicker	4.00
wood	4.00
TV Tray Table Set	
metal, 4 folding tables and storage cart, floral design	2.00
wood, 4 tables	
folding tables and storage cart	4.00
nesting tables	5.00

TYPEWRITERS

Typewriters are getting harder and harder to sell. Home computers are drastically reducing the demand for them. This is bad news for the seller but great for the buyer. If you're shopping for a second-hand typewriter, take a look at the electronic models. Their special features like built-in dictionaries, memory, and bold type make them far more versatile than the older electric and manual models. Be sure the instruction book is included – without it you'll be lost. Also, ask the owner if there are any additional ribbon cartridges. If you decide to buy an older manual or electric typewriter, be aware that new ribbons may no longer be available.

Electric	
office model	2.50
portable	5.00
Electronic, word processing	20.00
Manual	
office model	1.00
portable	2.00

Electric Typewriter, IBM, daisy wheel, $2.50.

UMBRELLAS

Large golf umbrellas are always in demand. If you plan to buy one to actually use on the golf course, make sure the shaft is made of either wood or fiberglass. Umbrellas with metal shafts make great lightning rods on open courses.

Many people prefer to pay garage sale prices for something they will probably misplace. While the folding umbrella's compact size makes it great for carrying, it also contributes to its high rate of loss. Older umbrellas with their interesting patterns and ornate handles are becoming increasingly popular, although they still tend to sell for less than the more practical Totes style.

Umbrella, older style, floral fabric, 28" l, $1.50.

Beach, weighted point for burying in sand	5.00
Folding, compact, Totes style	2.50
Golf	
fiberglass or wood shaft	5.00
metal shaft	3.00
Patio Table, $7^1/_2$' diameter, tilting, sand filled base	12.00
Standard, handle does not retract	
adult's	
fabric	
ornate handle	4.00
plain	1.50
plastic	1.00
child's, plastic	1.00

VASES

Vases are another form of decorative accessory that sells well at garages sales. You can never have too many vases, especially if the one you see at a sale is priced right. The same guidelines apply to ceramic vases as were mentioned in the flowerpots and planters category. Take a look at the bottom of the vase. Is there a maker's name? If so, look in a price guide for further information as to age and price. Common names to be on the lookout for are Abingdon, Fiesta (Homer Laughlin), Hull, McCoy, Roseville, and Weller. Vases made by these companies are very collectible and prices range from a low $12 to several hundred dollars.

The majority of vases found at garage sales will be inexpensive glass varieties, the type received with a delivered floral arrangement. A common example is a white milk glass bud vase. These types should be priced low in order to sell.

Ceramic, unmarked	
bud vase	3.00
full size	
6" high	2.50
12" high	5.00
18" high	7.50
lady head	10.00
Glass	
bud vase	
crystal, etched design	2.00
pressed glass design	1.00
ruby glass	2.00
white milk glass	1.00

Vase, green glass, 8½" h, $1.00.

full size	
6" high	
crystal, etched design	2.00
pressed glass design	1.00
ruby glass	2.00
white milk glass	1.00
12" high	
crystal, etched design	5.00
pressed glass design	2.00
ruby glass	4.00
white milk glass	2.00
18" high	
crystal, etched design	10.00
pressed glass design	4.00
Plastic	
bud vase	.25
full size	.50

VIBRATORS/MASSAGERS

Found that old back or foot massager in the corner of the closet? Check to see if it still works, give some thought to how seldom you used it, then seriously consider pricing it low. Personal appliances like this are very difficult to sell.

Foot, vibrating, water tub	2.00
General, various attachments	1.00
Neck, shaped headrest, kneading motion	5.00

VIDEO GAME SYSTEMS & CARTRIDGES

Video game systems are the most popular toys on the market today. As new systems are developed, more and more of the earlier versions are finding their way to the resale market. Once Super Nintendo improved upon the original Nintendo the first models lost favor. They can now be found at garage sales and flea markets at greatly discounted prices.

Video game base units and controllers are made to survive plenty of use and abuse, but everything has its limits. While most games found at garage sales probably work fine, be aware that the systems do fail occasionally. Base units eventually wear out, making it difficult, if not impossible, to start the game. Controller wires are often damaged due to over-exuberant play. Some of these defects are easy to spot – others are impossible to detect until the game is tested.

Not all video game cartridges are created equal. The more complex the game, the higher its price, both retail and resale. Used cartridges generally sell for between $^1/_7$th and $^1/_{10}$th of their original price. Buy used games with confidence. They rarely malfunction, even after many hours of play.

Finally, when purchasing a system, be sure all the necessary installation wires and directions are present.

Game Cartridge	
Atari	3.00
Nintendo	5.00
Nintendo Game Boy	3.00
Sega Game Gear	5.00
Sega Genesis	7.50
Sega Super CD, CD-ROM	10.00
Super Nintendo	7.50
Game Cartridge Case	
hard plastic	1.00
nylon, zippered	1.50
Game System	
full size	
Atari, base unit, 2 controllers, and hook-up accessories	15.00
Nintendo, base unit, 2 controllers, Duck Hunt gun, and hook-up accessories	20.00
Sega Genesis, base unit, controller, and hookup accessories	30.00

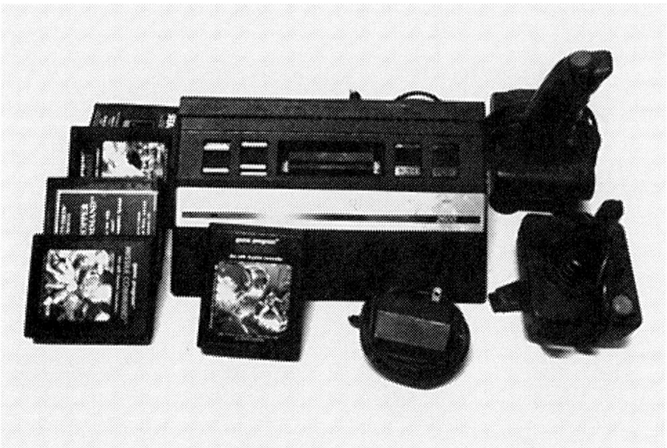

Atari 2600 Game System, base unit, 2 controllers, and hookup accessories, $15.00; Atari game cartridges, $3.00 each.

Sega Super CD, CD-ROM format, connects to Sega Genesis base unit . . . 75.00
Super Nintendo, base unit, 2 controllers, and hookup accessories . . . 30.00

hand held
Lynx, color, includes AC adapter . . 10.00
Nintendo Game Boy, monochromatic dot matrix screen, includes headphones and AC adapter 15.00
Sega Game Gear, hand held, high resolution color screen, stereo sound, includes AC adapter . . . 25.00

Video Game Cartridges, left: Nintendo's Double Dragon, $5.00; right front: Nintendo Game Boy's Tetris, $3.00; right back: Super Nintendo's The Legend of Zelda, $7.50.

Game System Accessories
AC adapter, hand held system 2.00
battery pack/recharger
Nintendo Game Boy 5.00
Sega Game Gear 7.50
carrying case, nylon, zippered
full size system 5.00
hand held system 3.00
cleaning kit, full size system 1.00
extra controller, full size system 2.50
Game Genie, any system, includes codes and instruction book 5.00
TV Tuner, turns Game Gear system into portable color television 20.00

WAGONS

If your child has outgrown his little red wagon try selling it at your garage sale. Clean it up and give the wheels a shot of oil. Arrange stuffed animals, dolls, or other toys in your wagon to add creativity to your display.

Metal
26" long 3.00
34" long 5.00
40" long 7.50
Wood, stake body sides, 40" long 10.00

WALL PLAQUES & POCKETS

Wall Plaque, dragon, self framed, imitation mother-of-pearl and glass, 5" x 7", $5.00.

Wall plaques, wall pockets, and other types of wall decorations make terrific garage sale items. The same companies that produced the now popular vases and planters also made wall pockets. Be on the lookout for their marks. The majority of wall pockets you encounter will be unmarked or made in Japan. Dust off plaques and pockets and, if possible, wash in a mild detergent. Keep facing pairs and matching items together and sell them as a set.

Wall Pocket, ceramic, made in Japan, 5½" high, $10.00.

Plaque	
brass, round, embossed colonial or European scene	1.00
ceramic (kittens, sports theme, etc.)	2.00
plaster (nursery rhyme character, animal, fruit, etc.)	2.50
plastic, (hot air balloon, car, Cupid, etc.)	1.00
twisted wire (peacock, fish, etc.)	2.50
Pocket, ceramic, unmarked or made in Japan	10.00

WALLETS

A wallet is the perfect gift to give someone when you have absolutely no idea what else to buy them. For the professionals and entrepeneurs on your shopping list, business card cases follow at a close second. No wonder so many of these gifts found at garage sales are brand new, still in the box. Genuine leather wallets will last longer and bring a better price than fabric, plastic, or vinyl examples.

Business Card Case	
brass	1.00
leather	1.00
plastic or vinyl	.25
Change Purse	
fabric, metal frame	1.00
leather, metal frame	2.00
plastic, squeeze type	.25
vinyl, zippered	.50
wristband, nylon, zippered	.50
Money Belt	2.00
Money Clip, metal	1.00
Wallet	
men's	
fabric	
bi-fold	.50
tri-fold	.50
imitation leather	
bi-fold	.50
tri-fold	.50
leather	
bi-fold	1.50
executive, fits in breast pocket	1.00
tri-fold	1.50
women's	
fabric	
bi-fold, with change pocket	.50
checkbook style, with change purse	.75
tri-fold, with change purse	.50
imitation leather	
bi-fold, with change pocket	.50
checkbook style, with change purse	.75
tri-fold, with change purse	.50
leather	
bi-fold, with change pocket	1.00
checkbook style, with change purse	2.00
tri-fold, with change purse	1.50

WASH BASKETS

Wash baskets can be found made of wicker, splint, or plastic. Wicker and splint baskets, because of their beauty and durability, are much more desirable than plastic, meaning higher resale values. Recycle or discard plastic baskets that are cracked or broken – you probably can't give them away.

Fabric, folding metal frame, wheels	4.00

Plastic 1.00
Splint 5.00
Wicker 3.00

WASH PROPS

Back in the olden days when clothes dryers were less popular, women hung their wash on clotheslines and then propped the lines up to catch the breeze. Wood and aluminum poles can still be found in a household that likes the smell of fresh sheets. Wash props are not expensive when new and should be priced reasonably at garage sales. Wood props are sturdier than metal and should be priced higher.

Clothespins, wood or plastic, any style, price
for bag of 50 . . . . 1.00
Clothespin Bag, hangs on wash line 50
Props
aluminum 1.00
wood 2.00

WASHING MACHINES

Clean and shine your used washing machine as you would any appliance. Making it look as new as possible will increase its saleability. Be honest about its condition. If the washer doesn't work it probably won't sell but if it should, you'll save yourself the trouble of a disgruntled buyer returning it and demanding a refund.

If you're selling a Maytag washer, price it slightly higher than other models. Maytag's reputation for dependability is well–earned. This is especially true of wringer washers. Believe it or not, there is still a market for these old workhorses, providing they are working and in very good condition.

Buyers, in addition to finding out that the washer works, also ask for the instruction booklet, hoses, and whether there are other accessories such as a fabric softener or bleach dispenser and small load basket. Be prepared to have help moving your new washer. A truck is necessary – a dolly would be helpful.

Full Size
large capacity
Maytag 150.00
other brands 125.00
standard size drum
Maytag 125.00
other brands 100.00
Portable, apartment size
Maytag 85.00
other brands 75.00
Stacking Unit
Maytag 115.00
other brands 100.00
Wash Tubs, galvanized, 2 tubs and stand . . 5.00
Wringer
Maytag
stainless steel 75.00
white porcelain 35.00
other brands, white 25.00

WHEELCHAIRS

Selling a wheelchair at a garage sale can be difficult. Like a pair of crutches or a hospital bed, no one wants to buy one unless he already has a need for it and then, chances are his insurance company has already provided a new one. Price your wheelchair extremely low – it will probably be bought only by an organization which provides free loaners to needy individuals. If it doesn't sell, consider donating it to a local ambulance corps or other similar charitable organization.

Wheelchair 5.00

WOOD & COAL STOVES

Wood and coal stoves are usually bought by energy cost–conscious people who don't mind the extra work needed to keep them running. There are four basic types of freestanding stoves available – coal, wood, coal/wood combination, and pellet. If you plan to buy a stove and you have small children or pets, consider buying a convection/radiant stove rather than a strictly radiant model.

Radiant heat is the direct warmth felt from a hot object. Cast iron stoves provide radiant heat only. Convection describes the flow of air around a hot stove caused by the transfer of heat to the air. Stoves with porcelainized cabinets provide both radiant and convection heat. Heat is always radiated directly from the door but the cabinet minimizes the intense heat directly around the stove and provides a safety shield against accidental burns to children and pets.

Be prepared to pay a professional to install your new stove according to local fire codes. Also, expect to buy new stove pipe to fit your home's installation requirements.

Wood Stove, cast iron, radiant heat, $35.00.

Accessories
- ash bucket, 5 gallon 2.00
- coal bucket, galvanized 2.50
- coal shovel 1.50
- draft gauge 2.00
- hearth rug, fire resistant 2.00
- leather gloves 4.00
- log carrier, wood and rope 2.50
- log holder, metal hoop 5.00
- slicing knife, coal 1.00

Stove
- coal
  - convection 75.00
  - radiant 50.00
- pellet 100.00
- wood
  - convection 50.00
  - radiant 35.00
- wood/coal combination
  - convection 75.00
  - radiant 50.00

WRISTWATCHES

Watches don't always need to be in running order to sell at a garage sale. If the watch is an expensive watch such as a Rollex, or if it has a high gold content, it will sell whether it works or not. Character watches, such as those featuring the likeness of Mickey Mouse or a favorite cowboy hero, vary in price according to condition and character. Check price guides for more specific information.

Most watches sold at garage sales will be inexpensive – originally bought for function rather than decoration. These watches must be working in order to sell. If your watch's only defect is its need of a new battery, replace it before you attempt to sell. Prospective buyers should only purchase watches such as Timex, Elgin, and Bulova if they run. Cost of repairs would most likely exceed the retail price of a new watch.

Children's
- character, modern
  - metal 5.00
  - plastic. 3.00
- digital, NFL team on dial, color coordinated vinyl strap 1.50
- game watch, Pac–Man, quartz LCD display, day/date on command, alarm, black plastic band. 3.00
- LCD, alarm, water resistant to 100', vinyl strap 50

Men's
- automatic analog, 17 jewel, water resistant, gold tone, luminous hands, day /date, self winding 10.00
- chronograph, musical alarm, LCD display, 24 hour repeat alarm, silvertone 1.50
- diver's, water resistant up to 30 meters, digital chronograph, 24 hour alarm, LCD display
  - black case, black plastic polyvinyl chloride strap 1.00
  - silvertone case 2.00
- quartz analog, 2 tone, dress watch, silvertone dial, goldtone and silvertone bracelet 7.50
- quartz LCD, sports watch, alarm/timer, rotating bezel indicates modes, day/date, water tested to 300', built-in illumination, rubber strap 5.00

Women's
- baguette, quartz LCD, narrow rectangular goldtone case, adjustable bracelet . 2.00
- bangle
  - acrylic and metal, burgundy dial and bracelet, clip closure. 2.50

- wire, goldtone dial, cable band . . . 2.00
- diver's, water resistant up to 30 meters, digital chronograph, 24 hour alarm, LCD display
  - black case, black plastic polyvinyl chloride strap 1.00
  - silvertone case 2.00
- quartz analog
  - 2 diamonds, oval goldtone case, adjustable bracelet 7.50
  - 10 diamonds, champagne colored dial, adjustable mesh bracelet . . 10.00

YARD ORNAMENTS

There are many types of "folk art" lawn decorations available at craft shows and lawn and garden stores. As a buyer, be aware that some of these, specifically bird houses, weathervanes, and whirligigs, are often replicas of antiques. If you can't be sure of an item's age and authenticity don't pay antiques' prices. If you are selling an ornament and are unsure of its origins do some research in order to avoid giving away a $500 weathervane at a fraction of its value.

Most yard decorations are easily recognized as modern. The prices listed below, unless otherwise noted, are for contemporary lawn ornaments.

- Barrel, wood, planter 5.00
- Bird Feeder, plastic 2.00
- Bird House, wood
  - "folky", ornate 10.00
  - plain, utilitarian 2.00
- Dummy Board, wood, painted (woman or man bending over in garden, cow, etc.) 10.00
- Kettle, cast iron, old, used as planter 20.00
- Pig Trough, cast iron, old, used as planter . . 20.00
- Pinwheel
  - plastic 50
  - wood 1.00
- Silhouette, wood, painted black, life size (golfer, man leaning against tree, etc.) . . 10.00
- Statue, cement, painted
  - animal
    - large (deer, dog, etc.) 20.00
    - small (squirrel, duck, rabbit, etc.) . . 2.50
  - gnome 10.00
- Stuffed Animal (bear, sheep, etc.) 2.50
- Wagon Wheel, old 15.00
- Weathervane, metal
  - 2–dimensional 15.00
  - 3–dimensional 30.00
- Whirligig, wood 20.00

CHARTS & SIGNS

CHARTS

SIGNS

TIPS FOR USING THESE SIGNS:

1. Photocopy, rather than cut, them from the book.
2. Consider enlarging the signs for easier reading.
3. Brightly colored paper is eye–catching.
4. Reinforce the signs with cardboard backing.

SUPPLIES CHECKLIST

SET-UP

- ❑ TABLES
- ❑ TABLECLOTHS
- ❑ CHAIRS
- ❑ DISPLAY CASES (OPTIONAL)
- ❑ BOXES
- ❑ CLOTHING RACKS OR CLOTHESLINES
- ❑ HANGERS
- ❑ PRICE TAGS
- ❑ DIFFERENT COLORED MARKERS OR STICKERS
- ❑ LABELING TAGS
- ❑ TAPE MEASURE
- ❑ SAFETY PINS (FOR ATTACHING LABELS TO FABRICS)
- ❑ EXTENSION CORDS
- ❑ TRASH CAN

ADVERTISING

- ❑ FLYERS
- ❑ SIGN MATERIALS

BOOKKEEPING

- ❑ CASH BOX
- ❑ CHANGE FOR CASH BOX
- ❑ CALCULATOR
- ❑ PENS AND PENCILS
- ❑ RECEIPT FORMS
- ❑ SALES RECORD FORMS
- ❑ CONSIGNMENT FORMS

PACKAGING

- ❑ BAGS
- ❑ OLD NEWSPAPERS AND WRAPPING MATERIALS

GARAGE SALE ADVERTISEMENT

NEWSPAPER ______________________________ PHONE # ( ) ____________________

ADVERTISING COPY:

_______ _______ _______ _______ _______ _______ _______ _______ _______ _______

_______ _______ _______ _______ _______ _______ _______ _______ _______ _______

_______ _______ _______ _______ _______ _______ _______ _______ _______ _______

_______ _______ _______ _______ _______ _______ _______ _______ _______ _______

Send Bill To:

____

____

____

PHONE # ( ) ____________________

Please run this ad in your Garage Sale section on the following dates:

____

____

____

PREPARATION CHECKLIST

1 MONTH BEFORE SALE

- ❑ **Pick Date and Rain Date** — Saturday is the best sale day. Schedule the rain date for the following Saturday.
- ❑ **Inform Family, Friends, and Neighbors** — They may want to join in. Plan a multi–family or neighborhood sale.
- ❑ **Get Permit** — Call your local government office for information.
- ❑ **Save Grocery Bags and Newspapers** — Ask family and friends to save bags, too.
- ❑ **Gather Merchandise** — Store smaller items in single location – larger items such as furniture can be moved at setup time.
- ❑ **Clean and Wash Merchandise** — Wash dishes and glassware. Launder clothing. Everything should look clean.
- ❑ **Price Merchandise** — Price individual items with removable tags. Do not write directly on merchandise with marking pen. Similar items can be displayed together with a single sign – "Everything on this table 50¢." Include seller identification codes for multi–family sales.
- ❑ **Label Merchandise** — Label clothing by size, linens by dimensions or sizes.
- ❑ **Make a General Listing for Advertisement** — List some specifics to attract interest – bedroom suite, fishing poles, washer/dryer. Generalize the remaining items – clothing, toys, household goods, furniture.
- ❑ **Make Flyers** — Include "Garage Sale" heading, date, rain date, time, place, and brief listing.

2 WEEKS BEFORE SALE

- ❑ **Distribute Flyers** — Place flyers in supermarkets, laundromats, community bulletin boards, etc.
- ❑ **Write Advertisement** — Check on advertising deadlines.
- ❑ **Submit Ad to Newspapers** — Most ads can be hand delivered, mailed, phoned in, or faxed.
- ❑ **Arrange for Help at Sale** — Have a minimum of three workers (including yourself).
- ❑ **Plan Sale Layout** — Decide where the sale will be held and the general arrangement of tables and merchandise. Tidy sale area.
- ❑ **Determine Setup Supplies Needed** — Determine the number of tables and/or racks needed for attractive, uncluttered displays.
- ❑ **Make Arrangements to Borrow Supplies** — Borrow folding tables, extension cords, calculator, tablecloths, etc. as needed. Try to improvise for items you don't have. Make extra tables from sawhorses and plywood or doors. Use bed sheets in place of tablecloths.

1 WEEK BEFORE SALE

- ❑ **Plan Sign Placement** — Plot directions from main roads. Determine the number of signs needed, directions of arrows, and method for hanging (telephone pole, stake driven in ground, etc.).
- ❑ **Pick Up Borrowed Supplies** — Check to be sure calculator and extension cords work.
- ❑ **Make Signs** — Create original signs or photocopy examples from book. Signs should be easily read from a distance. Use large, bold letters on brightly colored paper.

3 DAYS BEFORE SALE

- ❑ **Prepare Bookkeeping Forms** — If needed, photocopy appropriate forms from book for multi–family sale.
- ❑ **Get Change for Cash Box** — One roll each of quarters, dimes, and nickels, 25 ones, 6 fives, and 4 tens should suffice ($112.00).
- ❑ **Remind Helpers of Sale Date and Time** — Double-check that workers are still available to help.

DAY BEFORE SALE

- ❑ **Set Up Tables and Racks** — If sale will be held outdoors, check weather forecast. Wait until morning if rain is predicted overnight.
- ❑ **Set Up Sale (Indoor Sale)** — A sale held in a garage or barn can be completely set up the day before. Cover or tag items that are not being sold. Be sure to lock the doors.

DAY OF SALE

- ❑ **Set Up Sale (Outdoor Sale)** — Display merchandise neatly and attractively.
- ❑ **Put Up Directional Signs** — Have extras. Don't forget your hammer, nails, string, scissors, stapler, etc.
- ❑ **Post On–Site Signs** — Place signs and balloons at front of property directing shoppers to sale site.
- ❑ **Secure House** — Lock doors. Keep pets inside.

DAY AFTER SALE

- ❑ **Complete Paperwork** — Make a copy of the Multi–Family Sales Record for each seller. Check to see that the Total Receipts = Total Earnings + Cash Box Change ($112.00).
- ❑ **Disburse Earnings** — Pay each seller his/her earnings. Remember to deduct each seller's share of expenses previously agreed upon, such as advertising, cost of sign materials, and copying expenses. Don't forget to reimburse yourself the amount of start-up change put in the cash box.
- ❑ **Take Down Signs** — Remove **all** signs. Leftover signs are both an eyesore and a form of littering. Many communities impose fines for signs left standing following a garage sale.
- ❑ **Return Borrowed Supplies** — Return tables, calculator, and other supplies promptly.
- ❑ **Celebrate!** — Sit back and relax. Go out to dinner. Plan to spend your earnings on your preset goal.

WEEK AFTER SALE

- ❑ **Pay Advertising Bills** — Most bills are invoiced the day the ad appears and are due upon receipt.
- ❑ **Dispose of Unsold Items** — Keep any treasures you really want. Consider donating the remaining items to a local charitable organization such as the Salvation Army or Good Will. Remember to get a receipt – donations are tax deductible.

Multi–Family Garage Sale
Sales Record

ITEM	SELLING PRICE				
	SELLER #1	SELLER #2	SELLER #3	SELLER #4	SELLER #5
	$	$	$	$	$
TOTALS	$	$	$	$	$

CONSIGNMENT INVENTORY SHEET

Consignor's Name ______________________

Date ______________ Commission Rate ________ %

Item	Price Desired	Price Rec'd
	$	$
Total Received		$
Less Commission		–
Balance Due Consignor		$

I accept full responsibility for any damage or loss while my goods are in the hands of the Seller.

____

Consignor's Signature

SALES RECEIPT

Name ______________________

Date ______________________

Item	Price
	$
Total	$

Cashier

No Smoking

PRICE ____________ SIZE ____________	PRICE ____________ SIZE ____________	PRICE ____________ SIZE ____________
PRICE ____________ SIZE ____________	PRICE ____________ SIZE ____________	PRICE ____________ SIZE ____________
PRICE ____________ SIZE ____________	PRICE ____________ SIZE ____________	PRICE ____________ SIZE ____________
PRICE ____________ SIZE ____________	PRICE ____________ SIZE ____________	PRICE ____________ SIZE ____________
PRICE ____________ SIZE ____________	PRICE ____________ SIZE ____________	PRICE ____________ SIZE ____________

DATE:

GARAGE SALE

AHEAD

TIME:

DATE TIME

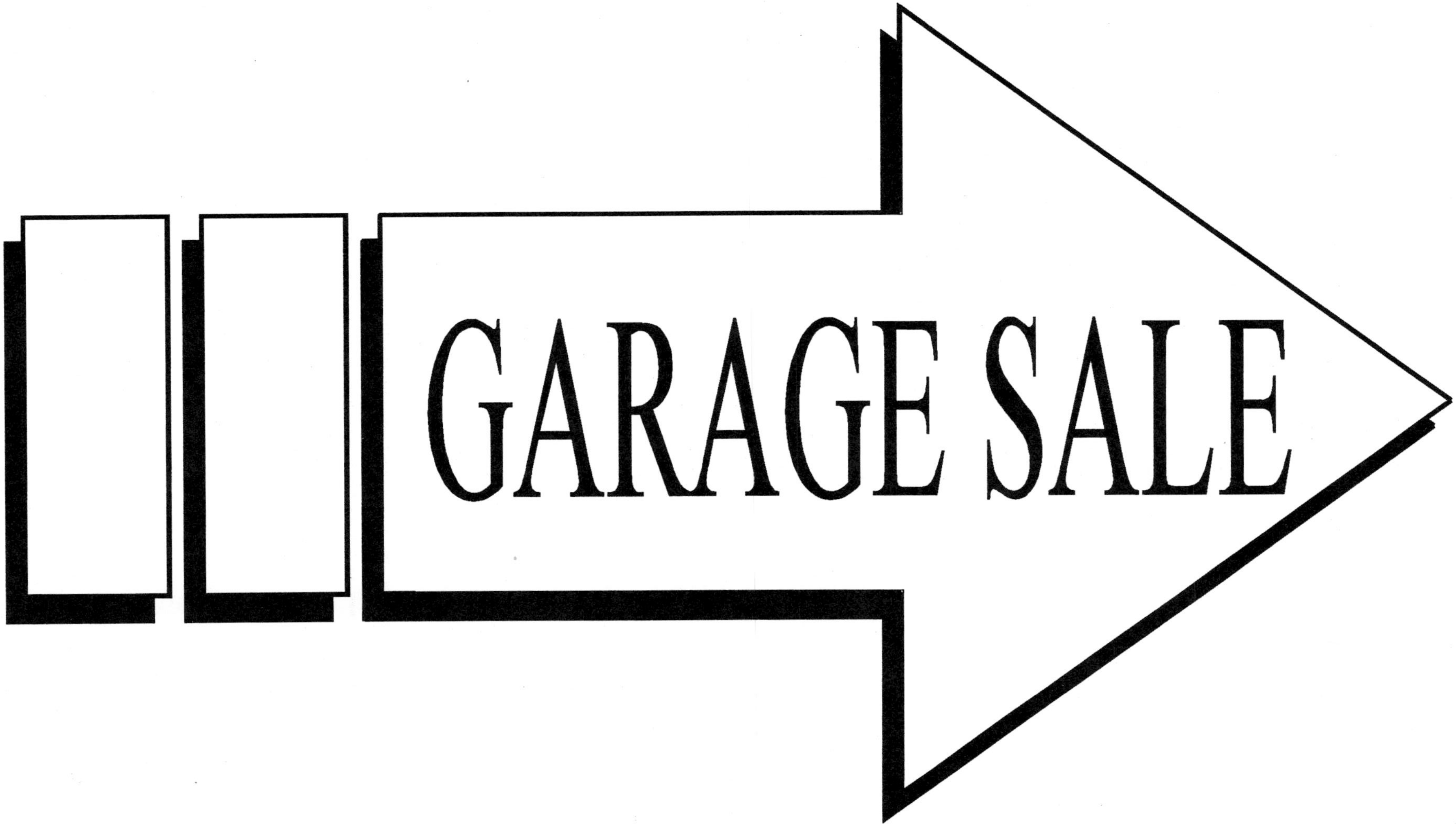

DATE TIME

GARAGE SALE

DATE: ______________ **TIME:** ______________

LOCATION: ______________________________

____

A Sampling Of The Goodies:

____

____

____

____

____

RAIN DATE: ______________

HOPE TO SEE YOU THERE!

date
date
time
Garage Sale
place

GARAGE SALE POSTPONED

RESCHEDULED FOR:

____

HOPE TO SEE YOU THERE!

ALL PRICES
FIRM

EVERYTHING
DISCOUNTED %

NOT
FOR SALE

Everything on this table

Everything on this rack

Everything in this box

SUBJECT INDEX

Note: Primary listings are indicated by bold type, secondary listings by regular type.